SOCIALITY

Wyse Series in Social Anthropology

Editors:
Maryon McDonald, Fellow and Director of Studies, Robinson College, University of Cambridge
Henrietta L. Moore, William Wyse Chair of Social Anthropology, University of Cambridge

Social Anthropology is a vibrant discipline of relevance to many areas – economics, politics, business, humanities, health and public policy. This series, published in association with the Cambridge William Wyse Chair in Social Anthropology, focuses on key interventions in Social Anthropology, based on innovative theory and research of relevance to contemporary social issues and debates. Former holders of the William Wyse Chair have included Meyer Fortes, Jack Goody, Ernest Gellner and Marilyn Strathern, all of whom have advanced the frontiers of the discipline. This series intends to develop and foster that tradition.

Volume 1
Sociality: New Directions
Edited by Nicholas J. Long and Henrietta L. Moore

Volume 2
The Social Life of Achievement
Edited by Nicholas J. Long and Henrietta L. Moore

SOCIALITY

New Directions

Edited by

Nicholas J. Long and Henrietta L. Moore

Berghahn Books
New York • Oxford

Published in 2013 by

Berghahn Books

www.berghahnbooks.com

©2013 Nicholas J. Long and Henrietta L. Moore

Library of Congress Cataloging-in-Publication Data

Sociality : new directions / edited by Nicholas J. Long and Henrietta L.
Moore.
    p. cm. -- (Wyse series in social anthropology)
  ISBN 978-0-85745-789-9 (hardback : alk. paper) 1. Ethnology. 2. Social
  groups--Cross-cultural studies. 3. Social action--Cross-cultural studies.
  4. Collective behavior--Cross-cultural studies. I. Long, Nicholas J. II. Moore,
  Henrietta L.
GN316.S63 2012
306--dc23
                                                                    2012019110

British Library Cataloguing in Publication Data

A catalogue record for this book is available from
the British Library.

Printed in the United States on acid-free paper

ISBN 978-0-85745-789-9 (hardback)

ISBN 978-0-85745-790-5 (ebook)

Contents

List of Figures

Acknowledgements

This book has its origins in a series of Senior Research Seminars that was staged in the Department of Social Anthropology at the University of Cambridge in the academic year 2009–2010. We are very grateful to the Department, and the Wyse Fund at Trinity College, for their financial support of that seminar series and of the present volume.

Whilst putting together this volume, we have benefited enormously from the advice and editorial assistance of Maryon McDonald, Ann Przyzycki DeVita, Mark Stanton and Lauren Weiss at Berghahn, and a team of anonymous peer reviewers who gave invaluable comments on both individual chapters and the volume as a whole. We would like to thank them, as well as Francesca Clouston, Ranald Clouston, and Connie Smith, for their generous help with preparing this volume for publication.

Introduction
Sociality's New Directions

*Nicholas J. Long, London School of Economics
and Political Science and
Henrietta L. Moore, University of Cambridge*

What would an anthropological theory of human sociality look like post-Strathern, post-affect theory, and post-actor-network theory (ANT)? It would certainly need to take on board the important insights and critiques that such paradigms have offered – but should also move beyond them to address their weaknesses. It would need to be able to account for the tremendous variety of forms that can be assumed by the sociality of humans – if not other entities – a variety that appears to be ever-burgeoning as new innovations in science and technology allow human beings to extend their imaginative and practical reach. It would need to engage with the ongoing problematic of virtuality – the fact that for all of human history, human beings have shown both a capacity to fantasize about forms of sociality that don't exist and an ability to remake the forms of sociality that they already have. As such, we argue, it would need to reject the flattening impulse within a great deal of recent critical theory, which, in a self-styled attempt to 'dethrone' the figure of 'the human subject' (e.g., Clough 2008), runs the danger of reducing human sociality to nothing more than the relationality between various beings or actants, or the transfer of affective energies between undifferentiated slabs of biological matter (Clough 2010; Venn 2010). Ironically, many of these ideas are inspired by precisely the kind of processual thinking that sparked an interest in the concept of human sociality, and might actually stand to enrich, rather than depose, its study if taken on board in an appropriate fashion.

Whether or not 'the human subject' should keep its throne is, as the papers in this volume reveal, a matter for ongoing and vibrant debate. But one conclusion is clear: dethroned or not, the human subject needs to remain in the palace. For, as we will argue in this introduction, and as is exemplified by the papers gathered in this volume, attending to the distinctiveness of humans (as well as that of other entities and materials) is not only the most profitable way to make sense of the plethora of new directions in which human sociality is unfolding in anthropological fieldsites around (and beyond) the world – it also does the greatest justice to those critical theories that would urge social scientists to develop symmetrical analyses or to pay attention to the biological dimensions of being human.

But what *is* sociality? You might well ask. The term has become increasingly prominent in sociocultural anthropology and the humanities over the last few decades – and it is easy to see why. The term has a lot of potential. Appealingly processual, it promises to overcome many of the drawbacks associated with the more static and bounded objects of enquiry that dominated many branches of twentieth century social science, such as 'society', or formal patterns of 'social relations'. The emphasis on *process* also offers advantages over approaches that seek to study 'the social', understood as the *product* of 'social relations' and/or 'social interaction' – an approach doomed to founder because, logically and existentially, sociality cannot 'precede' its articulations, but is rather co-extensive with, and as, articulation (Haver 1996: xiv).

Yet the full implications of what sociality actually *is*, and how it might most profitably be conceptualized and deployed, are often left obscure. The term has been used in a startlingly divergent number of ways by anthropologists – not to mention philosophers, animal behaviourists, evolutionary biologists, developmental psychologists, and literary theorists. For all its intuitive appeal, a quick survey of the literature might suggest, dispiritingly, that 'sociality' is capable of standing for anything and nothing. Yet this very problem of definitional haziness could be looked at differently, as evidence of human sociality's capacity to take many forms. What is in order, therefore, is not a highly specific, circumscribed definition of sociality, nor loose talk of a generic 'sociality' or 'capacities to "be social"', but rather a *theory* of human sociality – which is to say any sociality involving humans – that can account for its diverse manifestations, its plasticity and fragility, and also its possible resilience. As such, a core aim of this volume is to help readers navigate this rather bewildering intellectual landscape – identifying the shortcomings of several definitions currently in circulation and thereby defending the rightful place of human sociality as an object of enquiry, when understood as a dynamic and interactive relational matrix through which human beings come to know the world they live in and to find their purpose and meaning within it. Moreover, by developing a rigorous theory of human sociality, in this way, we also open up avenues for thinking about how to conceptualize other types of sociality (such as that of animals or of materials), thereby broadening the scope of the term without loosening its analytic horizons.

The papers in this collection, whilst inspired by different philosophical traditions and advocating their own subtly different and ethnographically tailored deployments of the sociality concept, support this contention in two distinct ways. Each paper demonstrates how a conception of sociality, taken in appropriate new directions, can be a powerful way of orienting anthropological enquiry. But this is not simply a case of using the category of 'sociality' to make sense of ethnographic materials: in each field setting, social actors themselves demonstrate an interest in the dynamic matrix of relations that we would term sociality, as well as desire (and sometimes refusal) to push it in new directions. The dynamic conception of human sociality that we propose is certainly helpful for understanding and theorizing these 'new directions' in real-world sociality. However, the fact that sociality is open to manipulation and transformation on the part of social actors (whether or not this is done consciously) also leads us to make a crucial theoretical intervention: human sociality cannot and must not be reduced to affectivity or relationality, much as these ideas might offer foundational concepts for understanding the world in which sociality unfolds. Instead we need to develop strong and rigorous theories of the motivations, desires, and ethics that shape such innovations; in short, the study of human sociality requires an explicit theory of human subjects.

Antecedents

> There is not a secret so aiding to the progress of sociality, as to get master of this *short hand*, and be quick in rendering the several turns of looks and limbs, with all their inflections and delineations, into plain words. For my own part, by long habitude, I do it so mechanically, that when I walk the streets of London, I go translating all the way; and have more than once stood behind in the circle, where not three words have been said, and have brought off twenty different dialogues with me. (Sterne 1768: 182, emphasis original)

One of the term's earliest recorded usages, Laurence Sterne's remarks on sociality in *A Sentimental Journey Through France and Italy* offer a productive point of departure for exploring both its promise and its (potential) pitfalls. Sociality is explicitly presented as an ongoing process, and not in the sense of its being a 'dynamic equilibrium' – the form of social process preferred by more stasis-oriented and structural-functionalist theoretical accounts – but rather a process that is at least capable of following a trajectory; of 'progressing'. Moreover, even practices that have become 'mechanical' are recognized as contributing to that trajectory on an ongoing and everyday basis. Yet this insight is bedevilled by an interpretive ambiguity over what exactly sociality is; or more precisely where its boundaries might lie.

We could, for example, follow John Mullan's interpretation of the passage to suggest that Sterne's 'sociality' refers to 'the pact between a knowing narrator and a knowing consumer of novels' (Mullan 2002: 34). For Mullan, sociality is what *we* enter into when we read Sterne's text; the term cannot encompass the relationship between the narrator and the French officer whose looks and limbs are observed, precisely because the distance inculcated by observation serves as an impediment to social relations (ibid.: 33–34). But a second reading is also possible. For just as a 'pact' might indeed be established between narrator and consumer, so a distinctive form of social relationship is created between observer and observed. Yorick's reflection on sociality is prompted by a sequence in which he enters an opera box, and a 'kindly old French officer' takes off his spectacles, an action Yorick translates as 'here's a poor stranger come into the box – he seems as if he knew nobody; and is never likely, was he to be seven years in Paris, if every man he comes near keeps his spectacles upon his nose'. In return, Yorick bows, to thank the officer for his attention (Sterne 1768: 179–182). These interpretations and responses are premised on a long history of social relations – the 'habitude' of which he writes – but also facilitate a new relational dynamic with the officer, and thereby a possible entry into the 'social world' of Paris. And the better Yorick gets to know Parisians, the better he stands to write about them for his readers; his social relations in France have a bearing on how he will go on to relate to his consuming public. Perhaps it will forge a 'pact' with them – or maybe they will find the text boring, or unconvincing. But in each of these eventualities, a dynamic matrix of relations is continually re-emerging, changing, evolving, or in Sterne's term 'progressing', thanks to the way the narrator is mastering (or not) his *'short hand'*: his entire, specific, way of being a social actor, understanding and interacting with the world around him. Is that not also the progress, and dynamic instantiation, of sociality?

These two interpretations speak to an ongoing confusion in academic usages of 'sociality', namely – as we shall illustrate shortly – how circumscribed the notion should or can be. Our position is that, while ethnographic or historical usages of the term may indeed be circumscribed (as suggested by Mullan's gloss of Sterne), its usage in anthropological analysis should be kept as open as possible, in keeping with the second interpretation outlined above. An approach that attends to an entire matrix of relations necessarily includes the study of what might be labelled 'pacts' or 'bonds', whilst avoiding the implication that these are the only forms of intersubjective engagement that prove meaningful for human beings over the course of their lives. Moreover, this approach highlights how the pursuit of certain forms of relation might be predicated upon others – a dynamic that could easily be overlooked if that form of relation were studied in isolation.

Our preferred approach to sociality would thus begin with its conceptualization as a dynamic relational matrix within which subjects are constantly interacting in ways that are co-productive, and continually plastic and malleable. This builds upon and extends the model of sociality championed by Marilyn Strathern and Christina Toren in the 1989 Manchester debate in anthropological theory, in which Strathern suggested that sociality should be understood as 'the relational matrix which constitutes the life of persons', who in turn should be apprehended as 'simultaneously containing the potential for relationships and always embedded in a matrix of relationships with others' (Strathern et al. 1990: 8–10).[1] The importance of this, according to Toren, is that sociality draws anthropologists' attention to 'dynamic social processes in which any person is inevitably engaged, rather than a set of rules or customs or structures or even meanings that exists *as a system* independently of the individual who is to be socialised' (ibid.: 19).

Such an approach has been powerful in generating more processual accounts of both stasis and change in settings as diverse as Melanesia (Hess 2009; Weiner 1988), Vietnam (Gammeltoft 2007), and Denmark (Bruun et al. 2011; Højlund 2011; Olwig 2011). Yet its original formulation now seems to present a number of conceptual ambiguities that need clarification in light of the developments and challenges posed within social, critical and anthropological theory over the past twenty years. What, for example, is 'a person'? What 'others' can and should be included within our understanding of the relational matrix? What is the place of non-humans, objects and 'things' in a theory of sociality? How can we best incorporate into the model an understanding of those situations in which humans appear to be affected by the presence or actions of others around them, despite the fact that they have no ostensible 'relationship' with them; a process Clough (2010: 224) describes as 'the sociality of the transmission of force or intensity across bodies'? And how can we account for the manifold forms of human sociality?

Two contemporary perspectives on these questions are provided in this volume's essays by Christina Toren and Henrietta Moore, both of whom underscore the analytical importance of ontogeny, intersubjectivity, human inherence in an environing world, and the developmental plasticity of human biology – including the brain. Toren's chapter sets out her own distinctive vision of the anthropological project, one in which sociality is taken as foundational because intersubjectivity – which she defines as 'the capacity for recursive thought that makes human learning a micro-historical process' – means that a human is always-already embedded in social relations lived within, and through, an environing world, and consequently the carrier of a unique collective-cum-personal history. Toren builds upon this argument to critique recent work that has sought to reify 'sociality' as a distinctive capacity or module of the human mind. Developing an approach informed by dynamic systems theory, she argues that no aspect of human development should be seen as being outside of sociality, and that anthropological attention should properly be directed to the full range of micro-historical processes by which persons are constituted over their entire lifespans. As such, she proposes a unified model of human being, in which distinctions such as those between matter and information, or biology and culture, are collapsed, but in which sociality stands at the core.

This raises the question of how uncritically we should engage with the category of 'the human', an issue taken up directly in Henrietta Moore's analysis of the socialities of the inorganic. Moore's approach to sociality adopts a more expansive notion of context than Toren's. While Toren argues that humans necessarily imagine and interact through an environing world, and that approaches such as actor-network theory, that would afford agency to non-human actants, are therefore unnecessary or unhelpful, Moore sees greater potential in analysing the vitalism and affectivity of matter, and its capacity to have formative influences on human lives and relations. Yet she is also adamant that this should not distract us from acknowledging the distinctiveness of human sociality. As she argues, the difficulties encountered by engineers when trying to successfully design a 'social robot' point to the significance of autopoiesis and humans' intersubjective development within a dynamic context for fostering a recognizably human sociality – one which involves the use of representation and signification to coordinate knowledge, higher order cognition, and affect. Anthropology's long-standing interest in humans' linguistic and representational abilities must therefore continue, provided it is seen that these emerge out of a 'biologically cultural engagement with an environment'. Secondly, she argues that the contemporary use of avatars, another 'inorganic sociality', reveals the distinctively human capacities to project notions of 'the environment' forwards and backwards in space and time, including into parallel, virtual realms, where things of the imagination can be ascribed with attributes, qualities and attachments. These projections constitute crucial dimensions of the matrices of relations in which humans are involved – and as such, even in a world understood to be replete with different agencies and affectivities, human sociality stands out as a distinctive and vibrant concern.

Alternatives

Before developing this position further, it is worth paying some attention to the relational matrix within which our own argument is embedded. For despite the conceptual and methodological advantages of the approach set out above, a large number of alternative understandings of sociality continue to circulate within the humanities, contributing to a lack of clarity over what is at stake in the term. It may thus be helpful to pause briefly, so as to review some of the major ways in which the concept has been employed by other authors, and to explain why we consider all of them to be inferior to approaches which would view sociality as a dynamic matrix.

One of the most frustrating has been offered by philosopher Margaret Gilbert, who, concerned that ideas about 'the social' are being invoked so disparately that the term lacks obvious importance, has argued that we can only speak of 'sociality proper' in cases that exhibit 'plural subjecthood' involving a type of 'mental connection' between people, that has been established by a 'joint commitment' (Gilbert 1997: 27–28). 'Plural subjecthood' refers to the phenomenon by which people come to refer to and think of an assemblage of themselves and others using a plural subject pronoun such as 'we' – and this is clearly a phenomenon worthy of investigation in any given context within which a researcher might be working. However, by definitionally privileging the phenomena that she considers 'most social', Gilbert has actually smuggled in unexamined a normative but unrealistic vision of harmonious and committed social relations. A similar problem occurs in the work of other philosophers who persistently equate 'sociality' with group living, or a 'we-mode' (e.g., Tuomela 2007) and thereby dismisses as asocial, or non-social, the experiences of those large numbers of people who for practical or ethical reasons conduct their lives amongst others, but in the absence of plural subjecthood, connection, or commitment (see, e.g., Haver 1996; also Allison, this volume).

This objection is particularly significant given that plural subjecthood itself is sketched very thinly in Gilbert's account. Placing such emphasis on putative mental connections and 'joint commitment' overlooks the ways in which even these kinds of social relations, by definition, contain the potential for their own termination and might thus be fraught with ambivalence and fear. In his contribution to this volume, Peter Geschiere analyses notions of witchcraft from twentieth and twenty-first century Africa to explore exactly how this capacity for betrayal and danger forces us to rethink dominant notions of intimacy and trust in the social sciences. Geschiere notes that the most frightening forms of witchcraft amongst the Maka of Cameroon are linked to 'the witchcraft of the house', in which witches betray their relatives to outsiders – a prospect that is imagined to generate moral dilemmas for witches but which also raises the question of how intimacy and trust can be sustained. Geschiere argues for the value of developing more nuanced notions of sociality, intimacy and trust, that can take into account the danger and aggression that might suffuse close social ties. In doing so, his analysis problematizes Gilbert's assumption that sociality is premised upon a 'real unity' between people (Gilbert 1997: 23). Rather, we suggest, building on Geschiere, that 'real unity' and trust should be seen as particular forms of human sociality which need to be accounted for through anthropological enquiry.

If connection, commitment and unity are, then, potentially emergent but potentially evanescent properties of all relations, rather than fixed attributes of those relations experienced as 'bonds' or 'ties', the most productive way forward is not to focus on those 'ties' in isolation, but rather to examine the dynamic matrix in which they are continually made, sustained or dissolved.[2] Such an undertaking necessarily involves attending to all relations in which a human being is embedded. This, we believe, offers a broad but strong notion of sociality.

It is not just philosophers who have put forward unhelpfully narrow conceptions of sociality; many anthropologists using the term have also deployed it as a substitute for a more specific process they are attempting to describe. Most of these accounts are *prima facie* highly appealing because they attend to aspects of the processuality of social interactions and social relations, and are also cognizant that the socialities they describe are contingent upon broader historical and spatial circumstances. The problem is that by limiting their understanding of sociality to the formation of very specific types of relation they neglect the broader relational context within which people are embedded. A case in point is the growing body of work on 'biosociality' – a term coined by Paul Rabinow (1996) to indicate the possibility that people might form groups based around particular diseases, symptoms, or genomic features. Kaushik

Sunder Rajan elaborates further to suggest that subjectivities become socialities when they 'transform into the locus of shared social identifications' (2008: 171). This focus on the group is worthwhile, and clearly important in certain ethnographic contexts, but underplays the extent to which a (historically situated) biomedical diagnosis can transform one's entire way of relating with the world, based on new apprehensions of factors such as one's mortality, historicity, vulnerability to infection, and capacity to infect others – as has been brilliantly explored by William Haver (1996) in his study of life 'in the time of AIDS'. To focus only on shared social identifications or the forming of politically motivated associational communities would be not only to neglect this extra dimension of sociality, it would be to ignore how a broader disposition of relating in the world following diagnosis both affected, and was affected by, these practices of group identification and association. As such, while Rabinow and his followers have identified an important phenomenon, we find no justification for its arbitrary delimitation as a concept, let alone as one that is described in terms of 'sociality'. To circumscribe the term in such a way would, in fact, obscure the central question of why human sociality is capable of taking many different forms.

A similar assessment applies to the many other attempts by anthropologists and cultural theorists to delimit 'sociality' as a specific phenomenon: Adam Chau's (2006: 147) definition of sociality as the 'condition of social co-presence', when humans (who may or may not be related or interact) gather in the same social space, such as a cinema or a crowd; John Monaghan's (1995) equation of sociality with Simmel's 'sociation' – the forms of being with and for one another 'in which individuals grow together into a unity and within which their interests are realized' (Simmel 1971: 24); or Peter Westoby's (2009: 93) suggestion that sociality is the purposeful and agentive process of creating new social relations. Each of these approaches has identified an important aspect of sociality, and crucially, an aspect that is of particular significance in the ethnographic settings in which they work. Chau's interlocutors in the Northern Chinese village of Shaanbei expressed an appetite for situations of crowdedness and 'red-hot sociality' (*honghuo*) that is clearly worthy of study; the Nuyooteco in Mesoamerica that Monaghan writes of are widely concerned with the question of how collectivities form and accomplish goals; and Westoby's idea of sociality as the agentive instigation of relations would of course be a paramount concern in the lives of South Sudanese refugees, who had few if any pre-existing social relations in their new home and whose sense of themselves as sovereign agents had been fundamentally challenged by the experiences of war. The problem, however, is that all of these texts equate a particular and ethnographically situated interest in certain forms of sociality with sociality per se; they convert an ethnographically interesting gloss, which needs to be accounted for, into an *analytic* gloss to be taken up within social theory, and in doing so, they cut the very phenomenon they are seeking to describe off from other important sources of insight.

This is not, of course, to say that ethnographically delimited understandings of sociality should not be scrutinized by anthropologists. They certainly should be. But rather than using those limits to create a definition of sociality, the historically and geographically situated, and politically inflected, processes by which a practice comes to be understood as the kind of sociality that one ought to have need to be carefully examined. As demonstrated by Chakrabarty's study of *adda* (friends getting together for long, informal and unrigorous conversations) in Calcutta, which, with a playful but appropriate nod to Foucault, he terms 'a history of sociality' (2000: 180), a genealogical approach can be helpful in revealing how understandings of what sociality is or should be might derive from broader contextual anxieties (as in the Bengali case, where the dominant concern is with how to engage with new categories of 'modernity'). This is a particularly important point to make, because social scientists' own approaches to sociality are not exempt from influence by historical, geographical and political context, and many of the ways in which the term has been delimited by scholars blur explicit or implicit ideas about how the world ought to be with claims about foundational philosophical principles.

A broader definition of sociality is thus in order. Some writers have found mileage in equating sociality with 'the capacity to be social'. This, for example, is the position of philosopher Frederic Schick (1984) who analyses examples of altruism, and tailoring conduct to the interests of others, to argue that sociality – having some form of 'involvement' between people – is logically antecedent to action. While his examples are reminiscent of the emphasis on cooperation, groups, and bonds, such a perspective could be extended to other relations as well, thereby reiterating and defending the oft-cited remark that humans are 'social beings' (e.g., Tuomela 2007: 1) and/or 'biologically social' (Strathern et al. 1990: 17). This contention, which in itself seems uncontroversial, has given rise to some important research programmes within biological anthropology, psychology and linguistics into the physiological and neurological underpinnings – and limitations – of that capacity (see for example Enfield and Levinson 2006), research which, although it should not necessarily be taken at face value, opens up a significant space of debate with which social anthropologists would be well advised to be familiar (see Toren 2012 and this volume). Work within occupational science and the anthropology of autism has also reminded us that capacities to be social are not just a matter of genetics or physiology, but are crucially dependent on the broader organization of the environment in which a person is emplaced (Ochs and Solomon 2010; see also Solomon, this volume). The 'capacity' definition has thus proven productive. However, to restrict sociality purely to this capacity strikes us as a problematic move because it either ignores or presumes an answer to the question of why that capacity is deployed in the first place.

The significance of this issue has been powerfully articulated by Leo Bersani in his essay 'Sociality and Sexuality'. Starting from the premise that relationality needs to be taken as foundational – there has never been any moment when we were not in relation, or when we did not have some form of capacity to be social – he notes that there is a further question to be asked:

> Why extend at all? Why do objects and living beings even begin to move? Again, there is no beginning of movement; nonetheless, relational movement requires an account of a foundational motor – in the case of human subjects, a fundamental motivation for all movement. 'Requires' in the sense that all particular motivations of all particular movements share a founding structure of desire, by which I mean a structure that accounts for the *will to be* in all things. (Bersani 2010: 104–105)

Biologically or cognitively oriented models quickly founder in the face of such a challenge. By presenting the desire to be social as instinctive, innate, or the product of natural selection (a formulation that frequently equates 'being social' with cooperation and altruism), they sidestep the complicated phenomenological realities in which human beings feel alternately compelled to engage and disengage with the world around them in ways that can be profoundly affecting and indeed formative. More nuanced models are required to address Bersani's challenge adequately – as well as the further questions that it raises, such as whether any such 'foundational motor' can span different historical, geographic, or even individual circumstances. This remains an area of vibrant and productive research. Bersani himself, for instance, rereads Plato's *Symposium* to reject psychoanalytic approaches in favour of his own notion of 'impersonal narcissism' in which desire is neither driven by a sense of lack, nor an impulse to master the world, but rather an appetite for sameness that is recognized in others. In this sense, he claims, all love is homoerotic (ibid.: 118).

We will leave readers to assess that argument on its own merits; however what makes it interesting for the present discussion is not its propositional force but rather the reasons for which it is made. Bersani frames his essay as a deliberate attempt to conceive, elaborate, and put into practice a 'new relational mode', following Foucault's (1997b: 138) suggestion that 'homosexuality is a historic occasion to reopen affective and relational virtualities'; his interest in the foundationality of being-in-relation stems from a frustration with the fact that most attempts to create new relational modes have hitherto been 'reactive' and premised on foundational notions of difference. He thus recognizes that the practice and experience of both sociality and desire is embedded in broader, but malleable, discursive contexts, and the recognition of human sociality as a dynamic matrix of relations is not just an ontological or theoretical question, but always contains both ethical and political dimensions – not least because human dynamic matrices are shot through with inequalities of resources and capacity, and with theories and ideas about those differentials.

This is not to discount the possible insights afforded by more 'foundational' ideas about the motivations or motors of sociality (see for example our discussion of affect theory below) – but to recognize that these need to be combined with ethnographically situated studies of the ethical practices by which humans might attempt to open (or shut down) virtualities. The significance of this point can be demonstrated through recourse to Foucault's characterization of the ethical practice of ascesis. He suggested that this offered a means of 'pulling myself free of myself ... preventing me from being the same' (Foucault and Trombadori 2000: 242), whilst Tuhkanen (2005: 26) describes it as 'an experience of immanence, a practice that begins from that which exists, yet elicits the unexpected, the unforeseen, from the plane of immanence'. Ethical practice, then, can form a basis for personal and social transformation – including in surprising or underdetermined ways. Theories of human sociality must therefore pay careful attention to the generativity of ethical practice, both because it moulds the discursive (and material) environments with which human beings engage from birth, and because it indicates that one's own sociality, and the impulses that underpin it, might be at least partly amenable to control. This need not only be via processes of conscious reflection and ascesis, however. It might also involve affective, fantasmic and highly embodied engagements with forms of unknowing and incomprehensibility, as Moore (2011: 17–18) highlights in her notion of the ethical imagination.

As such, it is clear that to equate sociality with an innate and/or environmental 'capacity to be social' would be an impoverished formulation because to understand how and why those capacities are used and directed over the lifecourse requires a sophisticated account of agency, motivation, intentionality and desire: in short, an understanding of the human subject as he or she exists in a given place and time. This is not because we wish to reinstate an ossified and universalizable theory of the human subject, nor because we wish to reduce human lives to states of discursive and linguistic subjectification (although this is certainly an extremely important dimension of living in the world). It is, rather, to recognize an important 'feature of human subjectivity: that we are born into and make ourselves under conditions that we may then choose to transform' (ibid.: 17). And a key aspect of this is how we manage relations to ourselves and to others – the human, the non-human and the inhuman (ibid.: 196) – how we act within, and attribute value to, the dynamic matrix of sociality.

The productivity of such an approach is well demonstrated by the papers in this volume. Sian Lazar's study of political collectivity amongst trade union members in Bolivia and Argentina reveals that locally significant tropes of sociality – '*vida orgánica*' and '*contención*' respectively – should be thought of as *ideologies* of collectivity, in that they help to construct (distinct) senses of collectivity, as well as ways of understanding and articulating what collectivity consists of. Her emphasis on the ideological is important here, for it underscores how collectivity is not 'natural' or 'spontaneous' (although it is often given the impression of being so) but rather requires conscious effort, understood in the form of well articulated organizational philosophies that themselves warrant ethnographic contextualization, reminding us that a study of the ethical imagination cannot and should not be divorced from questions of politicality, or the discursive relations in which a human subject is embedded. Moreover, as she demonstrates, even in cases where forms of sociality are heavily associated with moral obligations, sociality should not be conceived of as participation in an 'external social order'. Rather, active social life is constituted by obligations, the subjects who participate in it are themselves constituted by the same obligations, and sociality (and the forms of identity and belonging that stem from group membership) is thus 'constituted by and through subjects actively engaged in a collective being-in-the-world'.

The significance of human subjectivity, and the need for a nuanced and multi-layered theory of the ethical imagination, is also evident from Nicholas Long's analysis of emergent forms of sociality in the online metaworld of *Ultima Online*. Inhabitants of *Ultima Online* regularly attest to their participation in, and enjoyment of, forms of communitarian sociality – but their claims are not supported by tracing the practices of social interaction that appear to generate their pleasure. Long argues that the affectively enabling sociality in *Ultima Online* would be better analysed in terms of Wilde's conception of sympathetic individualism rather than the commonality suggested by idioms of friendship or community, but that the resonance of these latter terms with users' established horizons of the good life makes those characterizations of the sociality an important element of its pleasure. His chapter thus underscores that the ethical imagination can be both affective and perversely contradictory in ways linked to its political, intellectual and historical context – and suggests that relational matrices that finesse these contradictions might be those most powerfully experienced as 'utopian'.

Anne Allison's chapter, by contrast, highlights what can happen when one loses the capacity to imagine the form of sociality one is used to, and is confronted headfirst with sociality's precarity. Tracing the unravelling of the sociality known as 'my-homeism' in post-war Japan, Allison shows how Japanese youth confronted with the 'hardship of life' have turned to violence, killing, and social withdrawal as the established horizons of their ethical imaginations are eroded and they struggle to find a new sense of purpose and completeness in the world. Allison's analysis reminds us of the fragility of wished-for sociality, and its dependence on both the recognition of others and the macrological structures of political economy, such as the flexibilization of labour or the limited reach of state welfare. Yet her chapter also traces emergent socialities that 'carry for the potential of both futurity and hope' and in doing so she attests the enduring significance of the human ethical imagination, and its capacity to remake forms of sociality – for better or worse. While this remains true, a theory of human sociality cannot do without an understanding of the human subject. Or can it?

Why Sociality is Not Reducible to Relationality

Over the past twenty years, a number of theoretical interventions have advocated the adoption of a strongly relational ontology within the humanities and social sciences. Actor-network theory (ANT), for example, implores us to recognize that humans live in a world replete with non-human entities, the agency of which plays a crucial role in the production of phenomena that might have hitherto been described in the frustratingly mercurial terms of 'social tie' or 'social force'. For Latour (2007: 75), 'ANT states that if we wish to be a bit more realistic about social ties than "reasonable" sociologists, then we have to accept that the continuity of any course of action will rarely consist of human-to-human connections ... or of object-object connections, but will probably zigzag from one to the other'; it is a way of exploring 'the mediators through which inertia, durability, asymmetry, extension, domination is produced' (ibid.: 85). Given this, actor-network theorists propose that the notion of 'social' be redefined: phenomena should be considered 'social' if they are 'intrinsically interactive' or 'result from processes of assemblage or arrangement of entities, of whatever kind' (Cook et al. 2009: 55). This inevitably raises the question of whether 'sociality' is equivalent to, or even better described as, a radical relationality, association, or assembly.

For some thinkers this would indeed be the case. Gabriel Tarde, now hailed by some as the forefather of actor-network theory (see Latour 2002), was adamant that intrinsically interactive physical systems, such as galaxies, solar systems, or atoms, should also be considered 'social' phenomena (Tarde 1893). Anthropologist Tim Ingold stops short of that particular claim, but *does* call for a dissolution of foundational distinctions between humans, animals, plants and objects. He argues that, whilst dealing with different types of being and entity involve different sensory registers, there is 'no register that escapes the domain of our sensory involvement in our environment, no discourse that does not subsist in the process of our bodily dwelling' and that therefore 'if some relations are social, then all are, and all life would be social life' (Ingold 1997: 249). He thus argues that anthropologists must reject the conceit that sociality lies in the distinctive way in which humans perceive resemblances across species and put them to work in their knowledge practices, instead arguing for a more inclusive notion that encompasses diverse entities and beings (ibid.: 240).

However, ideas such as these need careful handling, as they can all too quickly conflate ontological interventions with cryptonormative programmes of how we, as analysts and subjects, should engage with a relational world. The idea that diverse entities are fellow participants in the same world, and co-constitute each others' environments – now widely acknowledged as a starting point for anthropological analysis[3] – is eminently persuasive to all but the most avowed solipsist. It can help delineate the nature and extent of the dynamic matrices with which our own conception of human sociality is concerned. But given that humans live in a world that is radically and dynamically relational, the questions of how and why that relationality is managed, directed, and operationalized remain a core concern. The two interests are not mutually exclusive conceptions of 'sociality' (cf. Ingold 1997: 240) but complementary concerns. This points to a significant analytical distinction between relationality as a particular intellectual problematization (following Foucault 1985, 1997a; Moore 2011:

19–20) of which contemporary humans (at least within the academy) are increasingly aware, and human sociality as a set of diverse ways in which that relationality is engaged with, each with their own form and character and always informed by historically and spatially particular practices of ethical imagination.

A number of works associated with the 'relational turn' in critical theory exemplify how ontological recognitions of relationality can slide into ethically imaginative programmes for sociality. In some cases these are set out very explicitly. The philosopher Glen Mazis (2008), for example, implores his readers to build on their recognition of relatedness to see themselves as 'earthbodies', enmeshed in the world with which we relate, such that they might develop a new and revitalized notion of environmental ethics. Similar notions, of course, are present in those analyses that present the positioning of animals within anthropological accounts as a political question (Kirksey and Helmreich 2010). Taking idioms of relatedness in a slightly different direction, members of the American Anthropological Association's biannual 'Multispecies Salon' and of the Matsutake Worlds Research Group appear to only be half joking when they respectively suggest that 'the swarm' and the 'rhizomic sociality' of mycorhizzal mushrooms might be appropriate or even 'tactical' means of organizing scholarly activity, collaboration, and writing (Choy et al. 2009; Kirksey et al. 2011). But even to the extent to which they *are* joking, and find such resonances playful and pleasurable (and the playfulness is evident in the ways in which they write), these scholars are still clearly engaged in the work of the ethical imagination, fuelled as it can be by affectivities, pleasures, and the intensity of cathartic release (Moore 2011: 204–205). Meanwhile, Haver has built upon the notion of sociality as a dynamic matrix of relations to suggest that:

> If we are serious here, it seems to me that we must therefore think sociality as vulnerability, as anonymity, and as a certain erotic nomadism. It is not, of course, that essence would precede existence, nor merely that existence would precede essence, but, perhaps more radically, that fucking precedes existence, rendering essence irrelevant … What is at stake here is the priority of a rendering oneself vulnerable to the risk of the stranger over any structure of intersubjective recognition in the quite literal multiplicity of 'the body' in orgiastic group sex, for example. (1996: xiv, see also 119–159)

The problem that bedevils each of these arguments, but which is made particularly explicit in Haver, is that the normative force of their models seems to stem from needing to be 'serious' about relational ontologies. But as the sheer diversity of templates illustrates, relationality in itself provides no directive force for how relations should be conceptualized, managed or experienced – even if the illusion of such is sometimes naturalized by contemporary ideologies of network capitalism (Boltanski and Chiapello 2005: 151). Rather, directive force stems from the ethical imagination's engagement with the problematic of relationality (Moore 2011: 136–205). Indeed, as has been brilliantly highlighted by Amanda Anderson (2001) and Matei Candea (2010), even those modalities of engaging with others that cultivate forms of detachment, or the simulation of non-relations, can be valuably understood as a particular ethical engagement with the very relations that they suppress. Given this, ethnographic accounts of ethically imaginative practice will always, we suggest, be a necessary supplement to accounts of relationality in and of itself.

The virtues of such an approach can be seen in this volume's chapter by Adam Yuet Chau. Following the Latourian and Deleuzian injunctions to pay close attention to how diverse entities adhere together in assemblages, Chau structures his analysis of Taiwan's Festival of the Righteous Martyrs around the concept of 'actants amassing', providing ethnographic snapshots of the roles (and perspectives) of both human and non-human actants – from pigs to betel nuts and local politicians – as they come together to form integral components of the ritual event. Yet as Chau notes, even if this can be theorized as a 'compositional assemblage' of actants amassing, there is still a question to be asked as to why it has achieved staying power.

In addressing this question, Chau makes an innovative theoretical advance in the study of the durability of assemblages. Moving away from early actor-network theory's interest in the (Machiavellian and human-centred) process of translation (Callon 1986a, 1986b), and drawing instead on Alfred Gell, he suggests that certain compositional principles and forms, 'once invented and tried and found useful (for all kinds of reasons, and not all conscious)' will exert a certain gravitational pull. In the Taiwanese case, these include idioms of hosting, competition, and rotation: all of which have distinguished genealogies in Taiwanese social life. Thus while Chau himself eschews the language of sociality, partly as a result of its already carrying so many alternative definitions (see above), two important points about sociality are demonstrated through his chapter. Firstly, he shows how the Latourian 'sociality' of a gallery of interactive actants warrants methodological innovation in how anthropologists define, study, and write about the field. But his material, we believe, also points to the relevance of a more closely delineated theory of human sociality of the kind we have been developing in this introduction, for his detection of compositional principles and forms that 'stick' could be seen as an ethnographic excavation of contemporary Taiwanese ethical imaginations. His paper thus points to some of the new directions – theoretical and methodological – that anthropology itself might take in a post-Latourian attention to the agencies and socialities of humans – and others.

Indeed, although actor-network approaches have often been caricatured as trying to dethrone the human (McLean and Hassard 2004), in our eyes they actually offer a perfect lead into a revitalized study of human sociality. Insisting that the human be embedded in a world of multifarious actants, the agency of which can indeed have powerful consequences for what happens in the world, they nevertheless recognize that diverse actants have their own incommensurable agencies which should be taken on their own terms (Latour 2007: 74). This, of course, includes the human. So when Latour (2010: 81) suggests it is time for

ANT to move on to be a 'fully colourised' rendering of associations, paying close attention to the world's many different *modes* of connection and *modes* of existence, we would agree, and argue that the ways in which human subjects engage with and drive forward human sociality will necessarily be central issues in any such account.

But what about non-humans? So much effort has been put into interrogating the validity of any boundary between human and non-human, that it might seem problematic for us to place so much weight on the supposedly distinctive features of 'human subjects'. But most of these interventions seek to problematize the asymmetrical *privileging* of humans over other animals or entities; and it is in no way our claim that humans are 'better' or 'more important' than these others. What we do believe, however, is that a truly symmetrical analysis needs to be honest and attentive regarding the specificities of the various entities it encompasses, even as it recognizes they may have co-evolved or exist in relations of symbiosis. Here, important insights are offered by Olga Solomon's chapter, which draws on the interactions between autistic children in the U.S. and their therapy dogs to critically interrogate existing theories of human sociality. Arguing that these theories have placed too great an emphasis on the role of language, theory of mind, and the primacy of human–human interactions, she reveals how interactions with therapy dogs might allow children diagnosed as autistic to recognize their own capacities to enjoy sustained and fulfilling relations with others: the dogs themselves, but also humans they go on to encounter at home and at school. Solomon employs the concept of 'worlding' to analyse this encounter, foregrounding how diverse entities co-shape each other in ongoing, and open-ended, processes of becoming to co-constitute 'figured worlds', thereby changing their grasps of the dynamic matrices in which they are emplaced.

It would therefore not be inaccurate to describe the coming together of child and dog (and therapists, parents, etc.) in terms of an assemblage or association, nor to theorize the dog as a non-human actant. But equating this with a generic sociality – of the kind that could be found in any instance of relations in an assemblage – strikes us as an impoverished formulation. It tells us nothing about those factors that allow the encounter to have the consequences that it does: the dog's disposition – a result of intensive training of the specific therapy dog, as well as millennia of selective breeding within its species; and the child's capacities to imagine a way of being other than that which it has experienced previously, to act upon that visualization, and to remember and project that encounter into future encounters with others – something that remains significant long after the assemblage has been dismantled. To understand these requires a theory of (autistic) human sociality, and a theory of (therapy) dog sociality.

The fact that anthropology has not yet developed a successful theory of non-human sociality is no reason to shut down a theory of specifically human sociality. Indeed, we thoroughly endorse Kirksey and Helmreich's (2010: 553) suggestion that anthropology should start engaging seriously with the 'alterworlds' of non-human entities – not only as a means of investigating what might be distinctive about *anthropos* (on which see Moore, this volume) but also in order to develop the theories of non-human sociality – and the impulses, motivations and practices that underpin it (if any) – that a full understanding of a dynamic relational matrix necessarily requires. Susanne Küchler's chapter offers a productive way forwards by discussing how new innovations in materials science might be usefully incorporated into anthropology to just such an end. Contemporary materials are emerging that are self-organizing, psychomotric, and electively affinitive. In contrast to most actor-network (and other) theorists' fixation with 'the entity', she argues that developing rich theories of the agency of *materials* in their specificity will be crucial for enhancing theories of sociality: it allows us to have a more sensitive grasp of the material agencies through which humans might conduct their relations; but it also helps us understand exactly *how* material objects (she gives the example of smart phones and iPads) might themselves engender, manage, or even dissolve relations in both anticipated and unpredictable ways. These properties, an analogue of the human capacity for ethical imagination, allow us to theorize what might be called the sociality of materials – a point which highlights once again why the dynamic matrix in which human subjects exist should not be reduced to the tracing of relations and/or recognition of present-anchored agencies. Such operations are important building blocks for theories of sociality, not substitutes for them.

Research on non-human animals, objects, and materials is thus clearly a field that promises to contribute much to our understanding of sociality in years to come. Ingoldian and Latourian interventions have set the human subject in a new context. But none of that should detract from the fact that human subjects, whether uniquely or not, possess an ethical imagination and intersubjective capacity, set within a material and multispecies world, that is of paramount importance for understanding the forms of sociality in which we are engaged, and one that is part of our materiality as biologically social beings.

Why Sociality is Not Reducible to Affect

Let's return to Adam Chau's (2006) example of red-hot sociality in Shaanbei, China (see also his study of Taiwan, this volume) – the 'red and fiery' sense associated with crowdedness that his interlocutors flocked to watch and consume – and thereby produced. While this cannot be, for reasons explained earlier, the sum total of 'sociality', such phenomena raise an important challenge for our conceptualization of a dynamic relational matrix. For the members of the crowd have no 'relationships' with each other; they do not interact; they have never met – and yet they affect each other in ways that might easily be formative. Comparably, Jo Vergunst and Anna Vermehren (this volume) offer a fascinating case of a 'social art' project in the Scottish town of Huntly that sought to 'slow down' the town, challenging participants to participate in events such as coordinated cycling through the town at a very slow speed. Vergunst and

Vermehren note that this raises important questions about the cadence, rhythm, and pace of sociality, since moving slowly together fostered an atmosphere of 'sociability' that stood in sharp contrast with more typical British socialities of cycling. As they note, the coordination of the speed of movement is a way to achieve a feeling of 'togetherness', while disjunctures in speed can allow someone walking in a crowd to feel she is alone. This affective and sensorial dimension of human experience clearly has implications for our understanding of sociality. The question we are presented with is why this should be the case.

A recent body of work, sometimes styling itself as 'affect theory', has attempted to offer some answers that, it claims, have profound consequences for the conceptualization of sociality. The approach has much in common with Deleuzian and Latourian ontologies of relationality in a material world. Affect theorists emphasize that the (human) body is itself an assemblage of materials – cells, nerves, fluids – that are constantly in a state of becoming; 'more assemblage than form, more associated milieu than being' (Manning 2010: 118). This emphasis on fluidity finds support in some recent neuroscience, and cellular biology – suggesting that what is being theorized are bodies in their biological specificity, beneath or before the level at which cognitive processes relating to language, representation, or consciousness might occur (Clough 2008; Connolly 2002; Massumi 2002; Thrift 2006). Within such a field of enquiry, affect is conceptualized as a set of as 'pre-individual bodily forces augmenting or diminishing a body's capacity to act' (Clough 2008: 130), arising either from dynamic, kinetic qualities of feeling attached to 'vital processes of life' (Venn 2010: 137) and/or 'discharges' from other bodies and environments with which one is in contact (Navaro-Yashin 2009); it is a 'relational force or energy, radically interior to the relation and not an outside force' (Venn 2010: 153), and frequently seen as autonomous and outside of social meaning (Hemmings 2005; Moore, this volume).

The reason this has a bearing on the question of sociality is that some theorists have suggested that biological matter is not only affectively interactive within a body, but also across boundaries between organisms and entities. Patricia Clough (2010: 227) invites us to consider phenomena such as trauma in ways that go 'beyond the individual subject and human sociality to an event of time in matter'. For her, sociality is a matter of affective transmissions across bodies in a machinic assemblage with technology and technical arrangements (ibid.: 225). A similar proposition is advanced by Couze Venn in a paper that, starting from the image of a flock of birds, asserts that it is 'rough-and-ready' to explain the phenomenon in terms of such concepts as 'instinct', 'imitation', or 'genetic programming'. Instead, he insists, we need to develop 'models that would not only allow us to better understand the mechanisms at work, but also show the proximity of *all living beings* at this level of processes that involve non-conscious, visceral, propriocentric, affective processes connecting bodies' (Venn 2010: 130, emphasis ours). And he really does mean all living beings, for a few sentences later he draws a parallel between swarming starlings and human behaviours such as social trends, *Zeitgeists*, moral panics, and the 'melding into a single organism', via the embodied forces or potentials of affect, of bodies, objects and technics in a financial trading firm. He thus proposes, drawing on Simondon (2005: 31), that we need a theory of the individuated subject, relational, and constantly in a state of becoming, that provides 'the foundation of participation to a much larger individuation, that of the collective' (Venn 2010: 145).

Part of the excitement of affect theory is that it redresses the problems that seem to bedevil a purely deconstructivist approach, principally that it leaves a residue or excess that is not socially produced outside of theoretical view: the very fabric of our being (Hemmings 2005: 549). But while this is a welcome development, affect theory needs to engage more directly with scientific debate over the neurology and cellular biology research findings on which it draws.[4] Moreover, reducing human sociality to the excitement of biological matter or a 'flock-like' phenomenon of collective individuation strikes us as extremely problematic. In an important article, Clare Hemmings (ibid.) questions the autonomy of affect through a re-reading of Audre Lorde's (1980, 1984) writings on race and the body. When 'white' people react with disgust and fear in the presence of Lorde, who identifies as 'black', Hemmings argues we can see affect's structured precision within a broader social world of associations and meanings. Some bodies are over-associated with affect; not everyone can experience it as autonomous. More importantly still, the sociality of affect can be manipulated and transformed through the work of the ethical imagination (Moore 2011: 170–205). As Hemmings (2005: 564) argues, 'Lorde's critical judgement of the ongoing spiral of smaller cycles of shame in response to her body and to racism is of such intensity that she is able to remake the relationship between her body, affect and judgement to inflect the social world with other meanings ... Lorde reinvents her body as hers not theirs, a body connected to other bodies by shared judgements of the social.'

From these arguments it is clear that a renewed attention to affect might be valuably incorporated into a theory of sociality, but that it cannot serve as an adequate analytic substitute for a conception of sociality as a dynamic matrix of relations through which persons are constituted in interactive and mutually constitutive ways. This is not just because affect is subjectively mediated but also because, as Hemmings' example of Audre Lorde illustrates, projection, imaginations and anticipations of affectivities *drive* formulations and practices of sociality.

Vergunst and Vermehren's analysis of the artistic attempt to 'Slow Down' Huntly offers some striking insights into how we might build on such realizations and develop affectively engaged theories of human sociality that improve upon those offered by much contemporary 'affect theory'. Unlike 'the flock' or 'the swarm', moving together slowly in the cycle parade had to be learned, and it required both advance political negotiation with local businesses, and ongoing reminders to 'slow down' from the artist on the day of the parade. As with the forms of collectivity described by Lazar (this volume), the affectivities of slow movement required hard work. Human subjectivity – and human understandings of their subjective and intersubjective relations projected forwards and backwards in time and space – thus remains a highly relevant concern. People participated in the artwork in Huntly because they were intrigued by the prospect of experiencing novel affectivities. The artwork's mundane setting – the participants' home town – meant that their bodily experiences opened up new possibilities for the town, and the prospect that its sociality might be changed for the better in years to come. Sociality – its affectivity included – was thus both generated by and generative of participants' ethical imaginations. Moreover, as Vergunst and Vermehren argue by drawing on Schutz's notion of consociation, these outcomes were underpinned by the capacity of shared (bodily) experience to foster shared understanding, meaning, and intersubjective knowledge. While attention to affective experience enriches our understanding of human sociality, it would be quite wrong to suggest that affect is 'pre-social' or generic; its role has to be understood in relation to the distinctive imaginative, ethical, and representative capacities of human subjects (see also Moore, this volume).

The importance of imagination and anticipation in all of the cases we have reviewed underscores that there is a crucial component element of human sociality that is very poorly captured by theories that emphasize material co-presence alone. This is what Moore (this volume) terms the 'human capacity for virtuality, for endowing things of the imagination and the mind with meaning and significance'. Indeed, as we have seen, this capacity is always being deployed, via practices of ethical imagination, in human sociality. This is why it is so problematic to offer any bounded 'definition' of what comprises human sociality, why human sociality has so many forms, and also why it is always being taken in new directions. This is also why the notion of dynamic relationality will not suffice as an anthropological theory of sociality; it needs to be combined with an attention to those aspects of existence within a relational matrix that are distinctively human.

Given this, we remain optimistic about both the value of retaining a notion of 'sociality' and the importance of exploring transformations, innovations, experiments and stasis in human sociality through in-depth ethnographic research. The contributions to this volume point to the promise of such work, embedding their portraits and accounts of the forms of sociality they describe in the ways human beings apprehend a world that is dynamic in terms of its materiality, its technological facilities, its inequalities and political economy, its affectivity, the others one encounters within it, and in its discursive formulation of ethical goods. These are essays that call attention to the multiplicity of ways in which sociality can be negotiated and mediated, and in doing so open up productive new routes for studying it, both theoretically and methodologically. To reappropriate the words of Laurence Sterne, then, we are confident that the ways the authors have 'rendered into words' the experiences of social actors from around the world, not to mention any 'pact' that these accounts might establish with their readers, could not be anything but aiding to 'the progress of sociality' – within anthropology and beyond.

Notes

1. It also builds upon a large legacy of work in developmental psychology. See Burman (2008) for an excellent critical review.
2. A comparable critique is emerging from within ethology, a field which has conventionally equated sociality with 'group living'. Reflecting on the adequacy of this approach, Lacey and Sherman (2007: 244) note that 'one reason that it is difficult to provide a precise definition of sociality is that "solitary" and "social" are not discrete alternatives but, rather, endpoints along a continuum of spatial and social interactions among conspecifics'. It is only a short logical step from this observation to the suggestion that what might be most profitably studied is the entire navigation of that continuum over an organism's lifecourse.
3. See for example the emphasis on co-production, co-habitation and co-evolution in Haraway's (2003, 2007) notion of the companion species; Miettinen's (1999) 'activity theory'; Kohn's (2007) 'anthropology of life'; and the burgeoning field of 'multispecies ethnography' (Kirksey et al. 2011; Kirksey and Helmreich 2010).
4. For discussion on this point see Barnett (2008); Hemmings (2005); and Papoulias and Callard (2010).

References

Anderson, A. 2001. *The Powers of Distance: Cosmopolitanism and the Cultivation of Detachment*. Princeton: Princeton University Press.
Barnett, C. 2008. Political Affects in Public Space: Normative Blind-Spots in Non-Representational Ontologies. *Transactions of the Institute of British Geographers* 33: 186–200.
Bersani, L. 2010. *Is the Rectum a Grave? And Other Essays*. Chicago: University of Chicago Press.
Boltanski, L., and E. Chiapello. 2005. *The New Spirit of Capitalism*. London: Verso.
Bruun, M.H., G.S. Jakobsen, and S. Krøijer. 2011. Introduction: The Concern for Sociality – Practicing Equality and Hierarchy in Denmark. *Social Analysis* 55, no. 2: 1–19.
Burman, E. 2008. *Deconstructing Developmental Psychology. Second Edition*. London: Routledge.
Callon, M. (1986a). The Sociology of an Actor-Network: The Case of the Electric Vehicle. In *Mapping the Dynamics of Science and Technology: Sociology of Science in the Real World* (eds.) M. Callon, J. Law and A. Rip, 19–34. Basingstoke: Macmillan Press.
——— (1986b). Some Elements of a Sociology of Translation: Domestication of the Scallops and the Fishermen of St Brieuc Bay. In *Power, Action and Belief: A New Sociology of Knowledge?* (ed.) J. Law, 196–233. London: Routledge.
Candea, M. 2010. 'I Fell in Love with Carlos the Meerkat': Engagement and Detachment in Human–Animal Relations. *American Ethnologist* 37, no. 2: 241–258.
Chakrabarty, D. 2000. *Provincializing Europe: Postcolonial Thought and Historical Difference*. Princeton: Princeton University Press.

Chau, A.Y. 2006. *Miraculous Response: Doing Popular Religion in Contemporary China*. Stanford: Stanford University Press.

Choy, T., L. Faier, M.J. Hathaway, M. Inoue, S. Satsuka, and A. Tsing. 2009. A New Form of Collaboration in Cultural Anthropology: Matsutake Worlds. *American Ethnologist* 36, no. 2: 380–403.

Clough, P.T. 2008. The Affective Turn: Political Economy, Biomedia and Bodies. *Theory Culture and Society* 25, no. 1: 1–22.

——— 2010. Afterword: The Future of Affect Studies. *Body and Society* 16, no. 1: 222–230.

Connolly, W. 2002. *Neuropolitics*. Minneapolis: University of Minnesota Press.

Cook, J., J. Laidlaw, and J. Mair. 2009. What If There Is No Elephant? Towards a Conception of an Un-Sited Field. In *Multi-Sited Ethnography: Theory, Praxis and Locality in Contemporary Social Research* (ed.) M.-A. Falzon, 47–72. Aldershot: Ashgate.

Enfield, N.J., and S.C. Levinson (eds.) 2006. *Roots of Human Sociality: Culture, Cognition and Interaction*. Oxford: Berg.

Foucault, M. 1985. *The History of Sexuality, Vol 2. The Use of Pleasure*. New York: Pantheon.

——— 1997a. *Essential Works of Michel Foucault, Vol. 1: Ethics: Subjectivity and Truth*. New York: The New Press.

——— 1997b. Friendship as a Way of Life. In *Essential Works of Michel Foucault, Vol. 1: Ethics: Subjectivity and Truth* (ed.) P. Rabinow, 135–140. New York: The New Press.

Foucault, M., and D. Trombadori. 2000. Interview with Michel Foucault. In *Essential Works of Michel Foucault, Vol 3: Power* (ed.) P. Rabinow, 239–297. New York: The New Press.

Gammeltoft, T. 2007. Sonography and Sociality: Obstetrical Ultrasound Imaging in Urban Vietnam. *Medical Anthropology Quarterly* 21, no. 2: 133–153.

Gilbert, M. 1997. Concerning Sociality: The Plural Subject as Paradigm. In *The Mark of the Social: Discovery or Invention?* (ed.) J.D. Greenwood, 17–36. Lanham: Rowman and Littlefield.

Haraway, D. 2003. *A Companion Species Manifesto: Dogs, People, and Significant Other-Ness*. Chicago: Prickly Paradigm.

——— 2007. Cyborgs to Companion Species: Reconfiguring Kinship in Technoscience. In *The Animals Reader* (eds.) L. Kalot and A. Fitzgerald, 362–374. Oxford: Berg.

Haver, W. 1996. *The Body of This Death: Historicity and Sociality in the Time of Aids*. Stanford: Stanford University Press.

Hemmings, C. 2005. Invoking Affect: Cultural Theory and the Ontological Turn. *Cultural Studies* 19, no. 5: 548–567.

Hess, S.C. 2009. *Person and Place: Ideas, Ideals and the Practice of Sociality on Vanua Lava, Vanuatu*. New York: Berghahn.

Højlund, S. 2011. Home as a Model for Sociality in Danish Children's Homes: A Question of Authenticity. *Social Analysis* 55, no. 2: 106–120.

Ingold, T. 1997. Life Beyond the Edge of Nature? Or, the Mirage of Society. In *The Mark of the Social: Discovery or Invention?*, (ed.) J.D. Greenwood, 231–252. Lanham: Rowman and Littlefield.

Kirksey, E., C. Schuetze, N. Shapiro, S. Satsuka, N. Myers, C. Lowe, J. Metcalf, and M. Candea. 2011. Poaching at the Multispecies Salon. *Kroeber Anthropological Society Papers* 100, no. 1: 129–153.

Kirksey, S.E., and S. Helmreich. 2010. The Emergence of Multispecies Ethnography. *Cultural Anthropology* 25, no. 4: 545–576.

Kohn, E. 2007. How Dogs Dream: Amazonian Natures and the Politics of Transspecies Engagement. *American Ethnologist* 34, no. 1: 3–24.

Lacey, E.A., and P.W. Sherman. 2007. The Ecology of Sociality in Rodents. In *Rodent Societies: An Ecological and Evolutionary Perspective* (eds.) J.O. Wolff and P.W. Sherman, 243–254. Chicago: University of Chicago Press.

Latour, B. 2002. Gabriel Tarde and the End of the Social. In *The Social in Question: New Bearings in History and the Social Sciences*, (ed.) P. Joyce, 117–132. London: Routledge.

——— 2007. *Reassembling the Social: An Introduction to Actor-Network Theory*. Oxford: Oxford University Press.

——— 2010. A Plea for Earthly Sciences. In *New Social Connections: Sociology's Subjects and Objects* (eds.) J. Burnett, S. Jeffers and G. Thomas, 72–84. New York: Palgrave Macmillan.

Lorde, A. 1980. *The Cancer Journals*. San Francisco: Aunt Lute Books.

——— 1984. *Sister Outsider: Essays and Speeches by Audre Lorde*. Freedom, CA: Crossing Press.

Manning, E. 2010. Always More Than One: The Collectivity of *a Life*. *Body and Society* 16, no. 1: 117–127.

Massumi, B. 2002. *Parables for the Virtual: Movement, Affect and Sensation*. Durham: Duke University Press.

Mazis, G.A. 2008. *Humans, Animals, Machines: Blurring Boundaries*. Albany: SUNY Press.

McLean, C., and J. Hassard. 2004. Symmetrical Absence/Symmetrical Absurdity: Critical Notes on the Production of Actor-Network Accounts. *Journal of Management Studies* 41, no. 3: 493–519.

Miettinen, R. 1999. The Riddle of Things: Activity Theory and Actor–Network Theory as Approaches to Studying Innovations. *Mind, Culture, and Activity* 6, no. 3: 170–195.

Monaghan, J. 1995. *The Covenants with Earth and Rain: Exchange, Sacrifice, and Revelation in Mixtec Sociality*. Norman: University of Oklahoma Press.

Moore, H.L. 2011. *Still Life: Hopes, Desires and Satisfactions*. Cambridge: Polity Press.

Mullan, J. 2002. Laurence Sterne and the 'Sociality' of the Novel. In *Laurence Sterne*, (ed.) M. Walsh, 33–45. London: Longman.

Navaro-Yashin, Y. 2009. Affective Spaces, Melancholic Objects: Ruination and the Production of Anthropological Knowledge. *Journal of the Royal Anthropological Institute* 15, no. 1: 1–18.

Ochs, E., and O. Solomon. 2010. Autistic Sociality. *Ethos* 38, no. 1: 69–92.

Olwig, K.F. 2011. Children's Sociality: The Civilizing Project in the Danish Kindergarten. *Social Analysis* 55, no. 2: 121–141.

Papoulias, C., and F. Callard. 2010. Biology's Gift: Interrogating the Turn to Affect. *Body and Society* 16, no. 1: 29–56.

Rabinow, P. 1996. *Essays on the Anthropology of Reason*. Princeton: Princeton University Press.

Schick, F. 1984. *Having Reasons: An Essay on Rationality and Sociality*. Princeton: Princeton University Press.

Simmel, G. 1971. The Problem of Sociology. In *Georg Simmel on Individuality and Social Forms*, (ed.) D. Levine, 23–35. Chicago: University of Chicago Press.

Simondon, G. 2005. *L'individuation à la lumière des notions de forme et d'information*. Grenoble: Millon.

Sterne, L. 1768. *A Sentimental Journey through France and Italy, by Mr. Yorick, Volume 1*. London: J. Creswick and Co.

Strathern, M., J. Peel, C. Toren, J. Spencer, and T. Ingold. 1990. *The Concept of Society Is Theoretically Obsolete.* Manchester: GDAT.

Sunder Rajan, K. 2008. Biocapital as an Emergent Form of Life: Speculations on the Figure of the Experimental Subject. In *Biosocialities, Genetics and the Social Sciences* (eds.) S. Gibbon and C. Novas, 157–187. London: Routledge.

Tarde, G. 1893. *Monadalogie et Sociologie.* Chicoutimi: Bibliothèque Paul-Émile-Boulet de l'Université de Québec à Chicoutimi.

Thrift, N. 2006. Space, Place and Time. In *The Oxford Handbook of Contextual Political Analysis* (eds.) R.E. Goodin and C. Tilly, 547–563. Oxford: Oxford University Press.

Toren, C. 2012. Anthropology and Psychology. In *The Sage Handbook of Social Anthropology* (ed.) R. Fardon, 42–78. New York: SAGE.

Tuhkanen, M. 2005. Foucault's Queer Virtualities. *rhizomes* 11. <http://www.rhizomes.net/issue11/tuhkanen.html>.

Tuomela, R. 2007. *The Philosophy of Sociality: The Shared Point of View.* Oxford: Oxford University Press.

Venn, C. 2010. Individuation, Relationality, Affect: Rethinking the Human in Relation to the Living. *Body and Society* 16, no. 1: 129–161.

Weiner, J. 1988. *The Heart of the Pearl Shell: The Mythological Dimensions of Foi Sociality.* Berkeley: University of California Press.

Westoby, P. 2009. *The Sociality of Refugee Healing: In Dialogue with Southern Sudanese Refugees Resettling in Australia.* Seaholme (Melbourne): Common Ground.

1

Avatars and Robots
The Imaginary Present and the Socialities of the Inorganic

Henrietta L. Moore, University of Cambridge

From time to time, particular ideas take hold in the academy and we feel closer to fully comprehending the world we live in and share with others. These ideas are most often a combination of periodizations with their attendant forms of progression, underpinned by organizing concepts which form the basis for models and guide critical thought by acting as quasi-organizing principles for certain pre-theoretical assumptions (Moore 2004). Where once we spoke of dialectics and structures of society and mind, we have now largely eschewed the world of scaffolded representations to embrace the digital, bio-informatic age where all talk is of potentialities, emergent properties, forms of becoming and modes of attachment and affect (e.g., Braidotti 2006; Thrift 2008; Bennett 2010; Connolly 2011). In this important and beguiling moment, questions of immense interest are thrown out as challenges: is agency restricted to humans; can we speak of cellular subjectivities; is social change the product of vital forces largely outside of human control (e.g., Deleuze and Guattari 1987; Massumi 2002; Latour 2004, 2005; Coole and Frost 2010)?

Two developments seem particularly salient. The first is the way that changing technologies enable new forms of data which are then turned into meaningful information through the application of new metaphors. These metaphors, in their turn, change the character of our objects of enquiry, our approaches to them, and the way we think about them. Once we assign scallops agency (Callon 1986) and claim to be able to hear yeast cells scream (Roosth 2009), it is inevitable that we see new connections, ask alternative questions. However, metaphors do not necessarily characterize the way the world is, but rather how we choose to talk about it. In the eighteenth century we fantasized about men as machines, and in the twenty-first we take a different tack and speak of assorted connections between humans and non-humans with novel propensities. Methodological and theoretical approaches redefine our objects of enquiry. One element in recent developments that illustrates this point well is how the boundaries between the human and the non-human are being breached – some would argue erased – through the extension of agency to non-human animals and to inanimate objects. In anthropology, the larger project of criticizing subject–object dualisms has perhaps been most salient in approaches to material things that argue against privileging language and representation, and seek instead to explore the intelligence of non-human 'actants' (e.g., Miller 2005; Henare et al. 2007). The dominant inspiration here is Latour, and Actor-Network Theory (ANT) more generally. The result is a series of interrogations about the category human, and its relation to, and difference from, the non-human:

> For the thing we are looking for is not a human thing, nor is it an inhuman thing. It offers, rather a continuous passage, a commerce, an interchange between what humans inscribe in it and what it prescribes to humans. It translates the one into the other. The thing is the nonhuman version of the people, it is the human version of things, twice displaced. What should it be called? Neither object nor subject. An instituted object, quasi-object, quasi-subject, a thing that possesses body and soul indissolubly. (Latour 1996: 23)

More broadly, however, such interrogations reconfigure the relation of humans to the natural world and to other living things, where embodiment involves a generative capacity as opposed to a finished form:

> Behaviour can no longer be localized in individuals conceived as preformed homunculi; but has to be treated epigenetically as a function of complex material systems which cut across individuals (assemblages) and which transverse phyletic lineages and organismic boundaries (rhizomes). This requires the articulation of a distributed conception of agency. The challenge is to show that nature consists of a field of multiplicities, assemblages of heterogeneous components (human, animal, viral, molecular etc) in which 'creative evolution' can be shown to involve blocks of becoming. (Ansell Pearson 1999: 171)

A focus on the agency of human and non-human actors in hybrid networks has in its turn stimulated ideas both about context and environment, and about interrelations and affects. Our worlds are full of encounters – moments of co-presence, affect and contagion – that involve many things that are non-human. The relational connection and movement between things conjoins with ideas about intensity and potentiality. The cornerstone in this approach is matter's capacity for self-organization: the potentiality of form that works through sets of intensities that come before, but are only realized in specific encounters between the human and the non-human, life and matter. As Massumi would have it: 'Affect is as good a general term as any for the interface between implicate and explicate order' (Massumi 2002: 37). The movement of affect is always indeterminate, vital, open to new possibilities, part of a series of potentialities that continually generate differences and divergences in what becomes actual. Affect as a term, and as an analytic concept, has diverse philosophical and disciplinary roots. But perhaps what is most significant about what has been called the 'affective turn' is that it wishes to inaugurate not just new theories, but new ontologies (Moore 2011: 170–205). At the present time, fields as apparently disparate as genetics, the biological sciences, astrophysics, neuroscience, narrative analysis, philosophy, media, informatics and cultural theory are all animated by the possibility of a common ontology that would link the social and the natural, the rational and the affective. The models and pre-theoretical commitments of this emerging ontology are grounded in ideas such as becoming, assemblage, relationality, autopoiesis, information and differentiation, its vitalism inhering in cellular capacities for replication.

The resultant impact is not just on our understanding of the category human, but also on the more fundamental issue of life itself. We have been used to thinking of the category human, and the notion of life, as foundational in the sense that they are conceived of as natural kinds. But, as the quest for new understandings of living things and life forms proceeds, we should recall that biology itself is not a natural kind and it has not always existed in its present form. As a 'grid of knowledge', it emerged in the eighteenth century (Foucault 1970: 139), and contemporary views of life are now overdetermined by the development of bio and information technologies that extract information and resources from bodies – human/non-human, organic/non-organic – and cast them into new frames. Life no longer has a single form or essence; it is not even necessarily the defining property of 'living' things (Helmreich 2011). Biological knowledge, biotechniques and biology 'itself' reshape each other. Life is changing as it gets remade, informatics have become constitutive of contemporary understandings of life and matter, and consequently the structure of our knowledge – its models, metaphors, frameworks – come more and more to resemble biological processes or 'life itself' (Moore 2011: 174). This has unhinged life from its self-evident manifestations, we are seduced by the realization that we do not know all the forms in which life might exist, and life has inexorably become something that can be abstracted from its forms (Helmreich 2011: 682–683). The result is that human capacities are no longer contained within the human, and life is no longer a feature only of organic things.

It is not surprising that how we think about the human is connected to how we think about life, but framings and classifications are always about politics. Politics, that is, in the sense of human purposes, and this is the second development that seems particularly salient. For example, when Donna Haraway (1991: 149–182) set out her cyborg manifesto, she envisioned a future when the cyborg's combination of the organic and the machinic would rupture the dichotomy between the human and the non-human, the natural and the artificial, and free the human subject from the imposed categories of biology, gender, and race. A developed version of that vision continues to underpin much recent work in feminist philosophy (e.g., Braidotti 2006; Colebrook 2010). Like Haraway, these theorists focus on an escape from the bounded individual body and/or subject, and on the opportunities provided by sets of new relations to transcend the human, and to build new kinds of networks and/or collectivities for enhanced agency and cooperation across lines of culture, language, race, and gender, as well as across the human, non-human, post-human, and inhuman. The ethical good in the vision of humanity operationalized here resides in the notion of radical relationality. Humans are envisaged as being at one with their world, but need to enter into relations with multiple others. In this project, the 'minoritarian', the 'other-than', women, gays, ethnic and racialized others, the natural, animal and environmental others – all that has been excluded from the rational, humanist subject – are the site or locale of political transformation (Braidotti 2010: 46–47). The transcendence of social categorizations and sedimented lines of power is one that is given particular imaginative force by the adherence to metaphors drawn directly and indirectly from biology: replication, cellular generativity, vitality, the limitless alterity of life as a form of becoming. This then is a theory of humanity at a particular moment in history, a theory taking form within a certain politics, where the social is reimagined for particular human purposes in the idiom of biological processes. William Connolly sums it up well, when he declares that neuropolitics is all about 'attachment to the earth and care for a protean diversity of being that is never actualized completely in any particular cultural setting' (2002: 197). Humanity, like life, is not a natural category, because our ontological categories are tied up with our representations, and regulatory ideals frame our descriptive and analytic languages (Moore 2011).

In a certain sense, and starting from a broad anthropology perspective, there is nothing new in any of this. The idea that humans are not the only things imbued with agency is a commonplace in many other cultures and philosophical systems where unstable connections between the human, the non-human and the inhuman can be equal sources of joy and concern. Anthropology has a large archive of communities of people whose ideas and beliefs extend the capacity for agency to non-human things and inhuman or post-human entities. In the 1940s, Maurice Leenhardt argued that the Canaque of New Caledonia regarded the person as being connected to other persons, both human and non-human, material and non-material (Leenhardt [1947] 1979), while Anne Strauss, for example, also suggested that for the Cheyenne the concept of the person extended beyond human beings to include other non-human persons (Strauss 1982: 124–125). Evidently, humanity has not always been synonymous with persons or agency, and humans are certainly not the only actants or agents shaping human/non-human relations. For example, in many contexts in Africa and Melanesia, artefacts are not just tools, but things that effect transformations through their agency. Constructions such as houses or the more famous Malanggan are regarded as extensions of bodies or persons, made up of parts of humans and animals, evidence (one might even say forms of mediated information) about the ways that bodies and things have affected each other in the world (e.g., Strathern 2001). In Latin America in recent years, new political actors have forced themselves onto the scene; these so-called earth-beings and/ or earth-practices embody and enact the respect and the affect between humans and non-humans, including animals, plants and landscapes, that maintain the possibility of a life-world. The 'things' (forces of nature, sentient mountains, etc.) that are now being made public in this form of politics are not simply non-humans, but sentient beings whose existence is threatened by the intersections between capital and the state, such as mining (de la Cadena 2010: 341–342). As de la Cadena makes clear, the public emergence of such earth-beings upsets the locus of politics (2010: 343), because having been excluded historically from nation-state institutions, defined, and thus confined, as little more than cultural beliefs, they are now becoming significant political agents within the emergence of a regional indigenous politics that both interacts with and makes claims upon the nation-state (Moore 2012). The decentring of the human subject and the notions of actant and affect in some ways hold no surprises, so why has contemporary anthropology turned to ANT, biology and informatics to re-theorize ideas about materiality, humanity, sociality and life, rather than to its own resources?

There are perhaps two reflections that might be relevant here. It's easy to comprehend that our accounts of what life or humanity are or could be are necessarily bound up with the stories we want or feel compelled to tell, but in the present moment those narratives have been both amplified and destabilized by the development of new bio and information technologies which provide new means of seeing and imagining, new ways of visualizing and recording the interiors of bodies and other spaces, and subsequently of categorizing and re-categorizing the information we uncover (Latour 2010). In this sense, new reproductive technologies, biology, evolutionary models, informatics have all been good to think with, they have enlarged our imaginations, provided new metaphors, reinvigorated our objects of study. This in itself is seductive, and most probably we find it particularly alluring because ideas about affect, oneness with the natural world, idioms of the shared planet, and the emancipatory pull of theories that privilege affective dispositions over rationalist thinking, are in tune with politics of the moment (Moore 2011: 170–205). The second reflection, however, concerns the appeal of moving definitely away from dominant models of language, signification and representation, where the postmodern transmogrifies into the post-human (Hemmings 2005; Leys 2011). The importance of human engagement with a world of non-humans, both organic and inorganic, cannot be overstated (see below), and key to these engagements is the body, as well as emotions and affects. Certainly, what is attractive about theories of affect is their attention to somatic experiences and forms of communication that are outside or below linguistic registers, their insistence on how bodies stay in touch with other bodies and attuned to the many 'others' who people the material worlds humans inhabit and share with others (Moore 2011: 180). But affect in the work of many writers is held to be prior to and external to all social meaning. Massumi defines it as both 'irreducibly bodily and autonomic'

(Massumi 2002: 28), and Barnett describes it as a form of practical attunement to a lived world that is autonomous of propositional intentionality (2008: 188–189). It is the autonomy of affect, its ceaseless escape, that is the guarantee of both its vitality and its changeability (Massumi 2002: 35). Social constructionism and the humanist subject now seem arrogant intellectual formulations/preoccupations, and suddenly we have a problem with anthropos being the centre of our world. The long history in anthropology of the critique of the subject–object distinction, and its immense archive of empirical data notwithstanding, we have slid away from the notion of 'others who are rational in context' since we no longer wish to make them or us the centre of explanation. While babies and bathwater come to mind, as has been cogently pointed out (Navaro-Yashin 2009), it seems impossible to resist the move away from social determinism towards the decentred freedom of affect, where the vitality of affect is confused with freedom itself (Moore 2011: 182).

What Can we Learn from Robots and Avatars?

I suggest that turning afresh to the notion of sociality is a productive way to consider what we might know about being human and being alive. One starting point for a renewed theory of sociality would be to ask ourselves what we have learnt about human sociality from the general gamut of theories of affect, co-presence, networks and assemblages. Is there something about a focus on anthropos that still requires a genuine anthropology? It may seem counterintuitive, but starting with robots and avatars is useful because it allows us to begin an enquiry without necessarily assuming a divide between the human and the non-human, the organic and the inorganic. Robotics is an especially provocative terrain because many of its practitioners believe that building robots tells us something both about how humans function, and also about what makes them distinctive. What is evident is that at the present time new personal relations are arising between humans and robots. New generations of robots, rather than being designed to replace humans – for example, by assembling cars or packing food in a factory – are being designed specifically to interact with humans, and to perform human tasks such as caring for children and the elderly, performing domestic tasks and providing companionship. Japan is the largest producer of robots in the world, and according to Jennifer Robertson there is already an established 'market for "intelligent," autonomous humanoid robots that can: operate power shovels and forklifts (Enryuu), patrol premises and extinguish fires (ReBorg-Q, Guardrobo D1), replace human service sector employees (Actroid, Asimo), babysit and tutor children (PaPeRo, Wakamaru), housesit (Nuvo), nurse the infirm and elderly (Ri-man), provide companionship and entertainment (ifbot, Pino, Posy, Robovie), and even provide sex (Kaori)' (Robertson 2007: 372–373; see also Sabanovic 2010). What is perhaps equally surprising is that robots and humans are co-developing in new ways. For example, Noby, short for 'nine-month-old baby', looks and feels like a human baby, with soft urethane skin and flexible joints. Developed by Yasuo Kuniyoshi and his team at Osaka University, Noby is powered by a powerful computer, and has 600 body sensors to feel touch, and cameras and microphones for vision and hearing. Research on child development enabled Noby's creation, but now researchers are using Noby to test theories of human development (e.g., Cowley and MacDorman 2006; Demiris and Meltzoff 2008).[2] We make the world as the world makes us.

Modern robots have to be designed to operate – not just function – in changing human societies. Key to this process is the question of embodiment. Both humans and robots are enabled and constrained by their particular morphologies. Physical constraints shape the dynamics of interactions between the embodied system and its environment; linked sensorimotor activity and body morphology (shapes of body and limbs, placement of sensors/organs) induces statistical regularities in sensory input and prioception. Biological systems respond to their environments and continuously improve their capabilities. There is a continuous and dynamic interplay of physical and information processes. Robotic engineers have taken inspiration from many biological systems – insects, lobsters, slime mould, salamanders, mice, dogs, monkeys, and human beings – in their quest to develop autonomous, self-organizing robots (Lindblom and Ziemke 2006; Pfeifer et al. 2007: 1088). One result is that many robots that need to operate in human environments and interact with humans have a human or anthropomorphic morphology. Yet humanoid resemblance is not quite enough (Lindblom and Ziemke 2006: 334). Real world contexts are uncertain and contingent, and while human embodiment actively promotes intelligent information processing for human purposes because sensorimotor coordination working alongside a specific body morphology shapes the resulting information structure, it does so in the context of the specific way in which human bodies and brains construct themselves into persons by attuning to patterns and norms in their social environment. Body and brain co-evolve.

Designing a robot that can do this is difficult for many reasons, but one is that social context or environment cannot be predefined, it emerges from interaction. This is why humans are so good at sensing – often without conscious thought – the feelings of others, or how to orient themselves in a particular context. Affect and emotion laid down through experience and interaction can precede conscious thought, as Damasio suggests (1994, 1999). Yet humans do more than simply react to social environments; they have biologically evolved capacities for linking affect to higher order cognitive states, and they can change and reflect on their cognitive states, as well as use others as cognitive resources to develop their capacities. One of the major challenges for social robotics is how to design a control architecture that can adapt in order to benefit from other agents' knowledge. Human babies develop these capacities long before they can talk. Touch, affect, and the carer's use of cultural values or norms prompts the infant to orient to what they value. Language use shapes adult interactions and so infants are immersed in a world of language before they can speak. The intersubjective nature of human sociality is built up through these processes; affect, emotion and touch play key roles where adults and others prompt infants to develop sensorimotor patterns and neurologically and biologically based routines that scaffold on intersubjective interaction, and they do so by drawing on cultural values and norms (Cowley et al. 2004; Cowley and MacDorman 2006; Cowley 2007). Human babies use affect to orient themselves to caregivers who respond by using verbal, vocal, tactile and expressive means. Certain patterns of behaviour become associated with affect and with visual and vocal stimuli that the baby later recognizes as symbols that are consistent, and around which the child can begin to organize actions and interactions with others. Human socialization is based on affective, neurological and biological development, but in ways that allow humans to augment their bodily and cognitive capacities. Biology becomes enmeshed with social life.[3] Human cognition and intelligence are not just embodied, but become embodied within a biologically cultural body (Enfield and Levison 2006). This formulation takes us well beyond theories of affect, and indeed phenomenology, as they are usually deployed in the humanities and social sciences.

What robotics demonstrates – perhaps unsurprisingly – is that human sociality as an emergent property of the interaction of biologically cultural bodies is foundational to social life and cognition. Humans are acutely aware of social and cultural norms, they identify with their conspecifics more deeply than other non-human primates do. The human child has a biologically inherited capacity for living culturally. One crucial difference between human infants and other non-human animals is 'the capacity to 'tune in' to others and to get others to tune into them (Lindblom and Ziemke 2006: 336). These capacities – part empathy and part discernment of motivation and intention – are developed intersubjectively, and are then gradually elaborated and ultimately form the basis for further coordination and communication. According to Tomasello (1999) only humans are able to understand other persons as intentional agents like themselves, and to use intentionality as a means of augmenting the capacity for changing both their cognitive states and the world. Key to this is that humans strategize, but also that they develop and share with others ways of paying attention to the world, and learn how to do this partly by interactive imitation, and the result is a unique human ability to identify with others and their objectives and desires.

If the ability to orient action to another's mental state is, as many now suggest, the defining feature of human sociality and cognition then clearly affect theories founded on cellular reproduction and/or swarms in nature are too thin to serve as adequate models for human sociality, and by extension human agency. This would apply also to those theoretical formulations that simply define sociality as a by-product or outcome of co-presence or interaction because to be powerful those theories would need to explain how and why affect links to intention and agency. ANT, with its emphasis on distributed forms of agency and actants (human and non-human) in assemblages returns us forcibly and profitably to a focus on the material world and to larger concerns with context and environment. When allied to general theories of affect, these ideas are persuasive because of their focus on emotion, embodiment, vitality and the movement of affect, but where their purchase is fragile is in understanding how and why human sociality – underpinned as it necessarily must be by affect – is nonetheless distinctive. There is a certain irony in the fact that it is those who make robots who should have most persuasively and powerfully found a means to understand how higher order cognition and values are linked to biological systems, neurological structures and affect in ways that are humanly distinctive.

One of the important aspects of this argument is to understand that affect is not autonomous in the way that Massumi (2002) and other theorists suggest. Cellular replication, vitality, life itself are processes that are constitutive of the human and non-human worlds, but biological systems are constituted as much through structures and hierarchies as they are through ceaseless vitality, and this is because they are emergent systems that develop in specific environments. Ants are well organized and live in large colonies, but it would be a mistake to imagine that their actions within their pheronomically constructed universe can best be explained by appeal to autonomous forms of affect. In much of the literature on affect, as explained earlier, its so-called autonomous character is held to be a consequence of the fact that emotion and affective processes occur independently of intention and meaning. Affect and cognition are held to be separate realms, with affect connecting to or operating, in the view of many, processes that are prior to language. However, work on animals demonstrates that affect and cognition are not separate realms. In humans, what binds them together is first that within a social world or environment affect is developmentally connected to language, norms and values from the earliest interactions of neonates and carers, and second that learning and the struggle for representation is productive of affect (Leys 2011: 122). Affect can potentially attach all over the place within a particular environment, but within human environments it does not do so randomly (Hemmings 2005; Navaro-Yashin 2009). Humans assign meaning to values, spaces, actions, gestures, objects, etc., and human environments are touched and formed through specific forms of human agency which can be recalled, reflected on and reinterpreted (Venn 2010). This does not mean that all affect is under human control, far from it, but it does mean that human patterns of intersubjective interaction assign values and meaning iteratively to patterns of affective response within particular environments, and so while affect may surprise, it equally often serves to drive and satisfy social norms, meanings and desires (Hemmings 2005: 559–562). Affect and its 'structured precision' (Hemmings 2005: 562) are part of what makes a human body biologically cultural.

In short, symbol recognition and manipulation emerge out of the child's history of coordinating and interacting with others; they are intersubjectively produced. In this process caregivers get babies to attend to particular aspects of the environment, and action-guided representations affect the developing brain. Certain patterns of behaviour are prompted and learned, then become salient and are saturated with affect. Over time, children learn to reflect on words and objects and stabilize their value, and this leads finally to speech-mediated communication and then context-free conversation (MacDorman 2007). Cowley (2007) argues that by four months, babies begin to use cultural capacities in response to caregiver wants (e.g., shut up!). Body–world interaction and sensorimotor coordination thus develop alongside social skills. The growing use of action regulated by social convention extends action-guided symbols. The infant observes – and begins to mimic – the fact that adults use gestures, voice, words and gaze to stand in for action, for things in the world, and for the intentions and motivations of others: as for example, when an adult shakes their head at a child to prevent them from performing a certain action. Gradually the infant learns to use action and symbols to get others to do things, and to get them to respond in particular ways. Consequently, infants develop styles of autonomy and agency that depend on value-guided actions accompanied by affect. The developing brain and neural systems of the infant become sensitized to arbitrary forms of signalling which incorporate cultural norms and expectations. Extraordinarily, human babies are able to exploit cultural signals and values even before they are capable of acting in self-directing ways (Cowley 2007). Infants at this stage do not understand language, leave alone cultural values or propositions, in the way that adults can, but are aligning themselves through mimetic action and affect to caregiver responses and demands. The result of this process of biological development through learning is an increasingly integrated neural system, body and brain that are closely attuned both to affect and to culture. Symbol systems as they are slowly acquired both stand in for aspects of the world, and also allow for recategorization of the environment and other people's motivations and responses.

Cognition and affect are bound together, and while sensorimotor skills and patterned perceptions allow humans to automate many tasks and responses so that they do not necessarily have to be thought about consciously, enabling us to act before we think, it is also the case that higher order cognitive tasks are scaffolded upon lower order ones. One of the things that is distinctive about human sociality is the way that humans use representation and signification to coordinate conscious and unconscious knowledge, higher order cognition and affect. Both verbal thought and meaning become increasingly systematic, generative and internally coherent over developmental time, and this is quite likely a consequence of biologically cultural brains aligning us to symbol systems and cultural norms as part of the process of becoming a human person (MacDorman 2007: 145). It is also likely that our ability to use such things as symbols, metaphor, allegory is a consequence of the way conscious and unconscious thought interpenetrate and combine. Much depends – even in academic life – on that fleeting sense of a connection, something half glimpsed, 'a sense sublime of something far more deeply interfused.'[4] The presumption that we are biologically – that is developmentally – cultural in no way vitiates cultural difference or distinctiveness, in fact it makes it essential to the process of becoming. Humans are world-oriented in a distinctive way, but symbol systems or cultural norms do not make persons in the way that cultural analysis has so often assumed – via some unspecified process of social or cultural determination – rather such systems and norms emerge out of a biologically cultural engagement with an environment.

If this is so, and if this is something that we have in part learnt from robotics, what is it that we might learn from avatars? One of the unique features of human sociality and cognition is its virtual character. It's not just that we learn to recognize that symbols stand for things in the world, but that we can also refer to those things when they are not there and bring them to mind. The character of our visual engagement with the world means that once we have an object in front of us, we can envisage doing a number of different things with it, actively visualize what might be the outcome of our actions, and decide not to pursue some or all of them. It is the symbolic nature of our engagement with the world that means that we do not just receive communications or other forms of stimuli, but we extract the intended meaning or significance through interpretation. Certainly, often when we do this we employ patterned behavioural responses, autonomic and affective responses to guide us and orient us, but we also have the capacity to use culture to amplify our capacities. For example, the oracle at Delphi exerted considerable influence throughout the Greek world, and no major decision was taken without consulting her. Yet after falling into a trance she is said to have uttered words incomprehensible to mere mortals, and even after the priests of the sanctuary had interpreted them they were always open to further interpretation, often containing dual and opposing meanings. Much effort was expended on the vagaries of the Gods, demonstrating, if nothing else, the human capacity for finding meaning in the world, as well as the all too human desire for attachment to the world through rendering it sensible to meaning. We make ourselves in social environments and within worlds of objects, and yet we dream of things we can only dimly discern, worry about things as abstract as fate, expend energy on the intentions of beings that do not exist and try to discern the meanings of fleeting utterances. The relationship of belief, intention and symbol to the world are also subject to theorization and problematization by individuals and communities. Cultural and historical variation in such things as theories of transcendence, divinity, and representation can and do have a profound effect on modes of perception, action and critical reflection: for example, Modernism's revolutionary assertion that imaginative representation was superior to merely imitative or mimetic art. It is said that when Picasso painted his portrait of Gertrude Stein, and he finally managed, after eighty or so failed sittings, to render her features through the planed features of an African ceremonial mask, he was asked whether it really looked like her, and he responded that in time, it would. He was right, in the sense that modern art did indeed make people see things differently, and not all forms of representation are merely mimetic or formal. The anthropological record is replete with examples.

Any view of human sociality has to take account of these capacities, not just their peculiar propensity for forward and backward projection in space and time (memory, regret, aspiration, hope) – thus extending any notion of 'environment' or 'cultural ecology' well beyond the presentism of many theoretical formulations of affect or assemblages of actants – but also crucially their ability to imaginatively ascribe attributes and qualities, and subsequently to form attachments, to things of the imagination. These may be Gods or myths, or more prosaic things such as communities, nations and other social imaginaries. This means that in the realm of human agency, there remains a question about what exactly constitutes an object, and indeed about the relation that objects have to acting, perceiving, affective, willed subjects. Avatars are instructive here because they are objects that we endow with meaning and value. Avatars come in many shapes and forms, and users have the ability to manipulate the appearance, attributes and characteristics of their avatars. In much of the literature on avatars the dominant discussion is about identity and identities. A lingering question remains about how avatars relate to the selves of their creators.[5] Some create their avatar in their own image, others engage in whimsical, bizarre and even outlandish constructions. For some individuals, the avatar is an idealized projection of self, while for others it is a way of experimenting with new identities. Some online users celebrate the fact that avatars allow their creators freedom from the constraints of biological, social and cultural determinants, such as disability, ethnicity, race and gender, while many analysts tend to demur, pointing out that avatar identities often reproduce and reinforce conventional and highly problematic ideas about social and cultural distinctions, such as race and gender (e.g., Nakamura 2002). Regulators in their turn worry about impostors, scammers and those intent on doing harm by misleading others. Sometimes, this results in a kind of moral panic, where commentators see paedophiles behind every virtual bush. Virtual worlds are often portrayed in the media as dangerous, addictive and escapist, a form of social pathology.

What do people do in virtual worlds? The short answer is that they drive cars, go shopping, take the dog for a walk, fall in love, have sex, fly, raise sheep, vanquish opponents, swim, go to gay bars, earn money – real money – dance, discuss and take university courses. Cybersociality is not insignificant; people create worlds and in the process create themselves. In February 2011, Farmville had 62 million active users, and 10 per cent of all Facebook users play the game.[6] World of Warcraft has 11.4 million subscribers, and Second Life 1.5 million. Some individuals already spend twenty-five hours a week in these virtual environments, roughly equivalent to a day per week. In the future, if you live to be seventy years old, you might have spent nearly ten years of your life in a virtual environment. Virtual reality is now part of life, and interestingly new research on university students shows that anonymity is not something they seek through online engagement: their current perception is that there is continuity between online and offline worlds, and that you will be held to account for what you do online just as much as you will be in the offline world.[7] Tom Boellstorff, who conducted ethnographic research in Second Life, regularly appears as himself in discussion fora in that world, and he is not alone, as many universities and companies move their activities online (Boellstorff 2008). Avatars are now much more likely in these contexts to be representations – even if augmented – of actual named individuals who are living a segment of their lives online. This blurring of the informatic and the biological, the virtual and the actual creates new contexts for human sociality, new kinds of social actors, new narratives for relations between self and world, and new languages in which to discuss such matters.

However, reframing the question of the relation between self and avatar requires further reflection. Recent research on violence in virtual worlds demonstrates that those whose avatars are stalked, killed, raped, assaulted and/ or tortured experience great distress. Being affected by online harm is most certainly a consequence of emotional engagement with the online world and the avatar (Wolfendale 2007). What is clear is that individuals form attachments to their avatars. In one particularly complex set of relations, a male individual created both a male and a female avatar who then fell in love with each other inside the virtual world. Media commentators poke fun at such situations, and indeed at those who get married in Second Life and divorced in Texas as a result of virtual infidelity. However, the partners involved do not always take these betrayals as virtual, or rather if they do, it is because betrayal always has a virtual character even in the actual world. Upright soccer mums who work as pole dancers in Second Life and Harvard-trained economists who pretend to be elves all raise questions about whether the online avatar is an aspect of self, a form of role playing, or an object like a doll or a puppet to be manipulated at the controller's whim. Individuals have many motivations for becoming involved in virtual worlds, and those motivations are becoming more complex and differentiated as more and more aspects of life move online or rather can be performed both online and offline. Many people now make a living in a virtual environment, and, of course, the vast majority of those do not actually inhabit a so-called virtual world.

Humans have historically always used objects and technology to extend their reach and to augment their cognitive and affective capacities. But what avatars reveal is that humans in their interactions with objects animate them, project through their interactions with them aspects and attributes of anthropos, seek out aspects of intentionality. Researchers working on humanoid robots report that provided the robots can perform tasks that mimic humans, individuals treat them as if they were sentient beings like themselves, even apologizing for standing too close to them (Shaw-Garlock 2009: 254). What is curious about avatars however is that they are involved in social interactions with other avatars in a symbolically rich world, and, as many participants report, actual world sociality does not completely explain virtual world sociality. This is because the sociality of the virtual world develops in its own terms, within its own cultural ecology, with avatars interacting with other avatars, and the results are unpredictable; they emerge from interaction in context. Many participants report instances of what has become known as the Proteus effect, where the actions or characteristics of the avatar produce changes in the creator/controller (Yee and Bailenson 2007). These may involve changes in self-esteem or in attitudes, but often involve a perception that the avatar is an independent agent or that rather than being the representation of a human self, the avatar is the locus of agency and the human the embodied referent of the avatar. Just as in the past, the puppets were said to control the puppeteers, and inanimate figures (Pinocchio, for example) were thought to come alive and revenge themselves on their makers. Sherry Turkle has discussed the ways humans use objects – many of them technologies – to develop and enhance a sense of self, to evoke affect, to find ways of engaging with the world, and to enhance cognitive functions (Turkle 2007). Such objects become closely intertwined with the self. Avatars exist on the boundary between the self and the object world, they implicate the forms of engagement and attachment that characterize human sociality, they draw on the pleasure of imaginative power for rethinking the world and our relations with others. The very fact that they are a virtual creation of our embodied engagement with objects and with the world – as we type them into existence on the computer – makes them imaginatively powerful for us. Virtual engagement is still a sensory experience (sights, sounds, touch), and our avatars as products of our imaginations are developmental objects: they develop over time as they acquire new appearances, powers, objects and experiences. They become the in-world embodiment of our in-world experience, and as such they generate affect and attachment.

Conclusion

Following Latour, we can agree that avatars are neither object nor subject, but if indeed they are things that possess 'body and soul indissolubly', it is because we animate them with these properties. Much of human sociality is and always has been virtual. Human life may be no longer confined to the organic, as people begin to live their lives – or part of them – in virtual worlds. However, people's ability to use digital representations of themselves depends on the much older human capacity for virtuality, for endowing things of the imagination and the mind with meaning and significance. What makes avatars distinctive arguably is that they create their own forms of sociality within online worlds in ways that are not completely under the control of their creators. However, as I have argued in this paper, while human sociality is underpinned by affect, it is nonetheless distinctive, and it is humans, not avatars, who hold views about social relations, values, and ideas, things that have to be brought into being through acts of the imagination. The avatar is a kind of extended metaphor, an allegory of the relation between images of the human body and actual human bodies, between the self and its relation to the world. What avatars demonstrate are many things of which we are already well aware: there is no fixed subject/object divide; humans form attachments to objects; objects, non-humans, and the inhuman are actants in the world. However, agency is not the same thing as sociality. I happily reserve judgement on slime mould, but certainly ants and the non-human primates – among many other organic things – have forms of agency and sociality. However, they do not have human sociality. The biologically evolved capacity for linking affect to higher order cognitive states ensures that in humans affect is not prior to and external to social meaning. Human representation and symbol-making are productive of affect, which is then imbued with value and meaning, as avatars themselves so amply demonstrate. The ceaseless vitality of cellular reproduction, the vitalism of the living world, may be seductive metaphors for our relations with the many non-human others with whom we share our world as we face the challenges of environmental and financial policies gone horribly awry. But we should not imagine that models and metaphors of biological processes profitably capture the character of human sociality, whose defining characteristic is that it depends on things that are not of this world.

Notes

1. John Donne, Meditation XVII.
2. <http://www.physorg.com/news195797609.html> (accessed 12 February 2011).
3. Biological systems are hierarchically organized, and a number of researchers from different disciplines have pointed out how higher order cognitive capacities and cultural norms/values/symbols are involved in scaffolding and augmenting lower order systems. For example, Damasio 1999, where he sets out to link non-conscious neural signalling with the experience of selfhood and consciousness.
4. William Wordsworth, *Tintern Abbey*.
5. Schultze and Leahy (2009) have identified eight different types of avatar–self relationship.
6. <http://www.onlinemarketing-trends.com/2011/02/top-5-farmville-economics-statistics.html> (accessed 12 February 2012).
7. <http://knightgarage.stanford.edu/2011/05/back-to-the-future-the-convergence-of-the-online-and-real-worlds/> (accessed 12 February 2012).

References

Ansell Pearson, K. 1999. *Germinal Life: The Difference and Repetition of Deleuze*. London: Routledge.
Bennett, J. 2010. *Vibrant Matter: A Political Ecology of Things*. Durham: Duke University Press.
Boellstorff, T. 2008 *Coming of Age in Second Life*. Princeton: Princeton University Press.
Braidotti, R. 2006. *Transpositions*. Cambridge: Polity.

———2010. On Putting the Active Back Into Activism. *New Formations* 68: 42–57.

Callon, M. 1986. Some Elements of a Sociology of Translation: Domestication of the Scallops and the Fishermen of St Brieuc Bay. In *Power, Action and Belief: A New Sociology of Knowledge* (ed.) J. Law, 196–233. London: Routledge and Kegan Paul.

Colebrook, C. 2010. Queer Vitalism. *New Formations* 68: 77–92.

Coole, D. and S. Frost (eds.) 2010. *New Materialisms: Ontogeny, Agency and Politics.* Durham: Duke University Press.

Connolly, W. 2002. *Neuropolitics: Thinking, Culture, Speed.* Minneapolis: University of Minnesota Press.

———2011. *A World of Becoming.* Durham: Duke University Press.

Cowley, S. 2007. How Infants Deal With Symbol Grounding. *Interaction Studies* 8, no. 1: 81–104.

———, and K. MacDorman. 2006. What Baboons, Babies and Tetris Players Tell Us about Interaction: A Biosocial View of Norm-Based Social Learning. *Connection Science* 18, no. 4: 363–378.

———, S. Moodley and A. Fiori-Cowley. 2004. Grounding Signs of Culture: Primary Intersubjectivity in Social Semiosis. *Mind, Culture, Activity* 11: 109–132.

Damasio, A. 1994. *Descartes' Error: Emotion, Reason and the Human Brain.* New York: Putnam.

———1999. *The Feeling of What Happens: Body and Emotion in the Making of Consciousness.* London: Heinemann.

De la Cadena, M. 2010. Indigenous Cosmopolitics in the Andes: Conceptual Reflections Beyond "Politics". *Cultural Anthropology* 25: 334–370. doi: 10.1111/j. 1548-1360.2010.01061.x.

Deleuze, G. and F. Guattari. 1987 *A Thousand Plateaus: Capitalism and Schizophrenia* (trans. B. Massumi). Minneapolis: University of Minnesota Press.

Demiris, Y. and A Meltzoff. 2008. The Robot in the Crib: A Developmental Analysis of Imitation Skills in Infants and Robots. *Infant and Child Development* 17: 43–53.

Enfield, N. and S. Levison. 2006. *Roots of Human Sociality: Culture, Cognition and Interaction.* London: Berg.

Foucault, M. 1970. *The Order of Things: An Archaeology of the Human Sciences.* London: Tavistock.

Haraway, D. 1991. *Simians, Cyborgs, and Women: The Reinvention of Nature.* New York: Routledge.

Helmreich, S. 2011. What Was Life? Answers from Three Limit Biologies. *Critical Inquiry* 37, no. 4: 671–696.

Hemmings, C. 2005. Invoking Affect. *Cultural Studies* 19, no. 5: 548–567.

Henare, A., M. Holbraad and S. Wastell (eds.) 2007. *Thinking Through Things: Theorising Artefacts Ethnographically.* London: Routledge.

Latour, B. 1996. *Aramis: Or the Love of Technology.* Cambridge: Harvard University Press.

———2004. *Politics of Nature: How to Bring the Sciences into Democracy.* Cambridge: Harvard University Press.

———2005. *Reassembling the Social: An Introduction to Actor-Network-Theory.* Oxford: Oxford University Press.

———2010. *On the Modern Cult of the Factish Gods.* Durham: Duke University Press.

Leenhardt, M. [1947] 1979. *Do Kamo: Person and Myth in the Melanesian World.* Chicago: University of Chicago Press.

Leys, R. 2011. The Turn to Affect: A Critique. *Critical Inquiry* 37, no. 3: 434–472.

Lindlom, J., and T. Ziemke. 2006. The Social Body in Motion: Cognitive Development in Infants and Androids. *Connection Science* 18, no. 4: 333–346.

MacDorman, K. 2007. Life After the Symbol System Metaphor. *Interaction Studies* 8, no. 1: 143–158.

—— and H. Ishiguro. 2006. The Uncanny Advantage of Using Androids in Cognitive and Social Science Research. *Interaction Studies* 7, no. 3: 297–337.

Massumi, B. 2002 *Parables for the Virtual: Movement, Affect, Sensation*. Durham: Duke University Press.

Miller D. (ed.) 2005. *Materiality*. Durham: Duke University Press.

Moore, H. L. 2004. Global Anxieties: Concept-Metaphors and Pre-Theoretical Commitments in Anthropology. *Anthropological Theory* 4, no. 1: 71–88.

—— 2011. *Still Life: Hopes, Desires and Satisfactions*. Cambridge: Polity Press.

—— 2012. Fantasies of Cosmopolitanism. In (eds.) R. Braidotti, P. Hanafin, B. Blaagaard *Cosmopolitanism: An Interdisciplinary Exploration*. London: Routledge.

Nakamura, L. 2002 *Cybertypes: Race, Ethnicity and Identity on the Internet*. London: Routledge.

Navaro-Yashin, Y. 2009. Affective Spaces, Melancholic Objects: Ruination and the Production of Anthropological Knowledge. *Journal of the Royal Anthropological Institute* 15, no. 1: 1–18.

Pfeifer, R., M. Lungarella and F. Iida. 2007. Self-Organization, Embodiment, and Biologically Inspired Robotics. *Science* 318, no. 5853: 1088–1093.

Robertson, J. 2007. Robo Sapiens Japanicus: Humanoid Robots and the Posthuman Family. *Critical Asian Studies* 39, no. 3: 369–398.

Roosth, S. 2009. Screaming Yeast: Sonocytology, Cytoplasmic Milieus, and Cellular Subjectivities. *Critical Inquiry* 35, no. 2: 332–350.

Sabanovic, S. 2010. Robots in Society, Society in Robots. *International Journal of Social Robotics* 2: 439–450.

Schultze, U. and M. Leahy. 2009. The Avatar–Self Relationship: Enacting Presence in Second Life. *International Conference on Information Systems 2009 Proceedings*. Paper 12.

Shaw-Garlock, G. 2009. Looking Forward to Sociable Robots. *International Journal of Social Robotics*. vol. 1, no. 3: 249–260. doi: 10.1007/s12369-009-0021-7

Strathern, M. 2001. The Patent and the Malanggan. *Theory, Culture and Society* 18, no. 4: 1–26.

Strauss, A. 1982. The Structure of the Self in Northern Cheyenne Culture. In *Psychosocial Theories of the Self* (ed.) B. Lee, 111–128. New York: Plenum Press.

Thrift, N. 2008. *Non-Representational Theory: Space, Politics, Affect*. London: Routledge.

Tomasello, M. 1999. *The Cultural Origins of Human Cognition*. Harvard: Harvard University Press.

Turkle, S. (ed.) 2007. *Evocative Objects: Things We Think With*. Boston: MIT Press.

Venn, C. 2010. Individuation, Relationality, Affect: Rethinking the Human in Relation to the Living. *Body and Society* 16, no. 1: 129–161.

Wolfendale, J. 2007. My Avatar, My Self: Virtual Harm and Attachment. *Ethics and Information Technology* 9: 111–119.

Yee, N. and J. Bailenson. 2007. The Proteus Effect: The Effect of Transformed Self-Representation on Behavior. *Human Communication Research* 33: 271–290.

2

Imagining the World that Warrants Our Imagination
The Revelation of Ontogeny

Christina Toren, University of St Andrews

Intersubjectivity is that capacity for recursive thought that makes human learning a micro-historical process. What are its consequences for our scientific models of humankind? Primarily, it forces recognition of what Husserl called 'historicity' – the fact that there is no aspect of anyone's humanity that is not historically constituted, from our genes to the very neurological processes that provide for brain function, to all our ideas of the peopled world. Historicity entails that all aspects of human being, including all perceptual processes (and thus every aspect of the world we imagine), at once evince a person's history and function to structure what the world can be for him or her. Intersubjectivity is at once the context for and the fundamental condition of being human and as such its specific character always remains to be found out.

The term 'intersubjectivity' is shorthand for: I know you are human like me, so I know that you know that I know that you know that I am too.[1] Intersubjectivity is the form of human sociality (as distinct from the sociality of, say, honey bees) and it is always historically prior because, whenever we encounter one another, we do so as carriers of our own, always unique, collective-cum-personal histories.[2] I make sense of what you are doing and saying in terms of what I already know: any experience is assimilated to my existing structures of knowing. This goes for us all, newborn babies and geriatric patients included.

Thus any human ontogeny – developmental history from conception to death – is informed by relations with others who are likewise products of their own lived histories.[3] When this realization is brought to bear on the succession of generations in time, we can see how, by virtue of intersubjectivity, what we think of as a collective (for example, regional) history continually informs our unique histories as particular persons. In respect of ontogenies of ideas, imagining and, in so doing, making sense of the world is for any one of us a material, self-organizing, historically structured, intersubjective process that at once transforms new experience in the course of its assimilation (to this extent conserving what I know) and transforms my existing structures of knowing in the course of their accommodation to new experience (to this extent changing what I know). Ideas of sociality, personhood and the self are, of course, crucial to who we are and to what we mean by what we say – the stuff of intersubjectivity and thus of the imagination. I am referring here to the very constitution of lived reality as this manifests itself in people's ideas and practices. The idea may be related to Castoriadis' concept of the 'radical imaginary' as 'literally, the ontological source of all human reality ... the creative matrix by virtue of which there is any given human cultural life-world' (Mimica 2009).

This view of intersubjectivity as an historical process is consistent with that of Castoriadis when he observes that:

> This existence with others ... is social and historical existence and, to us, this is the essential dimension of the problem. In a way the intersubjective is the material out of which the social is made but this material exists only as a part and a moment of the social, which it composes but which it also presupposes. (Castoriadis 1987: 108)

What Castoriadis characterizes as 'the social historical' is, however, more than the sum of its parts:

> The social historical is the anonymous collective whole, the impersonal human element, that fills every given social formation but also engulfs it, setting each society in the midst of others, inscribing them all within a continuity in which those who are no longer, those who are elsewhere, and even those yet to be born are in a certain sense present. (Castoriadis 1987: 108)

For all my admiration for Castoriadis, this view seems to me to be the product of our inability as particular human beings, and perhaps especially as particular analysts of the human condition, to grasp the whole; we are condemned to abstractions because we can have direct access only to our own experience as we live it; even our own lived past escapes us.

Nevertheless, one might argue, with justice, that human historicity is obvious, taken for granted by philosophers and human scientists. What is taken for granted, however, is often poorly understood. With the exception of certain anthropologists, human scientists in general tend to assume not only that people's concepts are at base pretty much the same, but that findings from studies conducted among Western populations can be generalized with little difficulty to people elsewhere.[4] So, for all it may seem obvious that our ideas of the world are uniquely constituted by every one of us, there are virtually no ethnographic studies of ontogenies of ideas – no histories of conceptual development throughout the lifespan – that investigate how this process manifests itself *as such* and what its importance might be for our understanding of humankind.[5] A fundamental problem here is that the models that dominate the human sciences cannot, for good reason, come to grips with our collective-cum-personal historicity: to do so challenges their taken-for-granted premise that the unity of humankind is given by human biology and that what differentiates us is culture. This idea of 'one unifying nature and many differentiating cultures' blinds us to historicity – our own as well as others' – and to understanding its consequences for what it is to be human.[6]

Consider the following observations from a fascinating review article in 2010 in *Behavioural and Brain Sciences*:

> [B]road claims about human psychology and behavior based on samples drawn entirely from Western, Educated, Industrialized, Rich, and Democratic (WEIRD) societies ... assume that there is little variation across human populations.... [R]eview of the comparative database from across the behavioral sciences suggests ... substantial variability in experimental results across populations ... WEIRD subjects are particularly unusual compared with the rest of the species – frequent outliers. (Henrich et al. 2010: 61)

Of course, the anthropologist reader may be inclined to assert that we have known this for a good long while. Even in the absence of a careful review, what we know of the considerable corpus of a century or so of ethnography from across all regions of the world suggests the likelihood that populations vary significantly across manifold cognitive domains. What actuated Henrich et al.'s review, however, was their concern that experiments on undergraduate psychologists could not properly be generalized to everyone else in the world. As evolutionary psychologists, Henrich et al. are keen to establish what humans have in common and, to this end, similarly keen to explain diversity, but for all they are concerned with spatiotemporal phenomena, they do not seem able to see that we humans have ourselves to be described *as such* precisely because it is we who make spatiotemporality so salient in our accounts of ourselves.

Evolutionary history figures strongly as an explanatory possibility in Henrich et al.'s account. Given the axiomatic distinction here between culture and biology there is, however, no explicit recognition that our evolutionary history is continuous with our collective-cum-personal histories. Nor is there any apparent awareness that literally all aspects of human being, notably all our perceptions and cognitions, are a function of, and thus manifest, the transforming history of social relations in which they are embedded and to which they continue to give rise. Moreover, the results of all the many studies included in Henrich et al.'s review are, I would argue, sufficient to demonstrate that, within and across 'populations', what humans have in common cannot be isolated from what makes them different: human diversity is a function of what we have in common and what we have in common emerges out of our diversity – they are aspects of the selfsame process. This is no mere paradoxical form of words. It makes no sense to theorize what it is to be human as if the disciplinary domains of neurobiology, biology, psychology, sociology, anthropology map neatly on to self-evidently separable aspects of human being: intersubjective sociality is implicated in everything about me – from my genetic makeup to my nationality and my personal likes and dislikes.

Once we recognize that our entire being (of which our physical make-up is but one aspect) is the product of a long, long history of social relations, it becomes possible to realize that intersubjective sociality is the fundamental condition of human autopoiesis – self-creation, self-organization, self-regulation.[7] In other words, our particular genetic inheritance cannot be properly understood outside the history of social relations that gave rise to us as the particular children of our particular parents, and so on back through the generations. Biologically speaking, autopoiesis is what characterizes living things; it makes us different from, for example, a computer or a robot which, for all its apparently remarkable abilities, does not bring itself into being by virtue of differentiating its own substance. Moreover, in the case of humans, this process of differentiation may be charted in respect of both physical and psychological development and it is tremendously important for sociality as at once the outcome and the condition of what it is to be a particular human being with a particular history.

Why Sociality Cannot Be a Research Domain

It seems useful here to refer back to a piece of intellectual history. In the Manchester Anthropology debate of 1989, I seconded the argument for the proposition put by Marilyn Strathern that 'the concept of society is theoretically obsolete'. In his introduction to his edited collection of the debates, Tim Ingold described our position as follows:

> Their plea is for an alternative conceptual vocabulary, anchored on the concept of sociality, that would enable us to express the way in which particular persons both come into being through relationships and forge them anew, without relegating both personhood and relationship to a domain of reified abstraction – epitomized by the concept of society. (Ingold 1996: 8)

The term sociality is derived from the same root as the term society (*socius*, 'companion') and twenty years ago it seemed to be mercifully free of any *determined* conceptual tethering to 'society and the individual' or 'culture and biology' or 'mind and body' and, because it implied processes that remained to be found out, it made no claim to being an analytical category. Likewise, relationship and personhood were heuristic devices which – like politics, gender, economy, kinship and so on – had the virtue of indicating ways in to the comparative investigation of what it is to be human. Moreover, in any geographical region, history was bound to come to the fore because any given anthropologist came face to face with the problem of how to analyse transformation over time. Sociality, however, could not in itself be a domain of investigation because, as I pointed out above, sociality pervades literally every aspect of being human. Or to put it another way, sociality is not part of what we are, but rather the sum total of human being – its entirety.

Strathern's observations in the 1989 debate were in part intended to show that the problem with 'society' as an analytical category is that it carries in its train the idea of the person as 'an individual'. We were then (and remain) in a situation where we cannot use the terms society and individual analytically because we know that while they are certainly taken for granted by large numbers of people, their apparent self-evident validity is challenged by other ideas of personhood and sociality held by large numbers of other people. Strathern's (1992) work on gender and the person shows how social process can be laid bare and understood through the use of obviation as an analytical device. Many of the younger scholarly generation at the time (myself included) were also trying to find alternative means of analysis. My own idea is that we should make the concepts in whose terms people talk about themselves and their lives work analytically by showing how, exactly, they are constituted (maintained and transformed) over time – a method we could easily turn on ourselves in order to analyse, for example, such ideas as 'society', 'the individual', 'culture' and 'biology'. Part of the problem here, however, is that we lack good ethnographic studies of ontogenies of ideas and we need them; for all that we can learn from theorists like Castoriadis and Strathern, we still know next to nothing about how exactly specific ideas of the person and social relations are actually constituted by the people whose lives they are said to inform.

A brief aside here for the sake of clarity. Given the continuing dominance in the human sciences (including anthropology) of the individual–society distinction, it seems important to point out that persons who are considered *a priori* to be individuals have to be rendered social by society – hence the continuing acceptance of ideas of learning as socialization or, because individual and society map neatly onto biology and culture, acculturation. Those of us who talk of 'social relations' are, however, by and large *not* invoking an idea of social and/or cultural construction in which individuals interact to produce (or negotiate) shared meanings. Rather, the analysis of social relations focuses on the processes that produce persons and relationships and political formations as always historically specific, and this is intended as a comparative project because the processes themselves are what are compared.

The phrase 'the transforming history of social relations' is intended to take in all domains of ideas and practice. In the human sciences these domains are indicated by heuristic terms such as 'kinship', 'politics', 'economy', 'religion', 'education', 'language', 'physiology', 'psychology', 'medicine' and so on and so on. It is worth noting too, in passing, that the recognition that transformation and continuity are given in the idea of human autopoiesis as an historical process strongly suggests that ethnographic analysis should be central to the human sciences. That is to say, precisely because science too is the transforming artefact of a continuing history of social relations, its most fundamental taken-for-granted ideas and practices want ethnographic analysis – not in order to gainsay them with some kind of social constructionist critique, but rather to show how they are constituted over time, and in the selfsame process, transformed.

It follows that a social analysis may take sociality for granted as the fundamental condition of human being, but how sociality evinces itself in personhood and other structuring ideas and practices – kinship, political economy, ritual and so on and so on – remains, always, to be found out. Moreover, since Strathern's seminal work in *The Gender of the Gift* (1992), we have seen the production of ethnographies whose object is to capture social relationships as they are lived and, concomitantly, 'relations between relationships' (McCallum 2001 provides an instructive example).

Recent years, however, have seen a retrograde move towards rendering 'sociality' as an analytical category – that is to say, one whose presuppositions and defining characteristics can, at least potentially, be precisely delineated and, as such, used across disciplines to make valid generalizations about what it is to be human. Moreover, taking it for granted that sociality is unproblematically a function of 'society', this move resuscitates the society–individual distinction as an aspect of the human condition rather than an historically constituted idea. Just when we might have supposed that anthropologists were ready to take on board the implications of an awareness of human historicity, we find in 'sociality' a new domain of reified abstraction foisted upon us. We have sociality as instinct, or as based in a fundamentally innate theory of mind, or as the artefact of actor-networks necessitating certain ideas of agency. All these ideas ultimately rest on the distinction between society and individual in which sociality is an attribute or defining *aspect* or *characteristic* of being human that provides for a domain of investigation that is distinct from, for example, the domain of perception.

It is important for us as anthropologists, however, to realize that human sociality cannot properly be biologically characterized as instinctive or as domain-specific – that is, a function of a dedicated cognitive module (irrespective of whether this is taken to be innate or a product of development in the foetus and early infancy). Indeed what happens in early infancy and to the developing foetus in the womb suggests that sociality as we find it in neonates and young infants is pervasive, a function of what Robert Lickliter (2011) has described as 'intersensory redundancy'. Lickliter's ideas are highly suggestive, because they are not based in any axiomatic distinction between matter and information and thus provide for an understanding of human development as a micro-historical process from which we cannot, at any point, exclude sociality.

[I]t is known that the sensory systems are strongly linked in the fetus and the neonate, such that alterations in sensory stimulation presented to one sense can result in changes in responsiveness not only in that modality but also in other sensory systems as well. It is also known that detection of amodal stimulus properties, such as synchrony, intensity, tempo, and rhythm, is promoted by redundancy across sensory modalities and is involved in the emergence of normal patterns of perceptual organization. Young infants must learn to selectively attend to relevant information, screen out irrelevant information, and efficiently detect which patterns of sensory stimulation constitute unitary multimodal events (e.g., the face and voice of a person speaking) and which patterns are unrelated. These emerging skills are facilitated by intersensory processing and the detection of redundant amodal information, including temporal synchrony, rhythm, tempo, and intensity. (Lickliter 2011: 597)

Lickliter's 'dynamic systems' approach to foetal and early infant development is useful to us in that, as anthropologists, we have to think about how sociality, as the condition of being human, is historically constituted. So, for example, when we think about prenatal development, we have to think about it as a process that is itself historically shaped by virtue of the shaping of the mother's own ideas and practices as a function of her own history, likewise those among whom the mother lives her life. So the 'prenatal environment' referred to by Lickliter itself has everything to do with the specific social relations that are informing what the pregnant woman does or does not do:

> Although little research has directly focused on this issue, the human fetus likely experiences a great deal of integrated multimodal stimulation across the auditory, vestibular, and tactile senses in utero. For example, when the mother walks, the sounds of her footsteps can be coordinated with tactile feedback as the fetus experiences changing pressure corresponding with the temporal patterning and shifting intensity of her movements, as well as accompanying and coordinated vestibular changes. In addition, the mother's speech sounds, laughter, heart beat, or sounds of breathing may create tactile stimulation that shares the temporal patterning of the sounds as a result of changes in the musculature involved in producing the sounds. (Lickliter 2011: 593)

The micro-historical development of intersubjectivity from birth onwards is charted in a revealing microgenetic study of a particular mother and child (one of thirteen mother–infant dyads videotaped weekly during the children's first year of life and bi-weekly during their second) by Fogel and DeKoeyer-Laros (2007). As developmental psychologists they are not, of course, concerned to produce a social analysis. In the paper to which I refer, their focus is the development of '[s]econdary intersubjectivity [which] implies that the infant is aware of co-affectivity and co-agency with another person in relation to something else' (2007: 64). The anthropologist reader, however, is likely to notice that the mother's specific ideas about what a baby is and should be are informing how she treats her child and the constructions she puts on the child's behaviour.

> At 39 weeks, [the mother] writes, 'Grandma marveled at how much [Baby] had grown, changed (physically and emotionally) since we had been home [at Grandma's] the two weeks.' At 40 weeks, mother describes a new game, '[Baby] likes to play a game shaking her head "no" when Mommy says "yes." She responds with a big smile and starts the game all over again. The beginnings of defiance? It's cute anyway.' This description indicates that [the infant's] sense of secondary intersubjectivity has spread ... to become a stable and more pervasive feature of different types of frames with mother and with other people. [The infant] seems to understand that her mother has a

different intention (yes) from her own (no) and creates a teasing game around that. (Fogel and DeKoeyer-Laros 2007: 80).

It seems clear enough even from this brief example that, were we able to embed such findings in a full-scale ethnographic study of ontogeny – that is to say, a study that focuses on the ideas and practices that are structuring, for example, the constitution of personhood, gender and kinship over time in middle-class American families – we could render these same ideas analytically useful by showing how they come to be taken for granted as given in the nature of things and thus as valid, because they have a purchase on the world as lived. This kind of study requires that historicity be built into our model of what it is to be human.[8]

Elsewhere I have proposed a unified model of human being in which mind is a function of the whole person in intersubjective relations with others in the environing world (Toren 1999). Implicit is a view of consciousness as an aspect of human autopoiesis. Here consciousness cannot be a 'domain' or a 'level of psychological functioning', rather it is that aspect of mind that posits the existence of the thinker and the conceptual self-evidentiality of the world as lived by the thinker. The implications of this proposed unified model are radical and far-reaching. It suggests that we cannot, in the absence of a social analysis, understand the nature of human development, especially conceptual development. It proposes a means for finding out the structures of intersubjectivity that are informing the development of conceptual processes in any given case. It enables analysis of the processes through which we come to take as self-evident – given in the nature of things – ideas we ourselves have made. It develops a dynamic-systems approach to the anthropology of human development to show how it comes to be the case that what unites and differentiates us is a function of the history that we have lived. Finally, the details of ethnographic studies of ontogeny as an historical process feed directly into the argument that the development of the neural processes that characterize conceptual development is an emergent aspect of the functioning of an embodied nervous system for which intersubjectivity is a necessary condition.[9]

Historicity as an Object of Analysis

I want to insist that the anthropological project – broadly defined – is best served when we put aside those theories in philosophy and in the human sciences that rest on the distinction between matter and information, between biology and culture.[10] In this connection, the *habitus*, which remains foundational for many an anthropologist and sociologist, might be taken as a telling example of a theory that promised much and failed to deliver.

By virtue of deftly side-stepping the problematic posed by the mind–body distinction, the idea of *habitus* at first sight looks reasonable, even seductive, in large part because it was produced in order to answer the fundamental question of how humans come to be enchanted by ideas they themselves have made. The anthropologist's task is to 'inquire into the mode of production and functioning of the practical mastery which makes possible both an objectively enchanted practice and also an objectively enchanted experience of that practice' (Bourdieu 1977: 4). The question remains fundamental, but in order to appeal to the *habitus* for help with the answer, you have first to make the *habitus* work.

There is a major problem here in that, as theorized by Bourdieu and his followers, the *habitus* never manages to escape the problems raised by the behaviourist theory of socialization that informed it from *Outline of a Theory of Practice* (1977) onwards. Bourdieu's theory of how *habitus* is produced was derived originally from a behaviourist 'common element' theory of concept attainment (see Bourdieu 1977: 88). Even twenty-five years later, the behaviourist model continues to reassert itself; take, for example, this characteristically slippery passage from *Pascalian Meditations*:

> the self-evidence of the isolated, distinguished body is what prevents the fact being realised that this body which indisputably functions as a principle of individuation (in as much as it localizes in space and time, separates, isolates etc.), ratified and reinforced by the legal definition of the individual as an abstract interchangeable being, without qualities, is also – as a real agent, that is to say, as a *habitus* with its history, its incorporated properties – a principle of 'collectivization' ... as Hegel puts it. Having the (biological) property of being open to the world and therefore exposed to the world and so capable of being conditioned by the world, shaped by the material and cultural conditions of existence in which it is placed from the beginning, it is subject to a process of socialization of which individuation is itself the product, with the singularity of the 'self' being fashioned in and by social relations (one might also speak, as Strawson does, but perhaps in a slightly different sense, of 'collective subjectivism'). (Bourdieu 2002: 134)

There is no viable theory of learning here or anywhere else in Bourdieu's work that shows how, exactly, social relations accomplish the 'fashioning' process. Neither is there, here or elsewhere, any recognition of the problem that 'conditioning' and/or 'socialization' pose for the *habitus*, depending as they do on taken-for-granted distinctions between body and mind, individual and society, biology and culture, material and ideal, and so on, all of which either appear or are implied in the above quote and all of which taken-for-granted entities, being separated, require to be brought together by dint of dialectical relations between the two component parts.

As described by Bourdieu, the *habitus* is not inherently transformational; change in the *habitus* can only be generated by exogenous forces (i.e., from outside the group in which the *habitus* under discussion was formed). In *Making Sense of Hierarchy* (1990) I showed how one can at once make the *habitus* inherently transformational (i.e., show how the *habitus*'s 'structured structures' come to work as 'structuring structures'), explain with some precision the intricacy of the social process in which schemes of thought are constituted, and understand something of the fundamentals of how continuity and transformation in social formations are given in this selfsame process. Despite my admiration for Bourdieu's many insights, however, I long ago became impatient with his analytical inconsistencies. At base, the idea of *habitus* depends on a theory of person and world that recruits a specifically Western ontology and entailed epistemology (or vice versa) which is more or less useless when it comes to understanding ideas of sociality, personhood, social relations, ways of knowing and so on that are not in accord with them.

I came to think that one can do without the *habitus*, having arrived at a simpler formulation: over time every one of us makes meaning for ourselves (i.e., autonomously) out of meanings that others have made and are making; this inherently social process manifests itself as a transformational process in which continuity resides. Or to put it another way, making meaning is the fundamental form of human sociality because we cannot make meaning independent of social relations whose history we transform by virtue of living it.[11] By these means we arrive at the point where at the very base of our research is the understanding that, if all our ideas of the world and human being are historically constituted, it is the historical process that is manifest in each and every human being that cries out for research and explanation.

It follows of course that the argument put forward here is itself an historical artefact, describing a particular intellectual trajectory, and given this awareness I can claim for it only this: that it is part of my continuing efforts to make an understanding of historicity central to the anthropological project of explaining what it is to be human. Moreover, considered as a theoretical proposition, the idea of autopoiesis as an historical process has the virtue of being objectively obvious. It is self-evident that in every aspect, living things continue over time as relatively autonomous systems of transformation – the life cycle of a tree or a dog is no more nor less autopoietic than the life cycle of a human being. The point is to comprehend the conditions and implications of autopoiesis in any given case.

These observations are germane to any theory concerning how we humans become who we are and, specifically, the place of others and things in this process. An epistemologically aware anthropology is necessarily alive to ontology and vice versa: ethnography provides good reason to argue that what exists for us is itself the outcome of an historically specific genetic epistemology, just as any ontology entails an epistemology that provides for its specific character. So from an anthropological point of view it makes sense always to stress that we cannot assume that the world as lived by other people is in all respects 'the same' as the world we ourselves take for granted. If cognitive schemes are 'self-regulating transformational systems' – that is, artefacts of an autopoietic process that is characterized by differentiation through functioning – then they must exhibit the history of their constitution over time.[12] These psychological structures are bound to become ever more highly differentiated in being brought to bear on the peopled world that is itself transforming as a function of autopoiesis.

Of course, human beings both think and come to be through an environing world of things as well as people – this seems to me to be uncontroversial; after all, we humans are highly evolved products-cum-producers of a long-evolving and highly differentiated environing world – a world in which, by virtue of this process, we inhere. Assuming that we all hold to some form of theory of evolution we can all agree that this is the case. As anthropologists, however, we want a theory that is capable of making evolutionary theory and the historical nature of human being bear on one another (see Robertson 1996). So, for example, we might take a developmental systems approach in which the fundamental unit of evolution is the life cycle:

> According to developmental systems theory, life cycles propagate from one generation to the next by constructing and reconstructing themselves (like a path laid down in walking), instead of unfolding according to any transmitted, genetic blueprint or program. The processes of reconstruction involve numerous, interdependent causal elements, which relate to each other reciprocally as process and product, rather than belonging to the dichotomous categories of genetic nature versus environmental nurture. (Thompson 2007: 188)

This idea is consistent with my proposed unified model of human being where mind is a function of the whole person that is intersubjectively constituted over time, and history – at once personal and collective – is the artefact of this process.

When we are theorizing how we humans come to think and be through people and things, it makes sense to recognize that we cannot fully understand specific instances, such as shamanism (Pedersen 2007) or the production of *malanggan* funerary sculptures (Küchler 2002), unless we are able to delineate the ontogenetic processes that give rise to them. There's no mystery here, I think, nor any need for additional ideas. Cognition is not to be conceived of as necessarily 'extended' or 'distributed' simply because humans make sense of properties of the world by means of these very properties themselves and technologies derived from them. In the case of actor-network theory, for example, the agency attributed to objects is a real problem, not because objects are objects, but because it is questionable whether 'agency' illuminates even our understanding of human beings.[13] And one only needs to extend or distribute cognition if mind is characterized as a function of the brain or, to be charitable, the embodied nervous system. A multiplicity of tools and technologies has long provided humans with ways of being/thinking/knowing that may lie beyond the confines of our bodies; indeed the body itself can be the lived basis of a 'cognitive system' such as number (see Mimica 1988). That we are able to conceive of cyborgs as a new means of extending our capabilities, even as a new way of being human, does not require so far as I can see a revolution in our thinking, for after all we have yet fully to come to grips with our historicity. Were we able to do so, that would be a revolution indeed, for it would enable us truly to analyse and understand the multiplicity of human being (potentially including cyborgs, for example, or what happens when humans are cloned).

By virtue of evolution, we humans, like other living things, inhere in the world, from which it follows that inevitably we make use of manifold aspects of the world in making sense of it. It is demonstrable that, with the exception of those who for one reason or another are profoundly cognitively disabled, we all grow up to conserve length, volume, number, space, time, and other physical properties of the world and routinely use these practical understandings to, for example, measure grain or build houses or find our way. But these abilities are not necessarily made explicit in standardized systems of measurement or even in a dedicated vocabulary and, where they are, are likely to be embedded in a complex of ideas whose logic may differ significantly from an idea – widespread among the generality of scientists and those educated in scientific traditions – that *requires* certain judgements to be distinguished as objective. Only by these means can they be held to be uncontaminated by historicity, 'valid' for scientific purposes and, in validating the scientist's own perspective on the world, make his or her status as scientist self-evident. As we all know, however (because the history of science makes it eminently clear) human consciousness is through and through historical, for all it is capable of finding out and making use of manifold aspects of the environing world in which we humans inhere.

It is important for us as anthropologists to understand that the peopled world provides for all our historically constituted descriptions of it, such that these always and inevitably partial descriptions are rendered objective in different ways.[14] Take, for example, numerosity as one form of rendering objective our descriptions of the world. For all they differ significantly from our own, Yagwoia people's ideas about number enable counting and other logical operations such as the projection of number into infinity (Mimica 1988). The fact that their number system is constituted in and through the body and as such has the base twenty ('two hands two legs' or 'one person'), and that they consider counting to be the artefact of a cosmogonic act that is played out over and over again in and through the lived bodies of human beings, does not obviate these logical operations. They do not, however, insist on making a distinction (as we try to do) between objective and qualitative perspectives on numerosity. Even so, our understanding of number can be rendered explicable to them, just as their understanding can be rendered explicable to us. This is possible not because certain concepts of number are universal, but because all of us have to come to terms with certain relatively invariant processes instantiated in the peopled world – for example, those that make unavoidable an apprehension of numerosity.

It is interesting to note in passing that, with respect to a person's constitution over time of the numerical system, Mimica's principal informant 'thought that the numerical significance of specifically fingers is already prefigured in a finger game' (1988: 24). The example is particularly suggestive:

When an infant is restless and cries it may be attended to by its mother ... She makes the little hands visible to the child, and then, by successively taking each finger starting with the thumb, she talks to it:

1. Me your mother will find one frog.
2. Me your mother will kill a mouse.
3. Me your mother will find an insect.
4. Me your mother will kill a lizard.
5. Me your mother will find an insect.
6. Me your mother will kill a bird.
7. Me your mother will find an insect.
8. Me your mother will find an insect.
9. Me your mother will find a worm.
10. Me your mother will kill a marsupial.

The informant commented. 'The child hears [understands] now. It doesn't cry any longer and it is happy now. This [game] purports to entice the thought of the child and later [the child] will learn to count. (Mimica 1988: 24–25)

While Mimica is not himself in a position to present us with an ontogenetic analysis of the constitution of the counting system over time by Yagwoia persons, this little game is suggestive. The child who is its object is being inducted into an intersubjective relation in which the specificity, the 'oneness', of each and every thing that is named and enumerated as one, implicates at once the mother and the child as specific entities and their assimilation to the oneness of the self-creating creator Omalyce who, as Mimica demonstrates in his monograph and elsewhere, is identical at once with the cosmos and every aspect of its differentiated being.

The Ethnographic Study of Ontogeny

I argue that cognitive processes are bound to manifest in human practices (including technologies) and that it is part of the anthropologist's task to find out those crucial cases that illuminate our knowledge of human possibilities. Understanding these cases is not, however, satisfied by looking at already highly differentiated adult ideas and practices. Here I feel it important to quote again from Henrich et al. (2010). For all their peculiarly ahistorical understanding of human beings, they do realize how important it is to find out more about children's perceptions and ideas:

The most compelling conclusions regarding universality would derive from comparative work among diverse human populations done with both adults and children, including infants if possible. Human work can then be properly compared with work among nonhuman species (including but not limited to primates), based on a combination of field and laboratory work. (ibid.: 80)

Henrich et al. are not, however, promoting the ethnographic studies of ontogeny that I think necessary. I argue that understanding ontogeny demands a social analysis and that this is indeed born out by Henrich et al.'s review. I would hazard a guess that the characteristics of WEIRD subjects have a good deal to do with the particular idea of the person as an individual that figures prominently in all aspect of their lives, and perhaps especially in their formal education. The idea of the person as an individual cries out for an ethnographic study of its ontogeny that can show how people come to be so enchanted by this idea that they come to take it for granted as self-evident, given in the nature of things. And it has been a good while now that anthropologists have been made aware that where we take for granted and project onto others our own ideas of personhood and relationality we have little chance of understanding and explaining historically divergent forms of sociality.

Tuomela's (2007) certainties concerning the I-mode and the we-mode are a case in point. I can agree, of course, that I differentiate between an I-mode and a we-mode in my own conscious functioning, but the fact is that this I-mode/we-mode distinction is already replete with the social relations that produced it even before I make my conscious distinctions.

> ... children acquire a rudimentary capacity for shared intentionality toward the end of their first year of life and for we-mode collective intentionality starting as early as in their second year of life. In this process the child learns to make-believe and pretend. This capacity is central, for example, to a person's understanding of institutional status. The disposition to have collectively intentional (we-mode) thoughts and to act in the we-mode seems to be a co-evolutionary adaptation (that is, based on a genetic and culturally evolutionary mechanism and history). The precise content of the collectively intentional mental state is nevertheless culturally and socially determined. (Tuomela 2007: 6)

Tuomela's argument, for all it proposes to advance a philosophy of sociality, depends on a theory of person and world that recruits a specifically Western ontology and entailed epistemology (or vice versa) which, like *habitus*, does not help in understanding ideas of sociality, personhood, social relations, ways of knowing and so on that are not in accord with them. Moreover, insofar as people everywhere operate differentially in terms of an I-mode and a we-mode, each mode is inevitably being transformed in the very process of its constitution over time from birth to death, such that the I-mode and the we-mode manifest as the two sides of the continuous surface given by a Moebius strip. So much for the axiomatic differentiation of collective intentionality and personal intentionality.

The burden of the present paper is that there is nothing we know of the world that can be divorced from the specific history of how we came to know it (up to and including this present moment). Sociality being all-pervasive for us, 'the social world' (so-called) cannot be distinguished from some other, as it were, non-social world. The challenge of ontology that the anthropologist faces is the tremendous difficulty of according validity to ideas of the world and what is in it that do not accord with his or her own. The problem is not solved by cultural relativism, which brings in its train all the problems of the taken-for-granted distinctions between biology–culture, body–mind, structure–process, universal–relative and so on that continue to bedevil ethnographic analysis. The problem is solved, I suggest, by giving full recognition to the following demonstrable propositions: (i) that each person's ideas (including those of the analyst) are historically constituted and, interestingly, (ii) that the world validates each and everyone's ideas (including those of the analyst) because what constitutes validity is a function of the epistemology-cum-ontology it appeals to. That is the remarkable thing about the way ontology and epistemology are bound to evince themselves as aspects of one another. Their workings can be laid bare, I suggest, by ethnographic studies of the ontogeny of sociality – that is to say, of the manifold processes in and through which we imagine the inexhaustible world that warrants our imagination.

Acknowledgements

An early version of this paper was presented to the 2009 workshop 'Materialising the Subject' organized by Gillian Evans, RCUK Fellow at Manchester University. The full version was written while I was Visiting Professor at ICS (*Instututo de Ciências Sociais*), Lisbon, funded by the project entitled 'The Territorial Web', reference FCT – PTDC/CS-ANT/102957/2008.

Notes

1. Intersubjectivity may of course take negative forms, or you may project onto me ideas of who I am that have little to do with my own ideas about myself. The point is that we bring to any encounter with another ideas about who that person is and about the relation that obtains between us.
2. I agree with Enfield and Levinson (2007) that intersubjectivity is the form taken by human sociality. Unlike them, however, I argue that sociality informs literally every aspect of human being and that ontogeny is an historical process (cf. Carrithers 1990; Ingold 2007).
3. 'Men make their own history, but they do not make it as they please; they make it under circumstances existing already, given and transmitted from the past.' See <http://www.marxists.org/archive/marx/works/1852/18th-brumaire/ch01.htm> (accessed 27 November 2011).
4. One might quote a whole list, no doubt, of anthropologists who have helped us to realize how fundamental may be conceptual differences across human populations; here I confine myself to two notable examples: Marilyn Strathern (1992) on the person in Melanesia and Jadran Mimica (1988) on Iqwaye number.
5. There are studies of learning in young people and adults, for example Lave and Wenger (1991) or Greg Downey (2005). I want to argue here, however, that ethnographies of infants' and young children's learning are crucial to our understanding of humankind.
6. It is interesting to think about what difference it might make were anthropologists like Viveiros de Castro's Amazonians for whom 'the original common condition of both humans and animals is not animality but rather humanity' (1998: 472). In *An Amazonian*

Myth and Its History (2001), Peter Gow considers what might be the historical trajectory of learning in the case of Piro people.

7. Sociality is the fundamental condition of autopoiesis for many animal species; intersubjectivity may be unique to humans, though one might want to argue the case in respect of certain non-human primates (see, for example, King 2002).

8. Rumsay (2003) provides elements of a study of children's language acquisition as a micro-historical process.

9. For an argument that shows why human sociality should not be predicated on the idea of a 'theory of mind module', see Toren (2012) and compare Enfield and Levinson (2006).

10. For an illuminating discussion, see Thompson (2007: 185).

11. My first formulation of the unified model (Toren 1999: 1–21) was derived from a synthesis of the works of neurobiologists Maturana and Varela (1980, 1988) on autopoiesis; Piaget's idea of the cognitive scheme as a 'self-regulating transformational system' (an autopoietic process) that provides for an idea of lifelong learning (1971: 113); Husserl's (1965, 1970) and Merleau-Ponty's (1962) phenomenology; and certain of Vygotsky's insights on language acquisition (1986). In its most recent development, my unified model makes reference to the neo-Piagetian-cum-neuroconstructivist work of Elman et al. (1996) even while it insists on intersubjectivity as analytically prior.

12. See, e.g., Toren (1990, 1999, 2011) etc.

13. 'Agency' is strongly associated with the idea of the person as an individual and with choice and free will. I find it, therefore, pretty much useless analytically.

14. See, e.g., Toren (2009).

References

Bourdieu, P.1977. *Outline of a Theory of Practice*. Cambridge: Cambridge University Press.

——— 2000. *Pascalian Meditations*. Cambridge: Polity.

Carrithers, M. 1990. Why Humans Have Cultures. *Man*. N.S. 25, no. 2: 189–206.

Castoriadis, C. 1987. *Imaginary Institution of Society*. London: Polity.

Downey, G. 2005. *Learning Capoeira: Lessons in Cunning from an Afro-Brazilian Art*. Oxford: Oxford University Press.

Elman, J. L., E. A. Bates, M. H. Johnson, A. Karmiloff-Smith, and D. Parisi 1996. *Rethinking Innateness. A Connectionist Perspective on Development*. Cambridge: MIT Press.

Enfield, N. J. and S. C. Levinson (eds.) 2006. *Roots of Human Sociality*. Oxford: Berg.

Fogel, A. and I. DeKoeyer-Laros 2007. The Developmental Transition to Secondary Intersubjectivity in the Second Half Year: A Microgenetic Case Study. *Journal of Developmental Psychology* 2, no. 2: 63–90.

Gow, P. 2001. *An Amazonian Myth and its History*. Oxford: Oxford University Press.

Henrich, J., S. J. Heine and A. Norenzayan. 2010. The Weirdest People in the World? *Behavioral and Brain Sciences* 33: 61–135.

Husserl, E. 1965. *Phenomenology and the Crisis of Philosophy* (trans. Q. Lauer). New York: Harper & Row.

——— [1954] 1970. *The Crisis of European Sciences and Transcendental Phenomenology* (trans D. Carr). Evanston: Northwestern University Press.

Ingold, T. (ed.) 1996. *Key Debates in Anthropology*. London: Routledge.

——— 2007. The Social Child. In *Human Development in the 21st Century. A Dynamic Systems Approach to the Life Sciences* (eds.) A. Fogel, B. King and S. Shanker, 112–118. Cambridge: Cambridge University Press.

King, B. J. 2002. On Patterned Interaction and Culture in Great Apes. In *Anthropology Beyond Culture* (eds.) R. G. Fox and B. J. King, 105–124. Oxford: Berg.

Küchler S. 2002. *Malanggan: Art, Memory and Sacrifice*. Oxford: Berg.

Lave, J. and E. Wenger. 1991. *Situated Learning: Legitimate Peripheral Participation*. Cambridge: Cambridge University Press.

Lickliter, R. 2011. The Integrated Development of Sensory Organization. *Clinics in Perinatology* 38: 591–602.

Marx, K. <marxists.org/archive/marx/works/1852/18th-brumaire/ch01.htm> (accessed 15 February 2012).

Maturana, H. P. and F. J.Varela [1972] 1980. *Autopoiesis and Cognition: The Realisation of the Living*. Dordrecht: D. Reidel.

——— 1988. *The Tree of Knowledge*. Boston: New Science Library.

McCallum, C. 2001. *Gender and Sociality in Amazonia. How Real People Are Made*. Oxford: Berg.

Merleau-Ponty, M. [1945] 1962. *Phenomenology of Perception*. London: Routledge & Kegan Paul.

Mimica, J. 1988. *Intimations of Infinity. The Cultural Meanings of Iqwaye Counting System and Number*. Oxford: Berg.

Piaget, J. [1969] 1971. *Structuralism*. London: Routledge & Kegan Paul.

Pedersen, M. A. 2007. Talismans of Thought: Shamanist Ontologies and Extended Cognition in Northern Mongolia. In *Thinking Through Things: Theorising Artefacts Ethnographically*, (eds.) A. J. M. Henare, M. Holbraad, S. Wastell, 141–166. London: Routledge.

Robertson, A. F. 1996. The Development of Meaning: Ontogeny and Culture. *Journal of the Royal Anthropological Institute* (N.S.) 2, no. 4: 591–610.

Rumsay, A. 2003. Language Desire and the Ontogenesis of Intersubjectivity. *Language and Communication* 23, no. 2: 169–187.

Strathern, M. 1992. *The Gender of the Gift: Problems With Women and Problems With Society in Melanesia*. Berkeley: University of California Press.

Thompson, E. 2007. *Mind in Life. Biology, Phenomenology and the Sciences of Mind*. Cambridge: Belknap Press.

Toren, C. 1990. *Making Sense of Hierarchy: Cognition as Social Process in Fiji*. London: Athlone Press.

——— 1999. *Mind, Materiality and History: Explorations in Fijian Ethnography*. London: Routledge.

——— 2009. Intersubjectivity as Epistemology. *Social Analysis* 53, no. 2: 130–146.

——— 2011. The Stuff of Imagination: What We Can Learn From Fijian Children's Ideas About Their Lives as Adults. *Social Analysis* 55, no. 1: 23–47.

——— 2012. Anthropology and Psychology. In *The SAGE Handbook of Social Anthropology*, (ed.) R. Fardon, 42–78. New York: SAGE.

Tuomela, R. 2007. *The Philosophy of Sociality: The Shared Point of View*. Oxford: Oxford University Press.

Viveiros de Castro, E. 1998. Cosmological Deixis and Amerindian Perspectivism. *Journal of the Royal Anthropological Institute* (N.S.) 4, no. 3: 469–488.

Vygotsky, L. S. [1934] 1986. *Thought and Language*. Cambridge: Harvard University Press.

3

Sociality and Its Dangers
Witchcraft, Intimacy and Trust

*Peter Geschiere, University of Amsterdam**

Witchcraft sits uneasily with sociality. Of course, in a Latourian sense, witchcraft has a sociality of its own – after all, it is 'intrinsically interactive' (even in optima forma).[1] Yet for many it constitutes a kind of anti-sociality. Anthropologists, confronted with the tenacity of ideas on secret conspiracies by witches in Africa (and elsewhere), tended to study it as the very denial of society. Compare the famous quote by Gluckman (1955: 94):

> An Anglican anthem demands 'See that ye love one another fervently.' Beliefs in the malice of witchcraft and in the wrath of ancestral spirits do more than ask this as an act of grace; they affirm that if you do not love one another fervently, misfortune will come.... Though a charge of witchcraft ... may exaggerate and exacerbate a quarrel, the belief emphasizes the threat to the wider social order which is contained in immoral sentiments. Hence the beliefs exert some pressure on men and women to observe the social virtues, and to feel the right sentiments, lest they be suspected of being witches.

In this view, witchcraft is seen as the antithesis of kinship, supposedly the backbone of social order in African societies. Gluckman and other anthropologists of his time certainly realized how closely the two are intertwined in everyday life. Yet, as in the quotation above, witchcraft was studied as the opposite of kinship, the very denial of its basic values. In recent decades anthropologists have analysed the close intertwinement of the two in a somewhat different perspective (Austen 1993; Geschiere 1997; Meyer 1999; *passim*). In my 1997 book on *The Modernity of Witchcraft* I characterized witchcraft as the 'dark side' of kinship. Rather than being outside kinship, it seemed to be seen by the Maka people, with whom I lived in Southeast Cameroun, as given with kinship – as part and parcel of the kinship order. This somewhat different accent is becoming particularly important with the increase in scale of kinship relations which are seen now as covering ever wider distances – between village and city or even transcontinentally with new forms of migrations.[2] The anthropologists of late colonial times worked mainly in smaller villages, where most people were relatives in one way or another; in such contexts the intertwinement of witchcraft and kinship was hardly surprising. Yet, with the increase of scale of social relations, the tenacity with which witchcraft rumours, despite all innovations, remain linked to the familiar truths of 'the house' and the family becomes ever more striking.[3]

The Maka are certainly not exceptional in stressing the close link between witchcraft and kinship. In many parts of the world, representations that are loosely grouped under 'witchcraft'[4] emphasize the close link between intimacy and occult aggression. The Maka speak with particular horror about the *djambe le ndjaw* [the witchcraft of the house] since this is supposed to be the most dangerous one. *Ndjaw* [house] has to be taken in a broad sense. In a concrete sense it does not refer just to one building, but rather to a sprawling family compound; in a social sense it includes all people who are in one way or another related to each other, but who do not necessarily live in the compound concerned. As said, in recent times, the *ndjaw* has become even more dispersed: it includes now also urbanites, who spend all their life in the city, and even transcontinental migrants. Even though these migrants may visit the compound most irregularly, they still belong to 'the house' – which implies that they are still in reach of this frightening *djambe le ndjaw*. As elsewhere, 'witchcraft' seems to be so unsettling because it is an attack that comes from within. Yet what might be special to many African contexts is the wide reach of these intimate relations, and hence of intimate dangers.

In this contribution I want to further develop the implications of this vision of the intimate – that is, of relations of proximity: with kin, fellow villagers and so on – as inherently dangerous.[5] What does this mean for notions of sociality? It may be clear that these implications can be quite subversive for current notions of community and family, as 'normally' constituting safe havens. Anthropology has been quite good at confirming such ideas. A classical example is Marshall Sahlins' famous model of concentric circles, to be found in many anthropology handbooks. The model's key is an arrow that starts in the centre, and moves from the inner core ('household') through the wider circles (from 'lineage sector' to 'village' to 'tribal sector' to 'intertribal sector'). The arrow goes from 'generalized reciprocity' in the inner circle, via 'balanced reciprocity' in the middle, to 'negative reciprocity' in the outer circles (Sahlins 1974a: 199). The message is clear: in the centre reigns trust, but this diminishes the wider the circle becomes. The emphasis on the dangers of intimacy that dominates many discourses on witchcraft and occult aggression conveys a completely opposite view. The Maka horror about the *djambe le ndjaw* – the witchcraft of the house – as the most frightening, is a graphic example of this. The implication seems to be that danger lurks especially within the very core of sociality; it is the attacks 'from within' that are the most dangerous.

As said, such a view is certainly not limited to Africans preoccupied with witchcraft. It is a recurrent premise of discourses on occult aggression in many parts of the world. Indeed, the realization that intimacy can not only bring protection but also danger might be universal. Yet in this text I want to stick to a few African examples. The aim is not so much to explore the wider relevance of this link between witchcraft and intimacy – to show that Africa is not that exceptional (for this see Geschiere in press) – but rather to follow the implications of this link for studying sociality. The question is what tools do we have to study sociality as inherently dangerous? This raises inevitably the related question of how, despite such a basic threat, trust can be established. If it is precisely your intimates that have such a dangerous hold over you, how then it is possible to nonetheless work and collaborate with them? These might be urgent questions for our understanding of sociality.

Witchcraft and Intimacy

Let me start by giving a more substantial image of this link between witchcraft and intimacy, notably within the family, that confused but also fascinated me so much during my fieldwork among the Maka in the forest region of Southeast Cameroon. The intrusion of *djambe* (witchcraft) into my research came as a sort of surprise. Arriving in the area in 1971, my plan as a political anthropologist was to study local effects of state formation. However, it soon became clear that whenever I wanted to discuss issues of authority and politics, my new Maka friends referred sooner or later to this *djambe*. Clearly to them, the politics in daylight were only understandable in relation to the nightly shadow-world of this occult force to which almost everybody seemed to have access in one way or another. Moreover, people also talked about the close link between *djambe* and kinship (the *djambe le ndjaw*, witchcraft of the house, mentioned before) as some sort of self-evident truth.[6] Rumours of witchcraft attacks – that in this region were only rarely translated into public accusations – always pointed to people of the same compound, or from within the same family. Urban elites complained that, despite all their commitment to their village of origin, they were really afraid to go back since 'those people will eat us'. Initially I thought such statements referred to the kind of sponging at which Maka villagers excel (as I knew only too well from personal experience), but I soon discovered that there was a deeper reference here to witches, who are supposed to 'eat' their own kin. *Nganga* [healers] would emphasize that they could only heal someone if the family wanted to cooperate and, indeed, they always discovered that the main source of danger lay 'inside'. My anthropological training had made me see kinship and witchcraft as opposites – witchcraft as an attack on the order imposed by kinship – but to my interlocutors they seemed to be completely intertwined: witchcraft as the flipside of kinship rather than its opposite. I learned also quite quickly that neither witchcraft nor kinship presented themselves as closed systems. The poly-interpretability of kinship relations – in practice each and every relation appeared to allow for contestation and different interpretations – matched the surprising dynamics of conceptions concerning the *djambe*. Precisely the relation between these two poles – each equally volatile and constantly changing, and even more uncertain in their mutual articulation – seems to give shape to the representations and practices of occult aggression, not as a fixed essence, but rather as an ongoing 'event'.

The link with kinship is central to the basic image of Maka notions of witchcraft: the nightly meeting of the witches. Elsewhere I have extensively described the Maka imaginary around *djambe*, the central notion in stories about witchcraft (Geschiere 1997), so a short sketch has to suffice here. People describe the *djambe* as an evil creature living in someone's belly which gives its owner (*djindjamb* – the one who has the *djambe)* special powers. The main power is the capacity to transform oneself into an animal or a spirit. Especially at night when the owl calls, the *djambe* will leave the body and fly off into the night – 'along the cobwebs of the *djambe*' – to the *sjoumbou*, the nightly meetings of the witches. There, terrible cannibalistic banquets are being staged. The stories about the debaucheries of these nightly meetings – marked by shocking transgressions, violent encounters and devious victories – are many.[7] But one element recurs all the time: each witch has to offer a relative in his or her turn to be devoured by the other witches; in daily life the victim of this nightly treason will fall ill and die unless the *nganga* [healer] is called in who can 'see' the guilty witches and force them out. Basic to Maka witchcraft discourse is that it is about the betrayal of one's kin to outsiders. In many respects witchcraft is at the interface of the private and the public: between the intimate world of kinship or the house, on the one hand, and the outer world and its fascinating opportunities for self-enhancement, on the other. Witches are supposed to have a special hold over their relatives but they use this in order to hand over their victims to outsiders.

The inherent link with kinship is cogently conveyed by a recurrent motif in witchcraft stories, as a kind of further elaboration of this basic scheme: it concerns the notion of the witch as a martyr who sacrifices him/herself rather than betraying another relative. The sad case of Eba's death was the first time I stumbled upon this kind of interpretation – a trope I was to encounter many more times. During one of the first months of my fieldwork in the village of Bagbeze in 1971, Eba (pseudonym), a man in the strength of his life, suddenly succumbed to a heavy attack of malaria. His family was in shock: one day Eba seemed to be still in good health and the next he was dying! So they made furious but as yet unspecific hints at witchcraft: they clearly were looking for someone to blame. However, other people said the very suddenness of his death showed that he must have been himself a witch. After all, everyone knows that when an 'innocent' – that is, someone who does not 'go out' in the *djambe* – is attacked, (s)he will die slowly. Only between witches does an attack lead to a sudden death: they can 'see' who is attacking them, and then it becomes a battle of life-and-death. Therefore, some people whispered that Eba must have been a witch himself who in his turn had the worst of the eternal fights among the witches; or, to put it differently: he got what he deserved.

But friends of Eba opted for another interpretation. Maybe he was a witch – after all, he had been very successful in the outlay of cocoa and coffee plantations and that suggested he knew how to defend himself against jealousy – but then it was clear that he had sacrificed himself since he did not want to offer yet another relative to his witch-companions. This image of the witch as a person of special courage returns in proverbs about the terrible loneliness of the witch who has neither 'brother nor sister, father nor mother'. If he refuses to give yet another relative, he has to face the wild crowd of witches all alone; people shudder before such an image. Eba might have been a witch but he was also a martyr who, despite earlier betrayals, had made a final stance by refusing to give up yet another kinsman.[8] His tragic courage offered again a powerful expression of the close link people make between witches and kin – witchcraft as the betrayal of kinship – which seemed to be self-evident to my spokesmen, but came to me as a shock.

Especially in present-day contexts, this continuing link with the local realities of kin and village is all the more striking since, at the same time, this imaginary shows a quite impressive ability to link up with modern developments that far exceed the limits of the village. As one of my Maka spokesmen told me back in 1973: 'We have our own planes, much quicker than yours – our witches fly to Paris and back within a single night.' The zombie spirits who in the 1960s and 70s were supposed to be put to work on 'invisible plantations' on Mount Kupe in West Cameroon by the nouveaux riches through a novel kind of witchcraft, are now said to be sold off to the mafia, Mount Kupe becoming only a relay station in global circuits of labour exploitation (see Geschiere 1997; de Rosny 1981). But, in the end, even such vertiginous speculations about dark global conspiracies are linked to the familiar, albeit shifting theme of the betrayal of kin to outsiders.

This new zombie witchcraft highlights the paradoxical combining of the global and the local in a particularly pregnant way. People tend to emphasize the novelty of this form of witchcraft, opposing it to older forms of witchcraft in which the witches would cannibalize their victims. Instead they are now supposed to turn them into zombies to exploit their labour or even, as people put it, 'sell' them. De Rosny traces the obvious link with traumatic memories of the slave trade, but he relates all the excitement over this new form of witchcraft also to people's bewilderment by the capriciousness of the new inequalities and the vagaries of the world market – why do a few people become so rich while all the others invariably fail in their plans? Rumours about zombies provide at least a possible explanation for the shocking wealth of the new elites. Yet even this 'modern' form of witchcraft is linked to similar ideas as the Maka obsession with the *djambe le ndjaw* [witchcraft of the house]. In his fascinating study of how the *nganga* [healers] try to deal with this new threat, Eric de Rosny shows that they always insist that the whole family has to be reunited. This is quite remarkable since it often concerns urbanites who have lived in the city for generations and sometimes really have to search for their kin in the faraway countryside. Despite all novelty and increase of scale, the most dangerous attack is still supposed to come from inside, and the family is still the obvious locus of this inside.[9]

This ongoing articulation of witchcraft and intimacy stands out all the more starkly with such an increase of scale. It is not a coincidence that among earlier anthropologists the one who formulated this link most tersely was Philip Mayer who mainly worked in a budding urban centre in South Africa: 'Witches and their accusers are people who ought to like each other, but in reality refuse to do so' (Mayer [1954] 1970: 55). One might wonder whether Mayer's statement leaves enough room for the full ambivalence of these ideas – mentioning witchcraft does certainly not exclude that the relation is continued: supposed attacks can be covered up and forgotten, at least for some time. But he did sum up most effectively the confusing balance between closeness and aggression that makes witchcraft such an uncomfortable threat.[10]

The link with intimacy – in this context especially with family – is certainly not an invariable or straightforward premise. For instance, at first sight the role of the *nganga* [healer] among the Maka and other groups in the forest of southern Cameroon seems to contradict this since they are supposed to work outside kinship. The *nganga* is supposed to use the forces of the *djambe* against the witches themselves and attack them from a distance. Sometimes people will even say that *nganga* should not live with their family since their powers are so frightening that they would be too much of a danger for their own kin.[11] In many respects they are beyond the framework of family. However at a deeper level kinship is significant as an essential condition for enhancing their occult powers. People will whisper that in order to be initiated into all this dangerous knowledge, a *nganga* had to sacrifice a close relative, who has to be 'given' to his/her 'professor' as reward for all the lessons.[12]

Even more important is the recent but quite general trend throughout the African continent to complain that witchcraft is breaking though the boundaries of kinship: supposedly in present times it has lost its old moorings in the family; hence a general worry about witchcraft 'running wild'. Indeed, the link between witchcraft and kinship may seem to become ever more stretched with modern changes and a constant increase of scale of social relations. New forms of witchcraft are seen as particularly shocking since they seem to be effective against anybody, kin or non-kin. For instance, in his recent study of *feymen* (Cameroon's equivalent to the Nigerian 419s, who are involved in global computer fraud, false money schemes and other illicit practices), Basile Ndjio (2006) emphasizes that the current association of the mysterious success of these swindlers – and some of them do become amazingly rich – with particular forms of witchcraft is no longer tied to kinship. Their *mokoagne moni* [magical money] rather helps them to find their victims – businessmen or politicians eager to invest in dubious schemes – on a much broader, even global scale: their *fronts* are in Europe, South Asia and the Gulf states far outside the reach of kinship. This is indeed a far cry from the idea that 'witchcraft never crosses the water [i.e., the ocean]' as people used to say in earlier decades.

Still, when one follows Ndjio's rich case studies in detail it is striking that references to witchcraft always seem to point back ultimately to the close environment of kin and locality: the helpers of a *feyman* are suddenly bewitched when they accompany him to the village, which in most effective ways takes revenge for the unwillingness of its ungrateful son to share his new wealth; a local community in Douala raises a magical barrier to another *feyman*'s activities by closing its ranks. This is symptomatic. Witchcraft may be supposed to work now in new circuits on a much wider, even global scale – this is one of the reasons for people's worries about it getting ever more out-of-bounds. Indeed, the capacity of this local discourse for grafting itself upon the opening up of new, global horizons is quite disconcerting. Yet in most of these global witchcraft stories there is ultimately a pointer back to the local realities of neighbourhood and family. 'The village' and its emotional intimacy may, at least in some respects, become an almost 'virtual' reality to many Cameroonians – modern urbanites with a global outlook – but it is still is deeply engraved in witchcraft visions.[13]

The Congolese anthropologist Joseph Tonda (now in Libreville) insists even more strongly that since the colonial encounter *la sorcellerie* largely surpasses the old lineage order (it is from then on 'beyond what is thinkable and possible in the lineage order' [Tonda 2002: 237]). Yet in his books the link with the family is everywhere. Even *Mammywata* – the beautiful lady, often white, with blond hair, who captures young men with evil promises of unheard riches – asks her followers to sacrifice a close relation, often a child (ibid.: 85; Tonda 2005: 177). *Mammywata* may be the very symbol of modernity and its promises of unlimited consumerism, but she is apparently not completely outside kinship. The general relevance of Tonda's insistence on a complete *déparentélisation* of society as a logical outcome of the colonial moment is problematic.[14] In many parts of Africa the remarkable elasticity of kinship claims grafting themselves upon completely novel relations remains quite striking (not to say worrying). Even African migrants in Europe and America fear the telephone calls from home with their endless demands that can be underlined with hidden threats. Precisely the ongoing association of family with witchcraft as a serious threat among migrants far away from home shows the impressive elasticity of the family-witchcraft complex. Tonda is certainly right that in such novel contexts witchcraft takes on new guises, but its precarious yet inherent link with kinship and the family is in many contexts constantly reaffirmed despite staggering distances. Apparently the map of intimacy can constantly be redrawn, stretching the witchcraft-family complex to a breaking point, yet without destroying its grasp.[15]

This basic link with intimacy – and in many African contexts this means the family from which one is born, and the soil in which one has to be buried – brings out the full horror of witchcraft. In most parts of Africa the family is still celebrated as the basic circle of sociability and trust – even though in practice things may be very different. Yet witchcraft introduces lethal aggression in the very heart of the community where only solidarity and serenity should reign. It expresses the shocking realization that there is not only harmony inside, but also jealousy and therefore aggression. Moreover, this aggression is all the more dangerous since there is hardly any protection against it. As said, this fear of aggression from close by is certainly not special to Africa or to other regions marked by poverty and crisis. On the contrary. I am always surprised that to Westerners this theme in many African stories of witchcraft – for instance on the betrayal of your own father or mother – is so shocking. After all, Freud warned us already that the family is not just a happy enclave in society, but also a primal hotbed of aggression. With their deep worries about witchcraft, Africans and others raise a universal issue: how to deal with aggression from close by – with intimacy that is not just a haven of peace but at the same time a lethal source of threat and betrayal?

A relational view of witchcraft as an event shaped by its ambiguous and volatile relation with intimacy may help to highlight the more general implications of Africans' continuing preoccupation with these occult forces – and also academics' continuing struggle over how to address it. The comparative possibilities of the witchcraft–intimacy dyad may be further enhanced by adding a third pole, trust, as a necessary complement. In all the examples above, the vital question is how people succeed – despite all the dangers implied by closeness – to nonetheless establish trust. It may be clear also from the preceding cases that this triangle of witchcraft, intimacy and trust allows for highly different patterns; the exact ways in which people link witchcraft to intimacy – in particular the modes in which they define the intimacy from which such worrying threats can emerge – varies constantly. So do the ways in which they try to establish trust nonetheless.

Clearly witchcraft discourse implies a view of sociality as a constant struggle. 'The collective' is never a given. It is internally undermined in most drastic ways and the establishment of trust against omnipresent threats is always precarious. To what extent can more theoretical explorations around the notions of intimacy and trust – both experiencing a recent renaissance in the social sciences – offer support for analysing this struggle?

Intimacy and the Uncanny

Can the close link with intimacy serve to get a grip on what shapes witchcraft in its ongoing transformations? A problem is that lately the concept of intimacy itself has become so fashionable among anthropologists and other social scientists – maybe as a potential answer to increasing feelings of alienation and isolation – that it risks becoming almost as empty as it is general. Apparently its currency does not stop it from being used in widely differing ways. Yet a common tendency, behind all these differences, is that a positive view seems to prevail. Reading intimacy from witchcraft suggests special attention to internal tensions. But references to potential dangers are conspicuously absent from recent explorations around this notion.

This positive trend remains implicit in the current, but also somewhat facile, use of the term as a euphemism for sexual relations, whether or not in a conjugal setting. A good example is American anthropologist Jankowiak's recent collection *Intimacies: Love and Sex across Cultures* (2008). Typically the notion of intimacy is not at all problematized throughout this voluminous book.[16] It seems mainly to function as a buzzword. Precisely because its meaning is taken for granted – no need to analyse it – it takes on quite happy implications: intimacy seen as a self-evidently comfortable niche, a domain of trust in a hostile society.

However, the prize for the most paradisiacal version of the notion goes without doubt to British sociologist Anthony Giddens. In *The Transformation of Intimacy* (1992), Giddens analyses intimacy between partners as the pinnacle of modernity, marking the transition from 'romantic' to 'confluent love'. He closely relates intimacy to autonomy and trust: in his version intimacy expresses the ideal of two adult persons who respect each other's differences and thus leave scope for the other's autonomy so that they can trust each other. Heavily leaning on psychotherapeutic literature, he poses intimacy cum autonomy as the opposite pole of addiction cum dependency – a view that is in striking contrast with basic elements of witchcraft discourse cited above. Any idea that intimacy can be fraught with special dangers and lead to stifling dependency is lacking here; the notion has only positive overtones, creating a safe haven of trust.[17]

A completely different view has been forwarded by the British-American anthropologist Michael Herzfeld in his publications on 'cultural intimacy' (1997).[18] For him this is certainly not the highest stage of modernity. It is rather the counterpoint for official nationalism. Herzfeld's main point seems to be that the formal truth of Benedict Anderson's 'imagined community' is complemented by more hidden everyday truths – he speaks of 'rueful self-recognition' (ibid.: 6) – that are at least as important to the reproduction of national sentiments. Examples are Greek jokes about their own machismo (and probably Dutch ironies about their stinginess) which create an informal or even ironic acceptance of one's identity. For anthropologists, this version of intimacy is certainly much more promising. In Herzfeld's use of the notion there is clear interest in its ambiguities – the tension between formal denial and implicit recognition of certain disreputable truths. Moreover, Herzfeld places his notion on the threshold of the private and the public: he refers to sentiments that are quite private, yet nonetheless half-heartedly publicized. Here there is indeed an interesting link to witchcraft as a discourse that brings out into the open what should remain private – that is, the hidden tensions within the family or community that become exposed to the public gaze. We are already further away from the vision of intimacy as a nice, protected sphere.

Clearly we need versions of the intimacy notion that go further in this direction if we want to address why to people in Africa – and certainly not only there – it is quite evident that there is a close link with witchcraft. We may have to look outside anthropology to find explorations that come closer to the idea of intimacy as a tension-ridden sphere. An interesting impulse comes from the American literary and cultural theorist Lauren Berlant who launched a whole project on the notion in *Critical Inquiry* (1998). For her, intimacy is full of ambiguity. It seems to belong to the private, but it is always on the border of the public: 'the inwardness of the intimate is met by a corresponding publicness' (ibid.: 281). For her intimacy is not necessarily related to the small scale. On the contrary, she speaks of the 'modern, mass-mediated sense of intimacy' and adds that 'intimacy builds worlds: it creates spaces and usurps places meant for other kinds of relation' (ibid: 282). She sees it as a notion intrinsically related to mobility: 'liberal society was founded on the migration of intimacy expectations between the public and the domestic' (ibid.: 284). All this may not seem to relate directly to the witchcraft examples above. Yet, her emphasis on intimacy 'usurping places meant for other kinds of relation' is surprisingly relevant for the new dynamics of witchcraft notions in changing circumstances. Even more relevant is Berlant's argument that 'in its expression through language, intimacy relies heavily on the shifting registers of unspoken ambivalence' (1998: 286). We are a lot closer here to the witchcraft vision of intimacy as a sphere of life that can be expanded in novel ways, and is full of deep tensions and ambiguities.

Another riddle is how so many recent authors with a quite positive – not to say paradisiacal – view of intimacy manage to completely ignore Sigmund Freud. After all, the latter, much criticized as he is now, did have basic things to say precisely on this point that are still highly relevant. Of course, Freud never used the term intimacy. Still, his insistence that the family is a hotbed of aggression and guilt remains highly relevant for the present discussion. In particular an essay by Freud, *Das Unheimliche* (The Uncanny), offers seminal starting points for exploring the tension between intimacy, trust and aggression ([1919] 2003).[19] This short essay can be seen as part of Freud's ongoing project to prove the relevance of psychoanalysis for gaining a deeper understanding of works of art. Indeed, the main purpose of the text seems to be to prove that Freud's approach allows him to discover a deeper meaning in the fairly enigmatic story 'The Sandman' (from 1816) by E.T.A. Hoffman, the king of the German *Romantik* storytellers. Freud focuses on the role of *das Unheimliche* [the uncanny] in the story in the figure of Coppelius alias Coppola – the 'Sandman' – who keeps appearing at unexpected moments and thus drives Nathaniel, the young man who is the story's main character, to madness and suicide – a fate that befell so many unhappy torchbearers of the *Sturm und Drang* [lit. tempest and drive] that haunted the German *Romantik*. However, Freud does not start with the story, but rather – in line with his general focus on language as a main tool to riddle-solving – with an extensive analysis of the central terms *heimlich* [homely] and *unheimlich* [lit. unhomely – ghastly, uncanny]. A major part of the text consists of a very long quote from a dictionary of the German language (by a certain Daniel Sanders, produced in1860) summing up all the different meanings of both terms. At the beginning this seems to be quite boring until one notes that the consecutive meanings of *heimlich* gradually verge towards their opposite, *unheimlich*! Indeed, the ambiguous meanings of *heimlich* emerging from Freud's long enumeration are quite intriguing: the term seems to have strong positive notions – since it is closely related to *Heim* [home]; but these more positive implications are balanced by another array of meanings centred around an association with secrecy (*Heim* as a place where things remain hidden, withdrawn from sight). Freud is not bothered by the fact that German is about the only language where this strange trend of *heimlich* switching into its very opposite gets linguistic expression. He does note that in English, French, Italian, Portuguese, Arabic and Hebrew the equivalent terms do not show this tendency, but apparently he feels that German expresses here a basic ambiguity on which he bases his further analysis.[20]

The central theme in Freud's analysis is that *das Unheimliche*, the uncanny – in this case the figure of Coppelius/Coppola – is so frightening since it is about repressed memories that come back with a vengeance. It is such repression that turns the familiar (*das Heimliche*) into the uncanny (*das Unheimliche*). Nathaniel is no longer capable of containing the fears that plague him from childhood when he unexpectedly sees emerge from the crowd an optician, Coppola, in whom he thinks he recognizes Dr Coppelius, an old friend of his father, but maybe also his father's murderer.

Hoffmann's haunting story and Freud's ambitious analysis have many more layers that are of interest to us. But of special importance is that Freud offers clear starting points for studying the uncomfortable link between intimacy and the uncanny: his leading question is how to understand the switch of *Heimlich* into its very opposite, *das Unheimliche*; and even more how to understand the reverse: how *das Unheimliche* can be turned again into *das Heimliche*. Or, to relate this to witchcraft discourse: when closeness breeds fears of hidden aggression, and how the threat of hidden aggression can be neutralized so that trust can be established. Of course, Freud himself wants to go a lot further than this. He also wants to offer a definitive explanation of such transitions, which in this case are seen as turning around repression. *Das Heimliche* – in Nathaniel's case a horrible childhood memory that was repressed – becomes *unheimlich* when it turns up later and is experienced as completely out of place.[21] It remains to be seen to what extent this specific explanation holds for witchcraft fears. The great merit of Freud is in any case that he definitely leaves behind the view of intimacy as a domain of harmony, and even more that he suggests steps for understanding the complex intertwinement of security and fear in people's experiences of intimacy. All the more surprising that so many social scientists after him continue to cling to the conception of intimacy as simply a sphere of security.

The Struggle over Trust

The above may already suggest that recent theorizing around the other corner of our triangle, trust, offers an equally positive image of proximity. In this respect the apparently obvious link of trust to intimacy remains very influential – including in anthropology. To optimistic authors like Giddens and the psychotherapists he quotes with such enthusiasm, it seems to be self-evident that intimacy and trust are complementary. Yet in witchcraft discourse it is instead a continuous challenge to combine the two. To my Maka friends, the particular dangers of the *djambe le ndjaw* (the witchcraft from inside the house) imply there is good reason to distrust one's intimates. Indeed, all over the world a key word in discussions on how to protect oneself against the witches seems to be closure. Among the Maka the key word is *bouima*, always translated as 'to armour oneself'. To them a good armouring is essential, preferably by a specialist (*nganga*) – even though contacting a *nganga* implies already that one is entering the *djambe* domain. Again, the Maka are certainly not exceptional in this. Favret-Saada (1977) describes farmers in the French countryside as obsessed with the need to magically close their compounds from the attacks of jealous or simply evil neighbours. The question all this raises is, of course, how one can ever fence oneself off from one's intimates, with whom one shares so much? The more general implication seems to be that trust is never a given, not even in kinship societies (or, rather, especially not there) – this in striking contrast to current stereotypes of what are sometimes called 'anthropological societies'.[22] Clearly, even within small-scale communities, trust is constantly tested and, therefore, it is of vital importance that it is time and again reaffirmed. To the Maka, the family is essential – it is highly questionable whether one can survive without it – yet it is at the same time the source of mortal threats. It might be precisely because of this absolute necessity of kinship that it is seen as fraught with dangers. The Douala, a group on the Cameroonian coast – the 'autochthons' of the huge city of the same name – have a saying that 'One has to learn to live with one's sorcerer' (de Rosny 1992: 114). This might be a much more common problem, also in so-called modern societies, than Giddens and the therapists he quotes are prepared to admit.

What has the general literature to say about such predicaments around trust in zones of intimacy? Recently, the very popularity of the notion of 'trust' risks turning it into another buzzword across the disciplines, just like the notion of intimacy, cropping up in the most unexpected places. Not only anthropologists evoke issues of trust as crucial to the quality of relations; representatives of the 'harder' social sciences have also become quite fond of the term. For many economists trust has become a black box invoked when the gap between their computer simulations and everyday developments becomes too big. Organizational sociologists and management experts have followed suit. When I decided to further explore the notion of trust I expected to stumble on the tenacious tendency of economists and others to stick to a rational choice model, explaining trust or its absence from the well-understood self-interests of the actors involved. Of course such starting points might raise problems in a field like witchcraft that is so strongly characterized by secrecy and ambiguous interpretations.

Yet somewhat to my surprise, certain anthropological ideas – or even premises – about trust were as much a stumbling block, notably the tenacity of many anthropologists, already highlighted above, to simply equate kinship with solidarity and reciprocity – and, therefore, with trust (see Sahlins 1974a; 1974b). This is quite striking in view of the discipline's long-standing interest in witchcraft, magic and such. However, these later aspects tended (and still tend) to be seen as exceptional moments of crisis after which reciprocity would be restored again (cf. Gluckman 1955: 94 [above]). Indeed, reciprocity – which in its more simplistic versions seems to imply automatic trust – has attained an almost sacred status in anthropology. In a critical essay, Chris Gregory (1994) discusses gift-giving with its obligation for reciprocity as the anthropological answer to theories of wealth as determined by commodities and capital (like the Marxian vision). It would certainly be interesting to do a genealogy of the notion of reciprocity and how it acquired such a central place in our discipline. Probably it would be necessary to go back even beyond our direct ancestors. Apparently Edward Tylor had already simply linked kindred to kindness, 'two words whose common derivation expresses in the happiest way one of the main principles of social life'.[23] But beyond him looms Tönnies – with his sympathy for a disappearing *Gemeinschaft* that was in everything the opposite of the *Gesellschaft* – and beyond this the German *Romantiker* with their nostalgia for a lost innocence due to progress and rationalism.[24]

However, in this context it may not be necessary to go so far back since Marshall Sahlins' by now classic text 'On the Sociology of Primitive Exchange', quoted at the beginning of this article, offers a convenient landmark for situating the heavy emphasis on reciprocity in anthropology.[25] In particular, the concentric circles model with the arrow going from the inner circle dominated by 'generalized reciprocity' to ever wider circles marked by 'balanced' to 'negative reciprocity' confirms the equation of the inside with reciprocal exchange. Or, as Sahlins himself neatly sums up the implications of this ambitious scheme: 'It follows that close kin tend to share, to enter into generalized exchanges, and distant and non-kin to deal in equivalents and guile' (Sahlins 1974a: 196 and 198). Family is trust, haggling is outside. Of course since then many anthropologists (notably feminists) have insisted on the tensions within this inner core. Still, it is striking how widespread the use of a notion like reciprocity remains in our discipline.

Sahlins presents this text as building on Marcel Mauss' famous *Essai sur le don: Forme et raison de l'échange dans les societies archaiques* [An essay on the gift: the form and reason of exchange in archaic societies] (1923–4).[26] Yet it is clear that Mauss' vision of the central role of gift-giving in 'archaic' societies was much more complicated. He strongly emphasized the dangers of the gift: if it was not properly returned in due time, it could kill the original receiver.[27] In his writings on 'The Spirit of the Gift', Sahlins (1974b) pays due attention to this aspect of Mauss' interpretations (and even to the close link between gift-giving and witchcraft in the case of the Maori, whose notion *hau* stood as the model for *le don* for Mauss). But apparently Sahlins preferred to omit this flipside of the gift in his more general text on 'primitive exchange' (1974a). This extrapolation helped to further reinforce his very positive image of 'generalized reciprocity' in the core sector, 'the house'. It fits in also with the general anthropological trend highlighted above to see witchcraft not as the dark side of kinship, but somehow outside of it – an exception rather than part and parcel of the kinship order. More recent commentators – notably Tim Ingold (1986) – tried to give reciprocity a more ambivalent meaning by pointing to different trends in exchange, even within the inner circles. Indeed, with the recent renaissance of interest in Mauss' work, especially in the U.S. and the U.K., it may be all the more important to emphasize that his version of exchange was much more ambiguous than is suggested by the incorrect translation of *rendre le don* as 'to reciprocate' in the 1990 English version of his essay. One may hope also that simplistic versions of the latter notion, like Sahlins' one – which had so much impact also outside anthropology – will continue to be relativized.

The general literature seems to leave us with a choice between, on the one hand, a rational choice approach or, on the other, accepting trust as an essence of 'anthropological societies' – neither of which are very helpful for understanding how witchcraft blossoms at the interface of the intimate and the public. Yet here, as well, a very useful lead comes from an older social scientist, whose work on trust seems again to be unjustly neglected in present-day debates on the concept – at least by anthropologists. Already in 1900, Georg Simmel – more or less Freud's contemporary – had published his challenging reflections on trust as containing, next to knowledge, 'a further element of ... quasi-religious faith'. This element may be 'hard to describe', since it concerns 'a state of mind which is both less and more than knowledge'; yet he sees it as crucial for understanding trust (Simmel [1900] 1990: 179). In a seminal contribution, Guido Möllering, a German organizational sociologist, tries to capture the complex interplay Simmel construes between knowledge, ignorance and trust by referring to the 'suspension of doubt' as crucial to any form of trust:

> Suspension can be defined as the mechanism that brackets out uncertainty and ignorance, thus making interpretative knowledge momentarily 'certain' and enabling the leap [of faith] to favourable (or unfavourable) expectation. (Möllering 2001: 414)[28]

This perspective of 'a leap of trust' requiring the 'suspension of doubt' may help to surpass both the rational choice and the anthropological vision of trust. Or to put it in more general terms: the tendency to understand trust as respectively just knowledge, or as an essence that is more or less given and only broken in exceptional circumstance. Simmel seems to speak directly to the Douala proverb quoted above that 'one has to learn to live with one's sorcerer'. If witchcraft discourse expresses the gruesome realization that the most dangerous form of aggression comes from inside, the main challenge it raises might be how one can suspend knowledge of this danger. What 'leap of faith' might help to re-establish trust in one's relatives? Clearly different answers are possible for dealing with this terrible challenge, varying from often desperate attempts to expel the threatening elements from the inner circle, to efforts to neutralize the dangerous forces or assuage jealousy by just redistribution of new forms of wealth (but what is just? [see Geschiere in press]). The conclusion must be that, as for intimacy, trust is never given or self-evident. It has to be studied as a product of specific historical circumstances, as a constantly emerging 'event'. All we can hope to attain is to indicate certain factors or settings that make for a possible 'suspension of doubt' as a condition for a trust that is never a given.

Back to Sociality

The dangers of intimacy, so strongly outlined by witchcraft discourse, can serve to highlight certain more or less implicit premises in current ideas about sociality (see Long and Moore, Introduction). It might be good to emphasize that pointing out the dangers of a vision of intimacy – whether within the community, the household, the family or 'confluent love' – as intrinsically based on reciprocity, à la Sahlins or Giddens, is doing more than flogging a dead horse. In Africa, for instance – as in other parts of the 'developing' world – this view is making an unexpected comeback with the imposition of neoliberal views on development. Neoliberal development experts seem to combine in quite unexpected ways a solid belief in the blessings of the market with an equally categorical appeal to the old idea of 'the' community as a starting point for new-style development projects.[29]

Against such romanticizing visions the candid view my Maka friends taught me of witchcraft – seen as part and parcel of kinship – might help to give notions of family or community a more realistic profile. An inspiring comment on my somewhat disappointing explorations of how theoretical approaches to the notion of intimacy could give me more insight into what was at stake in witchcraft imaginaries came from Jan-Georg Deutsch when I presented some of my ideas to the Africa seminar at Oxford University. As a good historian he sternly admonished me to stop theorizing about the witchcraft–intimacy link, but to instead try to study its changing articulations historically. If both poles of the relation are constantly shifting, like their mutual articulations, it might indeed be history that could bring more clarity.

Following up on this sound advice I tried to summarize the changes in the intimacy–witchcraft link in the Maka area, where I have done fieldwork since 1971. It is striking indeed that even over this relative short period of forty years people's definitions of this link keep changing. In the 1970s the distance between village and city was supposed to bring substantial protection against the jealousy of the villagers and their witchcraft. One of the new elites of the village where I lived, who had made his career in the city, decided to return and live again with his 'brothers' in the village. However he immediately fell ill, and was only cured by a powerful *nganga*, who admonished him to return immediately to the city, and thereafter keep his distance from village life. Other people commented that, of course, he had been most imprudent venturing again into the intimacy of his family 'at home'. Yet in the 1990s a cousin of this *évolué* became also involved in a witchcraft affair. But this time people supposed that he had brought an urban form of witchcraft into the village. By now, village and city have become so intertwined that the geographical distance between the two is certainly no longer seen as an effective protection against witchcraft attacks. Above I referred already briefly to a saying, popular in the 1980s, from another part of Cameroon – the Southwest, colonized by the British and therefore Anglophone – that 'witchcraft does not cross the water'.[30] Yet since the 1990s people in this area have become obsessed with the idea of 'bush-falling' – a new and quite surprising notion since 'bush' stands for Europe (or in general the richer parts of the world) while people relate 'falling' to the image of a hunter who has luck and returns with large amounts of booty.[31] However, the metaphor of the hunter has its ambiguities since everybody also knows the stories of hunters who stumbled upon an attractive spot in the forest and chose to create a new village there. So the families who are often very actively involved in enabling younger members to leave for 'bush' set great store on making sure 'they will not forget' (Alpes 2011). Talliani's seminal article (in press) on the heavy pressure on Nigerian prostitutes in Italy not to 'forget' the family at home shows how heavy the burden can become. In a study on Ghanaians in Tel Aviv, Galli Sabar (2010) shows most graphically how transcontinental migrants can come to fear angry phone calls from home reminding them of their obligations to share. Apparently witchcraft threats are now supposed – and most emphatically so – to cross the ocean. Clearly, the scope attributed to witchcraft threats can change over time in important ways, marking people's changing perceptions of what counts as intimacy.

The comparison with Europe – both with the historical studies of the witchcraft trials of the sixteenth and seventeenth centuries, and with Favret-Saada's seminal study of the Bocage in France in the 1970s – highlight again different variations. Favret-Saada (1977 and 2009) and others (for instance, Briggs 1996) emphasize that witches in Europe are not relatives, like in Africa, but rather neighbours. Compare Favret-Saada's mesmerizing image, invoked above, of French farmers who desperately try to close off their farm – often with the help of a healer – against dark threats emanating from neighbouring farms. Yet it is quite clear that she – like historians for earlier periods – applies a very restricted definition of kinship. Even cousins who do not live in the same compound are seen as neighbours rather than as relatives (Favret-Saada 1977: 322). An important difference with African contexts, also emerging from historical studies, might be a more strict localizing delimitation of 'the house'.

The contrast with the very elastic conception of the house in these African settings is striking. As illustrated by the examples just mentioned, the house now easily bridges the distance between village and city – and one can even say that the house has acquired transcontinental allures with the increasing migration overseas. Such a context might explain the strong resilience of witchcraft ideas and the ease with which they graft themselves upon globalization and increasing mobility.

The varying delimitations of what count as intimacy are crucial for understanding how the balancing between danger and support – that is, between witchcraft and trust – will work out. But it is quite clear that the ambiguity is always there. Or to put it in more concrete terms: in some contexts – as in many African societies – family networks may be extremely resilient, bridging new distances and new inequalities. But they are never the haven of safety and reciprocity that some development organizations and even some anthropologists believe them to be.

A related – but more general – implication of the above may be that a major challenge for turning sociality into an incisive analytical notion is to get rid of moralizing associations that apparently creep in quite easily. The notion's attraction might be an implicit positive tenor: sociality, in the sense of 'being social', as a human endeavour. This implication may have been particularly appealing to anthropologists. Witchcraft discourse rather highlights the fundamentally ambiguous character of social relations as such.

Notes

* This text contains elements that are further developed in my book *Witchcraft, Intimacy and Trust – Africa in Comparison*, now in press with University of Chicago Press.

1. See the Introduction to this volume.
2. Of course, kinship is in such context not a biological given but a social concept: the use of kinship terms is an attempt to order social relations with all the claims, obligations and emotions that these terms imply.
3. Neither of the poles in this nexus are fixed: kinship or people's ideas about 'the house' are also constantly evolving with this increase of scale.
4. It is worth noting that popular ideas on 'witches' exhibit surprising correspondences in very different parts of the world: 'witches' are mostly supposed to have acquired a special ability to transform themselves; they can leave their bodies at night and fly away to secret meetings with their fellow-conspirators to plot attacks on people in their immediate environment (see Hutton 2004).
5. Thus the aim of this text is not to work towards an analytical definition of the notion of intimacy. My interest is rather in following the changing ways in which people demarcate an intimate sphere. Through an ethnography of such changes, I hope to map the changing context in which witchcraft suspicions thrive.
6. As said, it is quite clear that this is not special to the Maka. See, for instance, Ralph Austen's emphasis that 'witchcraft efficacy is held to be a direct function of the intimacy between witch and victim' (Austen 1993: 90). It may not be by accident that this aspect is so heavily emphasised in Austen's text since his was one of the first contributions that addresses, in a

most pioneering way, the link between witchcraft and globalization. Indeed, it was precisely when witchcraft studies in Africa began to address the role of this imaginary in wider contexts than the village that the continuing emphasis of intimacy became all the more striking. See also also the central place of this aspect in historian Hutton's attempt at a 'global definition' of witchcraft, covering both the historical data on Europe and anthropological studies elsewhere (Hutton 2004).

7   Another recurrent theme, briefly mentioned above, in the Maka stories about the *sjoumbou* is same-sex intercourse: these nightly encounters are marked not only by cannibalism but also by sexual debauchery. Yet in the nightly world everything is turned upside down. So sex is same-sex intercourse, which according to most Maka is unheard of in everyday life (although that remains to be seen): in the *sjoumbou* men do 'it' with men and 'even' women with women. This equation of homosexuality with witchcraft has taken on new vigour with quite dramatic effects now that recently (especially since 2005) not only the state and the Catholic Church but also the population at large have embarked – as elsewhere in Africa – on ferocious witch-hunts against homosexuals. One reason that homosexuality has quite suddenly become a burning issue all over the African continent might be the propagation of a challenging global gay/lesbian identity over the Internet; but the backlash against international human rights missions insisting that homosexuality should no longer be a criminal offence also plays an important role. 'Who are these people that they come here to impose the depravities of the West on Africa?', as a Cameroonian prosecutor asked me in a fit of rage during a private dinner – on the very day he had also received a delegation from the Canadian Human Rights mission (see Geschiere 2009a).

8. This trope of the witch-as-a-martyr is certainly not restricted to the Maka.

9. See also the film *Le Cercle des Pouvoirs* by Daniel Kamwa. Also from Douala, he is inspired by similar ideas – notably the betrayal of intimates as the crucial condition for getting access to the new magic of wealth (see also Alexei Tcheuyap's [2009] sharp analysis of this film).

10. Cf. also Isak Niehaus' insightful work (2001) on often violent accusations of witchcraft and the complex articulation between, on the one hand, tensions within the family/ neighbourhood and, on the other, a longer history of migrant labour in the South African Lowveld; he shows also that recently accusations concern direct kin more often than in the past. Florence Bernault (2006) offers a challenging extension of the witchcraft/intimacy theme by developing the idea that under colonial rule there emerged 'destructive understandings' (rather than distance and opposition) between colonials and locals – the first becoming even 'intimate partners in the remaking of local cosmologies'.

11. See also Elisabeth Copet-Rougier (1986) on the Mkako of Eastern Cameroon.

12. See the seminal account by Eric de Rosny, a French Jesuit who was initiated as an *nganga* in Douala in the 1960s. The climax in his initiation was when his master demanded of him 'a hairless animal' (i.e. a human being). However, in view of his special position, de Rosny was allowed to offer a goat – hence the title of his beautiful book *Les yeux de ma chèvre* (1981).

13. The notion of the village becoming a 'virtual reality' for Africans comes from Wim van Binsbergen (2001).

14. Regional differences may play an important role in this context. It is striking, for instance, that – as Tonda shows in rich detail (2005: 223) – in Brazzaville and Kinshasa (and probably in other cities in Congo) there is hardly any question of bringing back deceased urbanites to their home village to be buried. This is a marked difference with other parts of the continent where the funeral at home – that is, in the village – is still a high point in the reaffirmation of belonging and the coherence of the family; it is also a moment deeply feared by many urbanites since their obligatory attendance at funerals in the village offers the villagers a moment of choice to get even with their 'brothers in town' who neglected their duty to redistribute (see further Geschiere 2009b: chapter 6). In both the DRC and Congo-Brazzaville the general practice of burying in the city itself (where funerals are

increasingly monopolised by unruly youths) might be a sign of a much further weakening of urban–rural ties: indeed a true *déparentélisation*? (see also de Boeck 2006 – and his recent film on funerals in Kinshasa).

15. See Benneduce (forthcoming) and Taliani (2010) on Nigerians and Cameroonians in Turin; and Sabar (2010) on Ghanaians in Tel Aviv.

16. In Jankowiak (2008) the only exception among the ten contributions is Daniel Smith's perceptive analysis of the intertwinement of different 'arenas of intimacy' among the Igbo in southeastern Nigeria. Smith shows how intimacy among (male) friends affects the intimacy of men with their (female) lovers and their wives (the last two spheres are also in constant interaction). The great merit of his analysis is that he thus shows that intimacy is never taken for granted, but continuously reshaped and under constant pressure. See also Povinelli (2006) who tends as well to associate intimacy with love, sex and the conjugal family (at least in the modern, liberal version of 'the intimate event'), but in a highly sophisticated argument shows what deep ramifications can be deduced from this: the liberal view of the intimate (love) is central to the disciplining of the subject; in contrast to what many observers think, this sphere of intimacy/love cannot be opposed to society's constraints as an area of relative freedom but is instead closely interwoven with the constraints of what Povinelli calls the 'genealogical society' (see especially ibid.: 3, 13, 182, 210). Apparently, even when intimacy is equated with love, it can still imply a more negative view of it.

17. The blandness with which the learned sociologist follows publications by psychotherapists – for instance a certain Jody Hayer who insists in his book *Smart Love* (1990) on the link between intimacy and autonomy – is a bit worrying (see also Bersani and Philips and their criticism of 'the pathological optimism of … ego psychology' that they see as 'a complete distortion' of Freudian ideas [2008:74]). Even in the modern West, that seems to be Giddens' only orientation point, people may be quite reluctant to become involved in any form of intimacy precisely because it is seen as entailing a growing dependency (and thus threatening one's autonomy). In this sense there is not much distance from the African view of intimacy as potentially dangerous precisely because it entails vulnerability. More attention to the ambiguities of modernity might have helped Giddens to do more justice to the flip side of intimate relations.

18. For an again completely different take on 'intimacy', see Richard Sennett's 1974 book – at the time quite famous – on *The Fall of Public Man*. For Sennett, the public space that was expanding during the nineteenth century becomes more recently invaded by considerations that rather fit with more intimate spheres of life. People tend to judge relations in the public sphere ever more on the basis of intimate experiences. This leads to a loss of autonomous public know-how, earlier forms of sociability in the public sphere being ever more undermined by what he calls 'the tyranny of intimacy'. Again, this is in striking contrast to Giddens' celebration of intimacy as some sort of pinnacle of modernity.

19. Many thanks to Susan van Zyl and Laia Soto Bermant for counselling me so wisely on Freud.

20. Dutch is of interest here since it has similar terms but splits up the double meaning of *heimlich*: this term can be translated in Dutch as *huiselijk* (from *huis*, home) in its more positive sense (homely), but also as *heimelijk* in its more negative sense (secretive). It is worth noting, however, that the Dutch *heimelijk* relates to *heim*, which in Dutch is an old-fashioned word for home. So despite the split between *huiselijk* and *heimelijk* there is some trace here of the double meaning of home (*huis/heim*) – more or less parallel to the surprising tendency of the German *heimlich* to turn into its very opposite, *unheimlich*.

21. There is an interesting parallel here with James Siegel's analysis of witchcraft as being experienced as particularly frightening since it makes impossible links between things (see Siegel 2006).

22. Even a sharp observer like Charles Tilley – in his 2005 book *Trust and Rule* – seems to take it for granted that trust only becomes a problem when society undergoes an increase of

scale and thus becomes increasingly complex. The flipside of this grand view is that apparently trust is not a problem within small scale societies (like the local communities in Europe's early Middles Ages).

23. This is quoted in Sahlins 1974a: 196 – who unfortunately does not give a reference for this quote.

24. Similarly, Hoffmann's *The Sandman* story can be read as a defence of the family (the father tried to protect Nathaniel against the terrible Dr Coppelius, and was maybe even killed for this). It is only when modern science, in the person of Dr Coppelius, invades the house that its intimacy becomes uncanny.

25. The text was first published in 1965 (in M. Banton's *The Relevance of Models for Social Anthropology*), but a slightly revised version published in *Stone Age Economics* (1972) became the standard source; I quote here from that version.

26. See also Sahlins' text in the same volume on *The Spirit of the Gift* (Sahlins 1974b: 149–185).

27. See Mauss [1923–4] 1950: 155–160, 254; see also Mauss' digression (ibid.: 255) on the double meaning of the word *gift* in German: 'gift' but also 'poison' (with parallels in other Germanic languages). At the very end of the text (ibid.: 279) Mauss gives an example of King Arthur and his *Table ronde* that approaches Sahlins' image of 'generalized reciprocity' in small-scale communities. Yet even here the trust is clearly balanced in Mauss' view by hidden competition. It might be significant that the word *réciprocité* is hardly present in the French original of Mauss' text (and *réciproque* occurs only a few times). In the most recent English translation (1990), on the contrary, the term reciprocity appears to be central to Mauss' work since *rendre le don* is consequently translated as 'to reciprocate the gift' (instead of the more adequate and more neutral 'to return the gift' – perhaps this particular translation was influenced by Sahlins' essays?). In the earlier 1954 translation, the English rendering of *rendre le don* is 'to repay the gift', which although inaccurate is less distorting than 'reciprocate'. Such distorting translations make it all the more interesting to follow up in more detail the genealogy of the notion of reciprocity in anthropology, and the implications this notion acquired. With many thanks to Patricia Spyer and Rafael Sanchez for reintroducing me to Mauss.

28. Many thanks to Mattijs van de Port for drawing my attention to this article.

29. Striking examples are to be found in Juan Obarrio's thesis (2007) on the emergence of what he calls the 'Structural Adjustment state' in Mozambique. He describes how, for instance, during a meeting a senior American UNDP official angrily replied to the doubts of a few social scientists about the ease with which he took 'the' local community as the starting point for projects: 'These communities know who they are and know also their boundaries perfectly well'. Similarly a British USAID consultant insisted that communities 'will be like corporations, unified single legal subjects under the new land law' (ibid.: 105).

30. Miriam Goheen drew my attention to this common saying.

31. See Maybritt Jill Alpes (2011) 'Bushfalling: How Young Cameroonians Dare to Migrate'.

References

Alpes, M.J. 2011. Bushfalling: How Young Cameroonians Dare to Migrate. Ph.D. diss., University of Amsterdam.

Austen, R.A. 1993. The Moral Economy of Witchcraft: An Essay in Comparative History. In *Modernity and Its Malcontents: Ritual and Power in Postcolonial Africa* (eds.) J. and J. Comaroff, 89–110. Chicago: University of Chicago Press

Beneduce, R. forthcoming. L'Imaginaire qui tue: Réflexions sur sorcellerie, violence et pouvoir (Cameroun et Mali). In *Sorcellerie, violence et pouvoir en Afrique* (eds.) J. Bouju, and C. Martinelli. Paris: Karthala,

Bersani, L. and A. Philips. 2008. *Intimacies*. Chicago: University of Chicago Press.

Berlant, L. 1998. Intimacy. *Critical Inquiry* 24, no. 2: 281–288.
Bernault, F. 2006. Body, Power and Sacrifice in Equatorial Africa. *Journal of African History* 47: 207–239.
—— 2009. De la modernité comme impuissance: Fétichisme et crise du politique en Afrique équatoriale et ailleurs. *Cahiers d'Etudes africaines* 49, no. 3: 747–774.
Bernault, F. and J. Tonda. 2000. Dynamiques de l'invisible en Afrique. *Politique africaine* 79: 5–17 (special issue on *Pouvoirs sorciers* (eds.) F. Bernault and J. Tonda).
van Binsbergen, W.M.J. 2001. Witchcraft in Modern Africa as Virtualised Boundary Conditions of the Kinship Order. In *Witchcraft Dialogues* (eds.) G.C. Bond and D.M. Ciekawy, 212–264, Athens: Ohio University Press.
de Boeck, F. 2006. Youth, Death and the Urban Imagination|: A Case from Kinshasa. *Bulletin des séances de l'académie royale des sciences d'outre-mer* 52, no. 2: 113–125.
Briggs, R. 1996. *Witches and Neighbours: The Social and Cultural Context of European Witchcraft*. London: Harper Collins.
Copet-Rougier, E. 1986. 'Le Mal Court': Visible and Invisible Violence in an Acephalous Society – Mkako of Cameroon. In *The Anthropology of Violence* (ed.) D. Riches, 50–69. Oxford: Blackwell.
Favret-Saada, J. 1977. *Les mots, la mort, les sors: La sorcellerie dans le Bocage*. Paris: Gallimard.
—— 2009. *Désorceler*. Paris: Seuil (Editions de l'Olivier).
Freud, S. [1919] 2003. The Uncanny. In *The Uncanny* (eds.) D. McClintock and H. Haughton, 121–161. London: Penguin.
Geschiere, P. 1997. *The Modernity of Witchcraft: Politics and the Occult in Postcolonial Africa*. Charlottesville: University of Virginia Press.
—— 2009a. Homosexuality in Africa: Identity and Persecution. In *Urgency Required – Gay and Lesbian Rights Are Human Rights* (eds.) I. Dubel and A. Hielkema, 126–132. The Hague: HIVOS.
—— 2009b. *The Perils of Belonging: Autochthony, Citizenship, and Exclusion in Africa and Europe*. Chicago: University of Chicago Press.
—— 2011. Witchcraft and Modernity: Perspectives from Africa and Beyond. In *Sorcery and the Black Atlantic* (eds.) L. Nicolau and R.Sansi, 233–259. Chicago: University of Chicago Press.
—— in press. *Witchcraft, Intimacy and Trust – Africa in Comparison*. Chicago: University of Chicago Press.
Giddens, A. 1992. *The Transformation of Intimacy: Sexuality, Love and Eroticism in Modern Societies*. Stanford: Stanford University Press.
Gluckman, M. 1955. *Custom and Conflict in Africa*. Oxford: Blackwell.
Gregory, C. 1994. Exchange and Reciprocity. In *Companion Encyclopaedia of Anthropology* (ed.) T. Ingold, 911–940. London: Routledge.
Herzfeld, M. 1997. *Cultural Intimacy: Social Poetics in the Nation-State*. London: Routledge.
Hutton, R. 2004. Anthropological and Historical Approaches to Witchcraft: Potential for a New Collaboration? *The Historical Journal* 47, no. 2: 413–434.
Ingold, T. 1986. *The Appropriation of Nature: Essays on Human Ecology and Social Relations*. Manchester: Manchester University Press.
Jankowiak, W.R. 2008. *Intimacies: Love and Sex across Cultures*. New York: Columbia University Press.
Mauss, M. [1923–4] 1950. Essai sur le don: Forme et raison de l'échange dans les sociétés archaiques. In M. Mauss, *Sociologie et antropologie*, 145–285. Paris: PUF.
Mayer, P. [1954] 1970. Witches. In *Witchcraft and Sorcery* (ed.) M. Marwick, 45–64. Harmondsworth: Penguin.

Meyer, B. 1999. *Translating the Devil: Religion and Modernity among the Ewe in Ghana.* Edinburgh: Edinburgh University Press.

Möllering, G. 2001. The Nature of Trust: From Georg Simmel to a Theory of Expectation, Interpretation and Suspension. *Sociology* 35, no.2: 403–420.

Ndjio, B. 2006. *Feymania*: New Wealth, Magic Money and Power in Contemporary Cameroon. Ph.D.diss., University of Amsterdam.

Niehaus, I. 2001. *Witchcraft, Power and Politics: Exploring the Occult in the South African Lowveld.* London: Pluto.

Obarrio, J. 2007. The Spirit of the Law in Mozambique. PhD diss., Columbia University.

Povinelli, E.A. 2006. *The Empire of Love: Towards a Theory of Intimacy, Genealogy and Carnality.* Durham: Duke University Press.

de Rosny, E. 1981. *Les yeux de ma chèvre: Sur les pas des maîtres de la nuit en pays douala.* Paris: Plon.

——— 1992. *L'Afrique des guérisons.* Paris: Karthala.

Sabar, G. 2010.Witchcraft and Concepts of Evil amongst African Migrants Workers in Israel. *Canadian Journal of African Studies* 44, no. 1: 110–141.

Sahlins, M. 1974a. On the Sociology of Primitive Exchange. In M. Sahlins, *Stone Age Economics,* 185–277. London: Tavistock

——— 1974b. The Spirit of the Gift. In M. Sahlins, *Stone Age Economics,* 149–185. London: Tavistock.

Sennett, R. 1974. *The Fall of Public Man.* Cambridge: Cambridge University Press.

Siegel, J. 2006. *Naming the Witch.* Stanford: Stanford Unversity Press.

Simmel, G. [1908] 1950. *The Sociology of Georg Simmel* (ed. and trans. K.H. Wolff). New York: Free Press.

——— [1900] 1990. *The Philosophy of Money.* London: Routledge.

Taliani, S. in press. Daughters of Evil, Subjects of Mercy: Symbolic Violence, Coercion and Suffering in Everyday Life of Young Nigerian and Cameroonian Women. *Africa.*

Tcheuyap, A. 2009. Exclusion et pouvoir: Formes et forces de l'occulte dans les cinémas d'Afrique. *Canadian Journal of African Studies* 43, no. 2: 367–398

Tilley, C. 2005. *Trust and Rule.* Cambridge: Cambridge University Press.

Tonda, J. 2002. *La guérison divine en Afrique centrale (Congo, Gabon).* Paris: Karthala.

——— 2005. *Le souverain moderne: Le corps du pouvoir en Afrique centrale (Congo, Gabon).* Paris: Karthala.

4

Group Belonging in Trade Unions
Idioms of Sociality in Bolivia and Argentina

Sian Lazar, University of Cambridge

In this chapter I discuss two sets of union leaders, of street vendors in El Alto, Bolivia, and public-sector workers in Buenos Aires, Argentina, and I examine the values that underpin the development of a sense of the collectivity among them and their affiliates. Specifically, I explore two contrasting practices of collective behaviour and belonging, called *vida orgánica* and *contención*. Among street vendors and other unionists in El Alto, dominant idioms of group belonging coalesce around the term *vida orgánica*, which translates directly as 'organic life', and articulates organizational life with respect both to collectivities and to individuals within a given collective. To 'do organic life' means to participate fully in the organizational activities that define the collectivity. Although similar understandings of the 'organic' exist in Buenos Aires, not so much premium is placed upon them. Instead, what was striking to me was a frequent referral to *contención*, or 'containment', which describes both a form of therapeutic practice and a political encompassment of the individual by the collectivity. As such, the material I present here points towards a study of collectivity as part of a process of formation of a politically motivated associational community (see Introduction) rather than sociality in a more expansive sense. However, I want to argue that ethnographic analysis of these particular forms of collectivity provide useful insights into how socialities are constructed and worked on very actively, through everyday practices of 'being social' and conscious reflection on the nature of collective belonging and being.

Thus, the processes underpinning any form of sociality entail considerable work. This recognition gives the lie to theories of sociality that assume its naturalness and, further, leads us to consider the importance of contestation and power relations within specific forms of sociality. For politically motivated communities, this is crucial. All the trade union groups I discuss here operate within a competitive environment: they compete with alternative organizations in their own area; there is always the danger of international factionalism and splitting; and often they have to take up an antagonistic position towards their employer or regulator – which is, both in Bolivia and Argentina, the state. Successful collective action enables each union to protect and serve its members, and thereby preserve itself, since people leave if they feel they are not part of the organization. In this chapter, I argue that the nature of that feeling of belonging differs between the two spaces: for the Bolivian street vendors, it is articulated and felt as a series of obligations that constitute political subjects and full persons, while for the Argentine public-sector unionists, belonging is about being cared for and given a political context by the organization. Both rest on different theories of the relationship between individuals and the collective – different theories of sociality.

The research presented here draws on fieldwork conducted with two sets of union activists: street traders in El Alto, Bolivia and public-sector workers in Buenos Aires, Argentina. Street traders in the city of El Alto are organized into associations which cover one street, a market or a part of a street market (say, fish vendors in one of the main street markets of the city, or traders in a particular neighbourhood market). The associations of vendors working in El Alto are grouped into the Federation of Organized Workers, Artisans, Small Traders and Food Sellers of the City of El Alto (hereafter, the Federation) that is responsible for the whole city. The Federation is affiliated to the local (city) workers' congress and the national confederation of street vendors. At the time of my research in the early 2000s, the local, city-level organizations were more active politically than the national confederation. I spent time with executive committee members of the Federation, and local association members, as well as ordinary inhabitants of the city, including street vendors. I attended informal discussions at the central Federation offices, conducted interviews with leaders, attended demonstrations, civic parades and fiestas, spent time in street markets, many hours at general assemblies of associations, meetings between associations, meetings between association and Federation leaders and government officials, and dispute resolution processes at the Federation offices.

In Argentina my main informants were union leaders from the two main unions of public-sector workers, Union del Personal Civil de la Nacion (National Union of Civil Servants, UPCN) and Asociación de Trabajadores del Estado (Association of State Workers, ATE). Both unions represent workers employed by the state, at varying levels of public administration, from civil servants in Ministries to researchers employed by the state in the Atomic Energy Service, hospital nurses and maintenance workers, stage hands, actors and musicians in state-run theatres, and so on.[1] UPCN is stronger among civil servants in administrative departments, and therefore perhaps more 'middle class', while ATE covers a wider demographic, with one of its most important sectors being health workers. Studying the two most important state workers' unions in Argentina enables a comparison between two important trends of unionism within the same occupational sector.[2] Whereas UPCN is bureaucratic, Peronist, and avowedly pro-government, ATE is attempting a much more social movement-like political project, which looks for inspiration to radical oppositional trends of 1960s Argentine unionism (known as '*clasismo*') as much as to contemporary Latin American social movements (Atzeni and Ghighliani 2009). My interlocutors were union delegates at the level of the administrative unit (e.g., government department) and those with positions in the central offices of the sections pertaining to the city of Buenos Aires. During fieldwork in 2009, I conducted extensive interviews with delegates and leaders from the two unions in both their workplace and the union offices, attended plenaries, assemblies (at the level of the Sectional office and at the workplace), and other meetings; attended classes for new delegates run by both organizations; and attended demonstrations, press conferences, and other public events associated with union activity.

Elsewhere (Lazar 2012), I have discussed the nature of comparison between informal-sector indigenous workers in one of the poorest cities of the region and middle-class state employees in one of the wealthiest. At first sight, they seem incommensurable groups of research subjects, but both are *sindicalistas* or trade unionists, operating in the context of a Latin American tradition of tension between corporatism and militant union activity. In this chapter I want to take that similarity as a departure point from which to discuss the kinds of socialities promoted within the political organizational form of the trade union as instantiated in these particular contexts.

Organic Life

Vida orgánica translates literally as 'organic life', but when used in this context 'organic' does not have the connections with healthy living and purity that it does in English; neither does it have the Gramscian overtones that one might also expect. In both research contexts, the adjective 'organic' referred to a more restricted definition of organic as having to do with living organisms (as opposed to inorganic matter). However, in both locations, the living organism referred to is the union. It is a conception of the group as a subset of society that bears similarities with 'thick' versions of the social, as an entity that is both an agglomeration of actors and external to or above them. 'Organic life' was an extremely important concept for the street-trader unionists of El Alto. Leaders continually assessed the extent to which an individual or association 'did' organic life (the translation is awkward, but the verb used is *hacer*, which can mean both to make and to do). This helped them to decide how to mediate conflicts, to promote correct action within the group, make sense of the group, negotiate with government, and so on. It may be considered both an idiom and a technique of collectivity.

The concept refers most fundamentally to participation in union activities. Organic life at an individual level consists, first, of fulfilling obligations of attending meetings, demonstration marches and civic parades called by the association. To be considered conscientious, individuals should also pay their affiliation quotas regularly and 'maintain' their stall, that is, ensure that the stall is staffed regularly. Further, stall-holders have the responsibility to clean the street around their stall, and contribute to the cleaning and policing of collective public spaces, through physical participation or contribution of quotas for private security. One level up, associations can be classified into those that do organic life and those that don't. When I asked for the number of associations affiliated to the Federation, people always made this distinction, so that although the Federation has about 350 affiliated organizations, only around 200 'do' organic life.

Federation leaders are more willing to defend associations that do organic life in conflicts with the authorities, and the Executive Secretary frequently upbraided petitioners who appeared in the office only when their association had problems that needed Federation help. The Federation has no directly coercive power to enforce organic life among its affiliated associations, but their central office is furnished with desks, bookshelves, chairs and benches that have been provided as fines by associations that did not fulfil organic life and subsequently wanted to return to the Federation. In their day-to-day activities the executive committee members tend to use positive methods to reinforce the value of organic life, such as mentioning the most conscientious associations at the official party to celebrate Independence Day. This gives considerable prestige to the leadership and is often marked by the giving of certificates; they also give certificates to those organizations who participate in civic parades.

A crucial part of organic life at individual and association level is participation in ritual events, which are embodied practices of collectivity with important ramifications for politics in El Alto (Lazar 2008). Ritual events such as civic parades and fiestas display the power of the Federation and associations to convene large numbers of people, which is a crucial aspect of their political clout within the city, especially when factional disputes have lead to the establishment of competing associations or Federations, or in the run-up to an election. They bring members together in a sociality of friendship and entertainment that encourages both group cohesion and the development of disputes. They also mediate the relationship between people and deities, as in the example of the Carnival festivities, which are organized by the street traders' unions, when people *ch'alla* their workplace for luck and prosperity over the coming year. The *ch'alla* is an Andean ritual libation involving – at carnival time – the decoration of the thing being blessed, whether that is the market stall, truck, house, shop, or, in the countryside, animals and fields. Beer is then sprayed over the stall or house, etc., and shared among the people present. As well as a ceremonial blessing at carnival time or other religious festivities, or when a new building is opened, and so on, a *ch'alla* happens every time a person drinks beer, alcohol or a soft drink. It indicates the sharing of alcohol with the earth (Pachamama), done by dropping a part of a drink onto the floor before draining the cup, and sometimes also at the end (see Lazar 2008). Catherine Allen (1988) argues that the *ch'alla* is about acknowledging the life force of the things that surround people, through sharing food and drink with them; and many Andean ethnographers have discussed this kind of commensality between deities and humans (Abercrombie 1998; Allen 1988; Carter and Mamani P 1989; Harvey 1994; Heath 1987: 25). The *ch'alla* in all its manifestations throughout the year is also an eminently social event, involving the consumption of often large amounts of alcohol, which has ritual efficacy, not least because it brings the ancestors and other spiritual beings into the network of social relations and sociality through commensality.

One of the most important obligations for association members is the structured sociality of the consumption of alcohol, especially as an aspect of ritual action. The consumption of alcohol is a highly complex practice of sociality. Since it is both pleasurable and an obligatory part of most ritual events, it exposes the play between spontaneous participation and obligation, understood as animating forces of sociality in tension with each other. While not an obligation that is enforced entirely or simply through coercion, it is difficult to avoid drinking a large amount of alcohol during ritual events and parties.[3] Most unions coordinate their members' participation in parades on important civic dates and in the dancing for the anniversary fiesta of their neighbourhood, as well as in demonstrations called by the Federation, and the end of the civic parade or demonstration is usually the cue for the participants to break up into their separate groups in order to mark attendance lists and/or to drink together. Dancing in anniversary fiestas usually involves drinking for up to three days, a sociality built on the sociality of alcohol consumption that is also a key part of the dance rehearsals in the few weeks prior to the fiesta itself. The dance, parade and demonstration are a means for individuals to define and physically experience the collectivity, creating a shared sense of identity through movement. Afterwards, they join together in small groups to drink, socialize, and *ch'alla*. As I explain in Lazar (2008), the conviviality associated with alcohol consumption is quite structured. The consumption of beer is a good example. Whoever has bought the bottle will pour out a small cup of beer for everyone. They then ask everyone to drink up (in Aymara, *umtasiñani*, which means 'let's drink up', in Spanish, just *salud*, or 'cheers'). At that point, everyone *ch'allas* Pachamama by dropping a small amount of beer on the ground, then either drains the beer entirely or drinks half the cup. Carter and Mamani say that alcohol consumption 'almost always occurs in a social context' (1989: 320); and this can be quite literal – you do not sip continually from your glass, but only drink up when others are drinking. This model is also followed for soft drinks, and stronger *tragos* [drinks made with burnt alcohol mixed with flavouring and drunk from shot-sized cups].

The sociality of drinking together also has a compulsory quality across the Andes (cf. Cowan 1990 for Northern Greece). I often heard people in El Alto saying 'they made me drink', which at first I thought was just an excuse for at times alarming levels of drunkenness. However, I soon realized that there was a strong element of empirical truth in this, since there is a lot of pressure around drinking. It is almost impossible to refuse a drink, because people just will not hear of it. If someone buys you a bottle of beer, you must reciprocate, that is buy them one and drink it that evening with them. If poured a drink, you must drink along with everyone else, and at the same rate, unless you are able to surreptitiously *ch'alla* larger amounts to Pachamama before drinking (Allen 1988). Drinking together is therefore a kind of active structured sociality, as with the more obviously ritualized political action of organic life as participation in demonstrations or parades. The two go together.

Conflict resolution is a key element of the negotiation of collectivity and group belonging, especially in such an organized setting as the trade union, and organic life matters when it comes to conflict resolution at multiple levels of the trade union structure. If one party to a conflict between individual vendors fulfils the obligations of organic life they have a greater call on the protection provided by that association; if one association is more conscientious than another, they have a greater call on the support of the Federation. Where both do organic life, then resolving the conflict is more complicated, because both are equally conscientious members of the collectivity. Fulfilling organic life can strengthen the hand of parties in a dispute, and we might therefore be inclined to analyse it as an external set of moral rules and regulations that encode a dynamic of obligations and rights between the association and its members. However, some care should be taken with this. For organic life is not generally spoken of as an exchange of duties and rights, or conscientious participation in return for protection. Rather, the overt discourse was one of taken-for-grantedness: there are certain things that one just does if one is a member of an association, certain things that associations just do as part of the Federation.

Thus a contract of rights and duties as in the Western legal tradition does not adequately describe the exchanges occurring under organic life. For one thing, the notion of organic life gives a sense of a gradation of rights that corresponds both to how conscientious the conflictual party has been, and in practice to how well they know the people mediating the conflict. The parties to the exchange are not contractual equals, or even stable entities; their relative call on their counterpart varies according to their actions, the perceptions of their actions, personal connections they are able to make, and so on. This kind of instability and fluctuation is, in practice, a constitutive part of Western legal contractual relations, but it is not constitutive of the very definition of the exchange, which is in contrast usually premised on relatively stable (if not equal) parties to a given contract.

For another, there is a general acceptance of what might appear to be coercive measures to enforce organic life. For example, affiliates are usually fined if they do not attend a general assembly of their association. At the end of the assembly, the leadership distribute paper tokens, and at the following market day they circulate around the stalls demanding to see each trader's token, and fining those who do not have one. Under normal circumstances, people also considered it an obligation to participate in civic parades, demonstrations and strikes, and this is often enforced by the practice of taking attendance and fining those who are absent. But it would be mistaken to see this as something entirely imposed from above, an external social order enforcing the rules of social control through obligation. In fact, there is a balance that leaders need to achieve: they are expected to fine those who do not participate in protest marches and other activities, but that fine should not be too heavy. This balance is a constant source of commentary, and if leaders overstep the mark too frequently then affiliates will complain and the leaders' position will become vulnerable. If the fine is set too high, people have no choice but to go on the march, whereas if it is reasonable, the fine becomes a form of participation, equivalent to physical participation. Whatever happens, participation will cost money – in lost income, for food, transport to the meeting point, etc. My interpretation is that some form of support, either through the fine or through physical participation, is considered to be obligatory.

The question at stake is how we understand that obligation, for the play between spontaneity and obligation (or structure) is an important aspect of how we understand sociality more generally. As for the Malawian case so perceptively discussed by Harri Englund (2008), even if buttressed by seemingly coercive provisions, the obligations to others encoded within practices of organic life are themselves constitutive of persons or selves. Englund argues that scholars have overlooked this possibility because of a tendency to equate morality with law, and he points out that the usual practice of 'linking the concept of obligation so closely to divine or social control' essentially overlooks 'the possibility that the compulsion at the heart of obligation is existential – that it is constitutive of, rather than external to, those who give and receive' (ibid.: 36). Olivia Harris makes a similar point in a discussion about the value of work in the Andes, where she argues that 'the *obligation* to work should not be equated with a notion of *coercion*' (Harris 2007: 159, emphasis in original). In both these ethnographic cases, as in my own, obligatory actions are not so much enforced from an external order but through a relationship between the self and sociality. The subject is constituted through the kinds of socialities that obtain in a given context. Organic life is not a moral law, but a way of being social – even a way of life, as underlined by the use of the Spanish word *vida*. That kind of active social life is constituted by obligations, and the subjects who participate in organic life are themselves constituted by the same obligations. This, then, suggests that sociality itself is not participation in some kind of external social order that can be taken for granted or envisaged as an inherently human quality, rather, it is constituted by and through subjects actively engaged in a collective being-in-the-world (Merleau-Ponty 1962).

Containment

Among public-sector unionists in Argentina, the concept of the *orgánico* does exist, and where used it usually refers to an organizational ethos of strong discipline, which is thought by many to lead to effective action.[4] However, it is not tied to a notion of collective life in the same way as in El Alto; nor does it have the same kind of prominence as an idiom of sociality. More prominent was a different idea, of *contención* or containment. This concept appeared in multiple contexts in my fieldwork, from informal conversations to interviews, in discussions about the role of the union leader (delegate), and with respect to the relationship between individual affiliate and their union.

The following quote from an anonymous delegate shows the importance of different forms of encompassment for some trade unionists; how passionately it can be felt (or at least expressed), using the language of family, protection, identity and containment:

> UPCN gave me identity, I feel part of UPCN, I don't feel alone, whatever happens, I'm from UPCN. And UPCN is everywhere, it's going to protect me, it helps me with my children in school, it gives me a summer camp [for the children], it gives me social coverage ... . UPCN gave me identity – wherever I am, or if there is a demonstration and although people come from other ministries, we're all from UPCN, and that's fantastic. UPCN embraced me [*me abrazó*], and it's a paternalistic figure.
>
> To me, UPCN gave me an identity, that I needed, and an embrace that I lost when I moved to the city of Buenos Aires, when I left the party, and UPCN gave me this peronist identity, that encompasses me [*que me abraza*]. I feel contained [*contenido*], it gave me identity, I am from UPCN.
>
> I'm part of UPCN, I'm part of an organization in an individualistic society. ... UPCN gave me a place where we're all equal, where it gives me everything that I need, or they give me everything they can give, and they protect me, that's what UPCN gives me.
>
> UPCN is like my family, I have my wife but UPCN is also my family. ... Perhaps it's difficult to explain with words, but UPCN is like a feeling [*un sentimiento*],[5] we're part of something, I'm not alone in the street or at work, UPCN is always there with me. (Interviews, anon., 13 April 2009)

In El Alto, the concept of organic life was brought into being through repetition, exhortation, and reward. This implicitly (and sometimes explicitly) acknowledged the work required to maintain collective life, as did the use of language – 'doing organic life' has a very active sense to it; the words contains within them the possibility that a person or a group might fail to 'do' organic life. In contrast, 'containment' as an idiom of sociality among the unionists I worked with in Buenos Aires named a technique of encompassment of the individual by the collectivity; it was a form of sociality enacted by the group on the individual, rather than one of the individual in the context of the group. However, in Buenos Aires, just as in El Alto, collective sociality requires considerable work; and that work is 'containment'. Although not quite such a dominant value as 'organic life' was in everyday evaluation of activities in El Alto, for the Buenos Aires unionists I worked with, containment as technique was a common term, one open to conscious reflection, especially during interviews.

Quite often I was told that part of the job of a delegate was 'to contain' (*contener*) the ordinary affiliate, or that 'there's a lot of containment' (*hay mucha contención*); this casual use of a term that was unfamiliar to me prompted me to explore it in greater depth in a series of interviews. I argue that containment has three dimensions: it can refer to a therapeutic practice of listening to individuals' problems, especially those that exceed ordinary workplace struggles; to a kind of politicized group encompassment of an individual that gives individual activists a context in which to act; and finally, the possibility that union delegates are containing their affiliates before their problems become serious enough or understood as structural or collective enough to warrant mobilization or some other form of politicized anger. So, for example, individualized strategies of therapeutic containment help people facing personal problems that have resulted from economic crisis, such as a house repossession; but some argue that this prevents them from a more explicitly politicized analysis of the crisis itself. For the purposes of this chapter I focus on the first two as most directly related to questions of sociality. I suggest that the notion of containment opens up an analysis of how the sociality of individual relationships between affiliate and delegate accompany more group-based socialities of passion, commitment and care. All are different forms of group encompassment of individuals through practices of interactive sociality. Differences between these practices and those of organic life in El Alto point to divergent conceptualizations of the self, choice and obligation.

The therapeutic practice of containment is a concept that originated in the work of Wilfred Bion, a British Kleinian psychoanalyst (Bion 1959; Douglas 2007; Hinshelwood 1989), and has entered into everyday language in Buenos Aires over the course of the twentieth century. Freudian psychoanalysis has been very popular in Argentina since the 1950s. Mariano Ben Plotkin has argued that 'a psychoanalytic culture' has developed in Argentina, to the point that 'since the 1960s, psychoanalysis has provided a framework of intelligibility to many Argentines for whom psychoanalysis still functions as a lens that filters reality' (Plotkin 2003: 229). He maintains that the 2000s have seen a banalization of psychoanalysis as it has permeated popular discourse. British Kleinian theories were the most influential in Argentina until the Lacanians began to dominate in the 1970s (Plotkin 2001), and so it is plausible that the notion of containment travelled from Britain to Argentina and entered into everyday speech through the influence of Kleinian psychoanalysts in Argentine society. The psychoanalyst Hazel Douglas provides the following definition:

> Containment is thought to occur when one person [the container] receives and understands the emotional communication of another [the contained] without being overwhelmed by it, processes it and then communicates understanding and recognition back to the other person. This process can restore the capacity to think in the other person. (Douglas 2007: 33)

The first container–contained relationship is that between the mother and infant, but in therapy that relationship is then replicated with the therapist being the container. The everyday understanding of containment in Argentina is heavily influenced by this, and some of my interlocutors spoke of it in very similar terms, or at least used the term to refer to the practice of listening to the affiliate and placing themselves in a quasi-therapeutic relationship. Sabrina Rodriguez argued that taking on a therapeutic role was one of the many tasks of a union delegate and she linked it to values of solidarity:

> There is a diverse set of jobs. Sometimes they are about containment, because a comrade [*compañero*] is overwhelmed with work and needs someone who listens to them, contains them, and calms them – the psychosocial situation. So, often it is just the theme of containment, from comrade to comrade, no?, and that's part of daily life. … You'll see here … always a climate of solidarity, of being concerned with the other comrade, of helping each other, within the delegation. … For example, when I leave this office and I see a comrade who is sat down with another comrade at 8, 9 at night, who is crying, in a situation that may even be personal, and she listens to him, she contains him, and that is the nice thing.[6] (Interview, Sabrina Rodriguez, 13 May 2009)

Ariel Negrete, another UPCN General Secretary, told me that in the delegate's job, 'there is a lot of containment' (*hay mucha contención*), and said that one was often like a psychologist. He argued that much of the union delegates' work was to do with workers' personal problems rather than explicitly work-related questions, saying that 'people have to go to someone who helps them rethink, recapacitate themselves' (Interview, Ariel Negrete, 17 June 2009). Informants also used the term containment just in passing, when referring for example to delegates' abilities to deal with affiliates' problems, using phrases such as 'capacity for containment' (*capacidad de contención*).

In addition, delegates would also often simply call the union a 'place of containment' (*lugar de contención*) and use containment to talk about a kind of group encompassment of an individual, the second aspect I discuss here. Containment can refer to the way that the union gives delegates a kind of context, both in the sense of a political context, which is constituted through particular politicized practices of sociality, and as a space for a structured sociality of care. An ATE delegate said:

> Well, the fact of belonging to a group, to a collective, at least it contains you [*te contiene*], it makes you feel good, because you might be with people, some more your friends, others less so, but you feel contained [*te sentís contenido*] in four or five small things you feel contained, you know that we're here for something in common.
>
> Let's say, of all those who are here – whether we're five or twenty-five, we all have some point in common with each other. Just today we were talking about this, about some of our affiliates, probably politically we just don't coincide at all, but they feel part [of the organization] and for them, belonging to the organization is very important. What I mean is, they say to you 'I'm from ATE', you hear them talk and you think 'I don't share anything' [laughs], of politics, of their vision of life, whatever, but

here they feel part [of something], we all feel part [of something] …. There's something that unifies us, and it's something that isn't material, rather it has something to do with living together [*convivencia*], with conceptions of life. (Interview, anon. ATE-Malbrán, 12 July 2009)

'Living together' takes multiple forms; for ATE delegates it is mostly associated with shared political work. That includes attendance at formal meetings and demonstrations as well as spending time in the local union office, answering workers' and affiliates' questions, preparing campaign materials and actions, granting interviews to visiting researchers, and so on. Much of the time in the local office is spent chatting with other delegates, over cigarettes and *mate*. *Mate* is considered by many to be the 'national drink' of Argentina, and is consumed in many contexts by Argentines from all walks of life. It is a herbal infusion prepared in a round cup: one person packs the cup with the *yerba mate* leaves and pours boiling water on from a flask. They sip from a metal straw until they have consumed all the liquid, and pass the cup and straw back to the person with the flask, who pours more water on and then passes the drink to the next person. Although people do also drink *mate* on their own, the conventions of sharing make drinking *mate* into a very social endeavour, rather like the Bolivian conventions around beer consumption. In the local ATE union office, drinking *mate* and smoking cigarettes is accompanied by wide ranging discussions, from matters of local gossip to very complex and passionate political discussions. Some of the interviews I conducted in these places tapped into what was evidently a common event, as activists took the opportunity to describe their political philosophy and analysis of the role of the union to a new audience. Often, interviews held in local union offices would fall into quite an easy sociality of political discussion, as one person might take the lead with others chipping in to back him (usually him) up, prompt him, contribute their own perspective. Activists knew the political positions that their colleagues tended to take, showing that these kinds of discussions were not entirely artificial events put on solely for the purposes of the interview, but part of everyday life.

Apart from day-to-day politicized discussion, general assemblies and demonstrations were also very social events. People met up with friends, enjoyed the effervescence of the moment, reaffirmed their views in conjunction with others. Activists acknowledged this entertaining aspect of the demonstrations explicitly, pointing out to me how everyone was friends, and saying that demonstrations are like a party. Either before or after the event, the organizers go to a nearby café to have coffee and a sandwich and discuss the progress of the campaign, future events, and so on. I found the number of demonstrations ATE delegates participate in quite tiring and draining, especially since they never seemed to resolve things in a final way. This is a kind of 'attritional time' of constant activity which – it is hoped – changes politics over the long term, but only very rarely erupts into a revolutionary event that holds the promise of significant change. This attritional aspect of political activity is part of what leads some to drop out and others to choose different unions or reject union membership entirely; but importantly many activists stay well into middle age. This may in part be because of the politicized sociality of participation in constant activity. For many, the entertaining aspect of the political activity is what keeps them active in the organization; for others, their passionate political commitment is repeatedly confirmed through participation in concert with other like-minded people, friends. The constant activity underlines the incompleteness of their mission and the necessity to keep going, maintain their commitment to the cause.[7] The activity itself is work, a way of life, which constitutes them as persons – defined politically.

UPCN delegates also participate in such explicitly political activities as street demonstrations and other mobilizations, although at nothing like the frequency of ATE. But they complement their political activities with a wide range of organizational activities revolving around encompassment as the provision of a space of protection and for self-actualization. They have a significant programme of professional training in public administration and a school for new delegates. They hold regular meetings of the delegates responsible for equality of opportunities, youth, culture and so on. They promote cultural activities, such as photography or creative writing competitions. They have a stand at the annual Buenos Aires book fair, where they hold debates and presentations. My interlocutors were very proud of these activities. Particularly active UPCN delegations also hold events at their place of work, for example to celebrate International Women's day. As with the ATE events, formal campaigning events are often followed by informal exclusive gatherings to gossip, have a sandwich, drink *mate* or coffee, discuss future events, and so on. The very structured sociality of a ceremonial event is combined with a more exclusive and less ritualized sociality of commensality and gossip as the organizers get together to chat about the event itself but also about their lives more generally. On a day-to-day basis, as with ATE, the shared time in the local union office conducting union business and discussing events of the day also creates an easy sociality of friends working together for similar goals.

In UPCN, a major practice of encompassment is enacted through care, specifically the care of the health of individual affiliates. UPCN is particularly proud of the fact that it controls the health insurance scheme for civil service workers, Union Personal. UP is widely considered to be a very effective health insurance scheme – unlike some of those controlled by unions – and it is open to all civil servants, whether affiliated to UPCN or not. One delegate called the health insurance scheme itself 'an important source of containment'. Delegates often saw one of their most important services to their affiliates as providing support and advice in managing the health care system: for example, they would help them through bureaucratic procedures, telephone clinics to make appointments or check up whether test results were back, and so on. In informal conversations, delegates advise each other on what they could expect from Union Personal, recommending it, advising what plan it might be necessary to sign up for, what one could expect, what the level of treatment was like, and so on. Sometimes, the union delegation will also take on wider responsibilities associated with the health of workers, for example, one delegate told me that he joined UPCN because when his baby daughter fell very seriously ill, it was only the UPCN activists who took care of him, even though he was not an affiliate at the time. They arranged for hospital treatment, and also ensured that he got paid leave from work to be with his daughter in hospital.

More widely, some particularly active delegations produce material and give advice for the workers in their office on a wide range of topics outside of the progress of political actions or collective bargaining, such as workplace bullying (*violencia laboral*), preventive health, or swine flu. UPCN also has a well-developed range of 'subsidies' (*subsidios*) for affiliates, which are gifts, mostly of a stay in a hotel, that mark particular life events from the birth of a child to weddings, wedding anniversaries and death of an affiliate. One of the day-to-day activities of the delegate in charge of Acción Social is to assist affiliates in applying for this support. UPCN also negotiates discounts with travel agents, kindergartens and other medical services; it provides school materials for preschool and primary school children each year; it also has three recreational facilities for its affiliates.[8] Through these activities, UPCN cares for its affiliates and their families at all stages of their life cycles, and for some delegates it can become a total institution, their whole life, as the quote at the beginning of this chapter shows.

Conclusions

In this chapter I have discussed a series of understandings of politicized socialities, often quite induced, which bring together disparate people and keep them together and acting – broadly – in concert. These include eating and drinking together; shared conversations on political and personal topics; other political activity such as campaigning, demonstrating, meeting; participation in ritual events, and the provision of practical assistance in social or health matters. They are quite structured, by which I mean both that they involve conventions or philosophies that are amenable to an anthropological gaze, and that they are often self-consciously constructed. In this concluding section, I bring an explicitly comparative perspective to bear on the differences between the two settings, and assess some of the implications of these for a more general approach to sociality.

In both El Alto and Buenos Aires, ritual action is an important kind of politicized sociality, and it is combined with a sociality of passion and shared political commitment, as well as day-to-day friendship. This could be analysed in a fairly functionalist way as repeated collective activity that creates effectiveness for the political unit. For example, the participation in demonstrations, parades and fiestas that is a crucial part of organic life in El Alto is central to the union's ability to negotiate with local authorities from a position of strength, where the latter depends crucially on being able to show that the union has large numbers of supporters. At the same time, participation in organic life as ritual activity is also often entertaining, exhilarating, fun. As with participation in various ritualized events in Argentina, from campaign meetings to political demonstrations, repeated collective activity may help to keep people's interest, passion and conviction from flagging.

Beyond the question of the relationship between sociality and the effectiveness of the political grouping, the discussion here illuminates questions about how membership of the group is created through particular understandings of the self and subject. To a greater or lesser degree in the two settings, participation is understood as obligatory – very obviously so in the case of El Alto, where the obligation to participate in organic life constitutes individual street vendors as well as political collectivities as subjects. In Buenos Aires, obligation is less emphasized in favour of passion, commitment, and shared belonging to a political ideal. Here, collectivity comes about more through practices of a sociality of care: quasi-therapeutic relationships of individualized containment, politicized group encompassment of the individual through providing them with a political context, and the provision of services and assistance for them and their families. The El Alto union does not provide the same level of individualized services for its members, but the content of organic life in El Alto hints at the content of the Federation's sociality of care conceived in this way. It revolves around the ability of the Federation leaders to resolve individual and group conflicts, to negotiate with local government, and supervise the commercial space of the city. Through enforcing organic life on a day-to-day basis, vendors associations ensure that people sell their products, maintain their stalls, clean the surrounding area; through enforcing organic life as participation in politics, the union maintains its position of strength as a negotiator able to protect its members.

Commensality plays an important role in the structured and less structured kinds of sociality within both sets of political organizations. The nature of shared consumption of food and drink shows quite well the interplay of structure, subjecthood and collective being-in-the-world that I argue is constitutive of sociality more generally. The conventions around drinking beer or *mate* are known to all and shape the kinds of interactions that occur between people. They therefore have an element of constructedness. The visit to a local café for a sandwich before or after a political demonstration would not occur without the highly organized ritual event that brings the group together. But they are also social events that are something we all recognize from our quotidian experience: gatherings of friends and colleagues, who gossip, exchange ideas, help each other out, and enjoy each other's company. Understanding these kinds of social actions through the concepts of organic life and containment illuminates their constructed nature but should not obscure the importance of the easy sociality of friendship that they bring forth over time. In turn, the structured aspect of these concepts points also to their fragility. Although organic life is talked about as something that one just does as a full member of the group, it is also often a source of frustration at both individual and associational level. It needs constant reiteration because people and groups do often fail to do organic life. Similarly, containment must be continually recreated through listening to affiliates' problems, helping them with administrative procedures, organizing campaigning activities, political meetings, demonstrations and informal gatherings, and so on. Both case studies show that the collectivity needs to be worked on; sociality cannot be taken for granted.

The exploration of a consciously created and politically motivated form of collectivity thus requires reflection on the relationship between collectivity and sociality. Stronger notions of sociality (such as those of Tuomela [2007] and Gilbert [1997]) tend to conflate the two. For Raimo Tuomela, for example, what he calls 'we-mode thinking, feeling and acting' (2007: 4) require the existence of a group, or group ethos, that humans are part of but that is something other than a mere assemblage, since it has agency and identity of its own and is therefore to an extent external. A kind of collective orientation, in this view, is inherent to humans, which he terms the 'collectivity condition' (ibid.: 5). This is, however, problematic because of a lack of theorization about the social construction of sociality understood in this way. Tuomela thus confirms the validity of Latour's critique of 'sociologists of the social' (2005b) for their circular reasoning: explaining 'the social' (society) by means of saying that something is social. His failure to deconstruct 'the group' or 'group ethos' thus simply explains collectivity through a propensity to collectivity. A contrasting perspective is the Latourian 'flattening' impulse that sees the social in any grouping, association or assemblage. According to this, since there is no society conceived of as a whole thing that could ultimately be known, even if through a piecemeal and layered intellectual process, the aim for social science research is to trace and describe associations, relations, interactions and so on that constitute assemblages of people and things (Cook et al. 2009; Latour 2005a, 2005b). Yet the widely critiqued evacuation of an analysis of power from this approach makes it equally unsatisfactory, especially for a study of explicitly political assemblages which are constructed for a particular cause.

We might, then, better approach politically motivated collectivity as one aspect of sociality and understand sociality in a broad sense as 'being social'. This seems reasonable, since reducing 'the social' merely to the ways that people group together represents an analytical impoverishment. Our understanding of the social needs to exceed a tracing of groups, networks, and so on, and incorporate questions of power, agency, subjectivity, consciousness and constructedness. However, there is a different meaning of 'sociality' that I have also explored in this chapter, of sociality as referring to the day-to-day practice of social relations, social behaviour understood as behaviour in groups (Candea 2010). The senses of collectivity achieved within activist groupings of Bolivian street vendors and Argentine public sector workers are attained partially by means of being social understood in this quotidian sense. By this I mean acting socially through physical co-presence: hanging out together, sharing cigarettes, drinks, having political discussions, attending demonstrations, parties, etc. 'Sociality' might then refer to these kinds of actions, and we might distinguish between different orders of sociality: sociality as 'the social' and sociality as (everyday practices of) being social. Thus we can argue that collectivity as part of sociality (as 'the social') is achieved through (everyday practices of) sociality.

Although true in my view, this statement is of course another circular argument. Nonetheless, an ethnographic exploration of the 'social' does need to take into account the interplay between collectivity and sociality without subsuming one within the other. Practices of everyday sociality (understood as forms of collective being-in-the-world) contribute to the creation of a sense of the wider group, and seem almost designed to do so. This is of particular importance when the group in question is one that must bring together diverse people for a set of political objectives. Unions in Bolivia and Argentina cannot take it for granted that their members will continue their membership. The dynamics are more complex than a contractual exchange between stable entities (union and self-interested individual) of duties towards the union for rights and protection from the union. Subjects, both individual and collective, are constituted through their participation in political activities and group socialities, although this process is differently conceptualized in each context. In Bolivia, the subject is expected to be constituted through the enactment of their obligations to the collective through participation, while in Argentina the idea is that the collective encompasses the individual through care.

Moreover, a focus solely on everyday practices of sociality would not fully explain the creation of senses of collectivity as belonging and political commitment that are the subject of this chapter, for one would also need to account for the conscious dimension of reflection on and construction of collective being and belonging. *Vida orgánica* and *contención* should, then, be thought of both as ideologies of collectivity, in the sense that the repeated injunction to live up to them helps to construct a feeling of group-ness, and as ways of understanding and articulating what given groups consist of. I have argued here that they are a form of collective self-fashioning into coherent but consciously constructed and not naturally given groups, each with some kind of sense of purpose and of identity. Importantly, the reiteration of techniques such as these indicates that that construction of the group is not the natural result of human social interaction (cf. Tuomela 2007); far from it. In fact it requires conscious effort, effort that has become understood in the form of well-articulated organizational philosophies. Indeed, the need to enforce these practices through a reiteration of their importance and naturalness demonstrates the fragility of the groups they make.

Acknowledgements

My thanks to the anonymous readers for their close and enormously helpful readings of an earlier draft of this chapter. Thanks also to Henrietta Moore for intellectual encouragement and discussion about comparison, but above all to Nick Long for his patience and flexibility as editor, and his perceptive reading and suggestions for improvement. The research for this chapter was funded by the Wenner Gren Foundation for Anthropological Research; the ESRC and the Centre of Latin American Studies at the University of Cambridge.

Notes

1. The teachers have separate unions. The main ones usually work in collaboration with ATE. Doctors have their own professional organizations.
2. The fact that several different unions operate in the public sector with full official recognition is atypical for Argentinean unionism, where the dominant model is a corporatist one of the monopoly of one officially recognized union representation per occupational activity.
3. One common – albeit quite drastic – way is by becoming an Evangelical Christian; and the avoidance of alcohol is one of the key features of Evangelical Christianity for many of its adherents.
4. See Lazar (n.d.) for a discussion about the different approaches to discipline of unionists in ATE and UPCN.
5. It is common to call Peronism a '*sentimiento*' like this.
6. Throughout the quotes in this paper, 'comrade' is used as a translation for '*compañero*', not '*camarada*', which is much more associated with communist parties, and not a common term for either UPCN or ATE activists.
7. My thanks to Sharika Thiranagama for pointing this out.
8. This last is quite common to most of the wealthiest unions, which run hotels, traditionally located in the beach resort of Mar del Plata. The union-run hotels boomed in the 1950s and gave members of the Argentine working class their first ever access to a vacation. UPCN's recreational centres are the remnants of this mid-twentieth-century trend.

References

Abercrombie, T.A. 1998. *Pathways of Memory and Power: Ethnography and History among an Andean People*. Madison: University of Wisconsin Press.

Allen, C.J. 1988. *The Hold Life Has: Coca and Cultural Identity in an Andean Community*. Washington: Smithsonian Institution Press.

Atzeni, M., and P. Ghighliani 2009. Labour Movement in Argentina since 1945: The Limits of Trade Union Reformism. In *Trade Unionism since 1945: Towards a Global History, Volume 2: The Americas, Asia and Australia* (ed.) C. Phelan, 223–248. Bern: Peter Lang.

Bion, W. 1959. Attacks on Linking. *The International Journal of Psychoanalysis* 40: 308–315.

Candea, M. 2010. 'I Fell in Love with Carlos the Meerkat': Engagement and Detachment in Human–Animal Relations. *American Ethnologist* 37, no. 2: 241–258.

Carter, W.E., and M. Mamani [1982] 1989. *Irpa Chico. Individuo Y Comunidad En La Cultural Aymara* (2nd ed.). La Paz: Libreria (Editorial 'Juventud').

Cook, J., J. Laidlaw, and J. Mair 2009. What If There Is No Elephant? Towards a Conception of an Un-Sited Field. In *Multi-Sited Ethnography: Theory, Praxis and Locality in Contemporary Social Research* (ed.) M. Falzon, 47–72. London: Ashgate.

Cowan, J.K. 1990. *Dance and the Body Politic in Northern Greece.* Princeton: Princeton University Press.

Douglas, H. 2007. *Containment and Reciprocity: Integrating Psychoanalytic Theory and Child Development Research for Work with Children.* London: Routledge.

Englund, H. 2008. Extreme Poverty and Existential Obligations: Beyond Morality in the Anthropology of Africa? *Social Analysis* 52, no. 3: 33–50.

Gilbert, M. 1997. Concerning Sociality: The Plural Subject as Paradigm. In *The Mark of the Social: Discovery or Invention?* (ed.) J.D. Greenwood, 17–36. Lanham, MD: Rowman and Littlefield.

Harris, O. 2007. What Makes People Work? In *Questions of Anthropology* (eds.) R. Astuti, J. Parry and C. Stafford, 137–166. Oxford: Berg.

Harvey, P. 1994. Gender, Community and Confrontation: Power Relations in Drunkenness in Ocongate (Southern Peru). In *Gender, Drink and Drugs* (ed.) M. McDonald, 209–233. Oxford: Berg.

Heath, D. 1987. A Decade of Development in the Anthropological Study of Alcohol Use, 1970–80. In *Constructive Drinking* (ed.) M. Douglas, 16–69. Cambridge: Cambridge University Press.

Hinshelwood, R.D. 1989. *A Dictionary of Kleinian Thought.* London: Free Association Books.

Latour, B. 2005a. From Realpolitik to Dingpolitik. Or How to Make Things Public. In *Making Things Public: Atmospheres of Democracy* (eds.) B. Latour and P. Weibel, 14–41. Cambridge: MIT Press.

——— 2005b. *Reassembling the Social: An Introduction to Actor-Network Theory.* Oxford: Oxford University Press.

Lazar, S. 2008. *El Alto, Rebel City: Self and Citizenship in Andean Bolivia.* Durham: Duke University Press.

——— 2012. Disjunctive Comparison: Citizenship and Trade Unionism in Bolivia and Argentina. *Journal of the Royal Anthropological Institute* 18, no. 2: 349–368.

——— n.d. Of Autocracy and Democracy, or Discipline and Anarchy: When Organizational Structure Meets Political Ideology in Argentinean Public Sector Trade Unions.

Merleau-Ponty, M. 1962. *Phenomenology of Perception* (trans. C. Smith). London: Routledge.

Plotkin, M. B. 2001. *Freud in the Pampas: The Emergence and Development of a Psychoanalytic Culture in Argentina.* Stanford: Stanford University Press

——— 2003. *Argentina on the Couch: Psychiatry, State, and Society, 1880 to the Present.* Albuquerque: University of New Mexico Press

Tuomela, R. 2007. *The Philosophy of Sociality: The Shared Point of View.* New York: Oxford University Press.

5

Utopian Sociality. Online

Nicholas J. Long,
London School of Economics and Political Science

These were dark days for WhiteKnight.[1] He had been a dedicated user of the massively multiplayer online role-playing game *Ultima Online* since the winter of 2000. Most evenings, and at least once a week, he would switch on his modem and log on to the fantasy-themed metaworld of Britannia – a world full of computer-animated creatures and landscapes, as well as hundreds of user-controlled avatars, of which WhiteKnight was but one. The opportunities that life in such a 'virtual world' offered him had once felt dizzying. He could enjoy the typical pursuits of a role-playing game, such as learning magic or battling hostile computer-controlled creatures, whilst simultaneously interacting with a large number of other people logged into the game at the same time as him. Moreover, Britannia was available to log into twenty-four hours a day, seven days a week – provided he kept paying his monthly subscription fee.[2]

But by March 2004 he was beginning to feel it might be time to move on. He logged on to the Stratics message boards – the principal online forum for *Ultima Online* users, where one could discuss all aspects of the Britannian experience – and started a new thread with the bleak heading 'Should I quit?' 2004 had been a bad year for WhiteKnight. An upgrade to the *Ultima Online* software had resulted in a series of bugs, inadvertently losing him several of his most treasured items and 5 million gold pieces. He also had serious worries about the game's future having heard that several senior programmers had resigned – a consequence (he speculated) of Electronic Arts, *Ultima Online*'s parent company, relocating premises. 'Frankly,' he wrote in his post, 'the game just isn't as much fun as it used to be, or as it *should* be.'

The responses he received were mixed. Some people encouraged him to leave, arguing that he shouldn't be paying money for something if he wasn't having fun. But others actively defended Britannia, suggesting instead that it was the player who needed a fresh approach. One suggestion was to create a new character from scratch: 'you will experience a freedom unlike that ever felt before … [and] get back the magic and fun of UO'. Another poster suggested he take a break, maybe even play another 'massively multiplayer' online game: 'you might find a wonderful new exciting virtual world out there *or* you might even discover that UO was best after all and return'. Several people tried to advise him, drawing on their own experiences: in each case they said that they, too, had tried giving up *Ultima Online* (either out of disillusionment or because of changing life circumstances, such as a new job or relationship) but had found that they could not stay away. One poster admitted that she had 'missed the camaraderie too much'.

WhiteKnight, persuaded to stay, decided to revitalize his experience online by starting up a character on a different 'shard' – one of the twenty-nine distinct copies of Britannia accessible via the Internet. The reason so many copies had been created was so that *Ultima Online*'s 250,000 users[3] could access Britannia via a server that was located geographically close to them, thereby speeding up connection time whilst also dividing bandwidth requirements. But for WhiteKnight, this manoeuvre also introduced an appealing degree of variety to life in Britannia. Each shard's version of Britannia had begun as an identical physical landscape, including large swathes of forest, caves and mountains full of wild animals and hostile creatures that users could choose to evade, attack, or domesticate, and towns created as 'safe areas' – from which attacking enemy creatures are blocked by the software code. But these had been transformed into uniquely differentiated versions of Britannia by user activity – most notably via the creation of secondary (and less safe) urban areas in expanses of open land across Britannia, where users had built and furnished their own houses: spaces that could be used for private conversations, public parties, or the solitary processes of decoration and housework. Furthermore, each shard played host to its own distinct collectivity of avatars.

This last point was a crucial factor in WhiteKnight's decision. He explained that he hoped moving shard would afford him exciting new social experiences and a chance to meet new people and make new friends. The way he anticipated the sociality of the new shard played a central role in his decision to maintain his *Ultima Online* subscription. And yet his ultimate course of action reveals how little weight the social relations that he had established over three years of living on his current shard actually carried. Those were relations that he was happy to sacrifice because the loss of five million virtual gold pieces had stopped life on his shard from being 'fun'. So what is actually at stake in ideas about, and practices of, online sociality in this incipient virtual world? And could this have anything to offer to the study of sociality more broadly?

The Sociality of Utopia

WhiteKnight's case exemplifies a broader puzzle presented by *Ultima Online*. Created in 1995, launched in 1997, and still on sale today, it had been specifically developed by its U.S.-based designer, Richard Garriott, to foster sociality infused with community spirit, friendship, and joy. In their account of Garriott's life and work, King and Borland (2003: 13–14) trace this back to his teenage experiences in a summer camp held at the University of Oklahoma, where he was invited to join a game of Dungeons and Dragons. This dissolved the 'miserable' feelings of 'awkwardness' that had characterized his initial experiences of the camp, replacing it with a 'feeling of community' that the young Garriott would be unable to forget. He would seek to cultivate it in his school, in his neighbourhood, and eventually – they suggest – throughout the world at large:

> Richard had hit on an essential truth: even if he spent long hours alone in front of his computer writing code, the games he was starting to create were essentially social in nature ... He'd spent most of his life in a family and a wider community of friends and neighbors who supported each other in the craziest projects they could come up with. His weekend role-playing games and the computer games he based on them created their own tight communities. As he grew older and his games touched hundreds of thousands instead of just dozens of people, those communities would be replicated on a larger scale. (ibid: 20)

Such a vision draws heavily on ideas that proved very powerful in the Europe and North America of the late twentieth century: that 'community' offered a desirable and fulfilling means by which human beings might interact with each other; that it was foundering in the face of an increasingly atomistic, individualized, and competitive culture – a phenomenon often attributed to 'neoliberal' variants of late capitalism; and that the Internet offered an important opportunity to 'bring people together' in one place, thereby revitalizing society and rekindling community (see, e.g., Star 1995). These were certainly tropes that played a prominent role in how *Ultima Online* was marketed by Electronic Arts. Their promotional material draws heavily on users' experiences in order to entice prospective consumers to take the plunge and enter Britannia – offering such testimonies as 'the magic of UO for me is the magic of all the friends I have made, and the new ones I meet every single day!'[4] People I interviewed within the metaworld echoed these sentiments, and academic analysts of *Ultima Online* who have worked with users of the software concur that the principal reason they both sign up and renew their subscriptions is, like WhiteKnight, to consume a 'social experience' (Taxén 2002; Kolo and Baur 2004; Aupers 2007).

But participant observation of life on the Europa shard told a different story.[5] This shard primarily serves the U.K. and Western Europe – but since most *Ultima Online* users log on in the evenings or at weekends, it also hosts a sizeable contingent of Americans who are at home during the day and access Europa when their local shard, several hours behind GMT, is quiet. Here, conversations were fleeting at best, life online was suffused with suspicion, trickery and crime, and the majority of users spent most of their time alone. Considerable importance was attached to making money, acquiring valuable objects, or developing advanced specializations in specific skills: these were sought out with great fervour; deep, enduring social relations were not.

This might sound like a case of social engineering that failed; indeed for cultural theorist Steven Shaviro (2008), *Ultima Online* – and metaworlds like it – represent the death of the internet's utopian potential and its subsumption to the logic of the market. Yet the story cannot be quite so simple – for inhabitants of Britannia describe it in terms that suggest they experience it as a form of 'lived' or 'actually enacted' utopia (see Foucault 1986; Sargisson 2010: 24). They told me that, even if it wasn't a perfect place, it was 'magical', 'the best world [they] could imagine' and certainly much better than the world they inhabited offline. Emily, an active *Ultima Online* user ever since the software was launched, explained that 'in UO, I'm free from the rat-race of the modern world … In Britannia, the world is always beautiful … who could ask for more than that?' These claims need to be taken seriously as empirical philosophies of the good. Moreover, whenever I asked users to describe what they liked about *Ultima Online*, their answers were strikingly uniform: they spoke of 'friendship', of 'the people', of 'the sense of community'. I asked them to elaborate what they meant by this; Titania said that *Ultima Online* 'fills all social needs I have' while Anubis, a self-styled 'sociopath' explained that 'nothing beats the conversations when everyone comes together'. Such glosses were close to the concepts that had infused Garriott's and Electronic Arts' vision for the software, concepts which users' own socialities appeared to deny.

This ethnographic puzzle raises broader conceptual questions about what it is that makes specific forms of sociality appealing and enjoyable, and the relationship between those factors and the way that sociality can be – and is – described. What is clear is that the case of *Ultima Online* and its users' testimonies to 'community' cannot be straightforwardly analysed in terms of conventional communitarian utopianism, of the kind that has been particularly prominent in European and North American social thought and social experimentation since the 1960s (although with influential philosophical antecedents stretching back at least as far as Rousseau and More, not to mention Durkheim and Marx) – and which remains the substantive bedrock for the interdisciplinary field of Utopian Studies (Levitas [1990] 2010: 180). While numerous studies of 'intentional communities' have shown that aspirations to harmony and commonality founder in the face of conflict, discomfort, and emergent hierarchies (e.g., Sargisson 2010), these obstacles are experienced as negative impediments to members' realizing their aspirations of 'community', which are nevertheless – in most cases – maintained. *Ultima Online* is different, because users do not generally seem to show a conscious ethical commitment to building 'community', and actively enjoy their fractious and atomized virtual lives. Yet their experience also cannot be reduced to enacting a 'libertarian capitalist fantasy' (cf. Shaviro 2008), since the presence of other users plays such a central role in how they describe and evaluate their experiences.

How, then, might one conceptualize the pleasurable socialities of online individualism? An important first point is that successful individualism might involve collective action, as highlighted by Fishman's study of how 'bourgeois utopias' (London suburbs) emerged in the eighteenth century. Living a private life was, he writes, a collective effort (1987: x). But shared practices of mutual boundary-setting do not translate easily into notions of camaraderie, friendship, or community. A further set of helpful conceptual resources thus comes from the utopian writings of Oscar Wilde ([1891] 1997), in which he describes the form of individualism that he imagined would be fostered under socialism. Wilde considered the sociality of his times to be tarnished by people 'spoil[ing] their lives by an unhealthy and exaggerated altruism' and 'the sordid necessity of living for others' (ibid.: 1), and pictured a world in which every individual could truly know themselves, be themselves, and as such, 'live' (ibid.: 5). This would be infused with 'unselfishness', by which he intends the acceptance and enjoyment of 'infinite varieties of type... [A] red rose is not selfish because it wants to be a red rose. It would be horribly selfish if it wanted all the other flowers in the garden to be both red and roses' (ibid.: 15). Consequently, Wilde believed individualism would afford a 'higher form' of 'sympathy' – a widely valorized ethic in Victorian literary circles – than had hitherto been achieved. This would be sympathy 'with the entirety of life ... with life's joy and beauty and energy and health and freedom.... Anybody can sympathize with the sufferings of a friend, but it requires ... the nature of a true Individualist to sympathize with a friend's success' (ibid.: 16). Sympathy was the cornerstone of Wilde's utopian sociality, but this meant that he, ultimately, and like communitarians, envisaged a world free of argument and dispute (ibid.: 5).

Such ideas can facilitate interpretive purchase on what *Ultima Online* players might mean when they talk of friendship, camaraderie, and community – although Wilde's original formulations of 'sympathy' and 'unselfishness' need adaptation for a setting in which conflict and dispute – and indeed combat – were both widespread and seemingly part of online sociality's pleasures. Yet the conundrum remains as to why figures such as WhiteKnight should sacrifice existing 'friendship' in the name of 'making new friends' on a new shard. We should thus also consider the possibility that the nature of online sociality is being mischaracterized or misrecognized by *Ultima Online* users – and that this might be an important dimension of its pleasure. This in turn opens up new horizons for theorizing human sociality, and the ethical imaginations that underpin it.

Sociality, Solitude, Sympathy

> Virtual worlds are not secondary representations of
> the actual world. They require actual world computers
> and bodies to exist, and draw upon many elements
> of actual-world sociality, but through *techne* residents
> reconfigure these elements in unforeseen ways.
> (Boellstorff 2008: 201)

The user world of *Ultima Online* is heterogeneous, and people play it for different reasons. This might be to maintain relations with a distant friend or relative from 'real life'. It might be as part of a role-play guild, in which the character spends all their time logged on acting the part of, e.g., a peasant militiaman. However, the dominant playstyle on the Europa shard was referred to as 'powergaming', a playstyle which seeks to develop the character's prowess in particular skills through repeated practice and the gaining of experience. Users could choose to specialize in a wide variety of skills, ranging from martial and magical combat (for which one would train by engaging in battles with the wild creatures that littered the landscape) to crafts such as blacksmithing, carpentry, and weaving. Developing these skills involved sourcing raw materials such as ore or timber from the landscape (or from another user) and turning them into ornate artefacts that could then be sold. The complexity of their design would develop as one's skill level increased, allowing them to fetch a higher price on the in-game market. A final popular specialism was animal taming, in which animals from around Britannia were turned into 'pets' that could be ridden or used as allies in combat. One tamer, Alicia, described feeling a 'sense of accomplishment' whenever she saw that her skill level had raised, and explained that she found animal taming particularly 'immersive' thanks to the opportunities for training her pets.

Powergaming could still be combined with social interaction and non-institutionalized role-play, and several of my interlocutors were quick to draw a distinction between *Ultima Online*'s 'players' – who appeared to treat it only as a game – and its 'inhabitants', who recognized, in one gamer's terms, that '*Ultima Online* was not just a game but a "virtual reality"'. (For this reason I do not use the term 'player' to refer to generic users of *Ultima Online*, even though many of my interlocutors, and the software infrastructure itself, did so.) Nevertheless, even for such inhabitants, 'powering-up' their characters was a widespread concern, because it was linked to the very fabric of how *Ultima Online* avatars were constructed and engaged with.

The virtual 'body' is measured in terms of a series of statistics, relating to bodily attributes such as Strength, and to proficiency in particular skills. The display of these statistics is generally restricted to windows only accessible to the user, with the exception of one's most proficient skill, which is appended to one's name in the 'paperdoll' – a character's public profile, which can be readily accessed by left-clicking on the avatar moving around the screen. However, users were usually at pains to disclose their skill levels, and the comparison of 'vital statistics' is a common topic of conversation. This is partly because parity in attributes such as strength and resistance to magic are prerequisites for embarking on shared adventures outside of Britannia's towns, and also because many seasoned users enjoy helping 'newbies' learn the most efficient ways to train in order to open up the advantages that come with higher skill levels. This in itself attests to the important role skill levels play in establishing in-game hierarchies, securing recognition and a sense of achievement.

```
Andronicus: DoomMaster, u have 79 parry
Andronicus: 84 swords
Andronicus: 85 tactics
DoomMaster: i do
Andronicus: 88 anatomy
Andronicus: 78 healing
DoomMaster: i win
Andronicus: mm
Andronicus: nice
DoomMaster: thanks :)
Andronicus: Mercury, what's your swords?
Mercury:    69.6
Andronicus: wow!!
```

Skill levels are a significant source of pride for many inhabitants of *Ultima Online*, and this is displayed publicly in a variety of ways. It is not uncommon for characters to 'boast' openly after accomplishing a skill/attribute gain. A particularly memorable example of this was a warrior character who ran around the crowded town of Britain shouting 'RAAAAAAR! 100 STR!!!!' for fifteen minutes to testify to his most recent achievement. Users frequently use the 'player profile' section of their paperdoll to list their attribute levels and the skills in which they have achieved 'GM' (grandmaster) status, or signal their experience and prowess through practices of conspicuous consumption. These typically involved replacing the more functional costumes of clothing and helmets with brightly coloured robes and hats, gold armour, and neon hair dye. These products, the only commodities which can be publicly consumed wherever one goes – because they are shown on the paperdoll – express aspects of identity that go beyond mere style or personality, because it is widely known that such items carry high price tags. Indeed, this is readily publicized by consumers themselves. One of my earliest in-game conversations was with a paladin who had bought a cloak he claimed was worth '30,000GP' – not an unlikely figure, and one which attracted praise from the various interlocutors in the vicinity: 'amazing', 'totally worth it', 'wow – it's cool'. To earn such money, however, requires many hours of monster killing or trading, and it was this skill and dedication that was implicitly being asserted. A trade in items known or thought to be expensive also fuels the powergaming strategies of the users who craft them, and who described their goals to me as 'making as much money as possible' or 'spreading my characters' names [which are inscribed on the items they craft] as far across Britannia as possible'.

The consequence of this emphasis on skill development was that many users spent large portions of their time online in solitude, training. When I first met Phoebe, who had been an inhabitant of Britannia for five months, it was in the town of Moonglow. She had come there for a social break, having spent 'all afternoon at the graveyard training [the spells] Provoke and Peace'. After just twenty minutes of role-playing, pretending that her ten-year old character was romantically interested in a muscular male lumberjack, she was back to the graveyard to boost her statistics. This was a routine she kept to every day. Likewise, at least on Europa shard, guilds – communities of supposedly like-minded characters that Taxén (2002: 5) has described as 'probably the game feature that is most important for producing veteran users and keeping newcomers interested' and as 'true virtual communities' – recognized that if they were to survive, their demands had to be subordinate to members' interest in training and powering up. When I met Shosa, the 'Leader of Paladins' in a medium-sized guild of elves (twenty-four members), I asked her what she did in the way of 'leading' them. 'To be quite honest', she replied, 'we all train as individuals, but sometimes we hunt together'. She later admitted it had been difficult to sustain much interest in the guild's activities more widely. Shosa, and another guild member, Peter, described how they had attempted to stage an 'Elven fair' in which members of the guild could sell their handmade produce. Not a single person turned up. Some had been on holiday. Others had logged on but had foregone the fair in order to train, alone.

There are good reasons why combat-focused powergamers usually prefer to train in (relative) solitude: it allows them a complete monopoly on all the gold, resources, and skill-building combat that they might encounter. Having other people around was a grave inconvenience – and one that could actually spoil the experience of being in Britannia. When the warrior Andronicus allowed me to join him out hunting, for example, he vetoed my suggestion of going to the Solen Mountains – home to gold-laden giant ants – because although he agreed that 'the Solen ants are fun', he felt that the mountains 'are always way too full'. The Troll Cave we eventually went to was quiet at first, but after half an hour, more people had begun to trickle in, to the point that there were at least seven of us on the second floor. Andronicus suggested this meant it was time for us to leave. 'It's getting a bit full now', he commented. 'When it's not full, it's a lot of fun'. 'Fun' presupposed having this online social space all to oneself.

In cases where social contact was unavoidable, a code of ethics had evolved to safeguard the 'right' of a combatant to deal the lethal blow on a creature he had begun attacking – thereby securing exclusive access to its corpse, for looting. Other players in the vicinity who wanted to assist with the attack were obliged to do so by casting healing spells on the attacker, rather than dealing any damage to the creature.[6] This protocol maximized in-game freedom: it allowed role-playing (or genuine) altruists to be altruistic, whilst letting powergamers level up uninterrupted. By 2003, it had spread across the Europa shard, and was actively taught to new users in towns; regular 'kill-stealers' acquired a terrible reputation and were often shunned. This emergent and shared dynamic of Britannian sociality served primarily to support individual users' own projects of self-formation.

The individuated process of skill levelling and training was a very important dimension of *Ultima Online*'s appeal. Many of my interlocutors considered it integral to the way that the metaworld allowed them to 'be their true selves'. This builds directly on Turkle's (1995) argument that online interaction would allow people to socialize without being overdetermined by physically visible traits such as gender, race or disability. For avid powergamers, what was empowering was, comparably, the capacity to defy structural obstacles such as class, status, age, and qualification levels that might hold them back in the real world. Berowne, whose offline occupation involved washing dishes in an Italian restaurant, valued the experience of being able to role-play as a crafter and sell 'handmade' furniture. Since Berowne could not be online all the time, he deposited objects in a 'store', allowing customers to buy products from the store, at any time, via a menu interface:

> I have always taken pride in my workmanship, whether it is doing machine work or washing dishes. When my father was alive he was determined not to be like his father, so he always let us know when we had done good. I like that sort of attention. I like for other players in UO to know that I can do good work, and I can do that by making things for them. With crafting, I can be recognized as one who plays UO hard, even when I am not around.

This account of self-fulfilment is particularly interesting because it hinges on social recognition (in that it requires the attention of others) that may nevertheless involve no direct interactions with other users. The act of purchasing, or even of viewing the goods, was enough for Berowne to feel assured that he had 'played hard' and 'done good', achieving the dream of self-propulsive excellence that his low-grade employment in the real world thwarted on a daily basis. Another shop-owner, Felicity, who primarily made and sold clothes, told me that 'I tend to play by myself mostly, and the shop takes up most of my time'. For her, the 'most satisfying' thing to do in Britannia was owning and running her shop, to which the pleasures of role-play, social interaction and exploration of 'alternative characters' only served as a supplement. These testimonies echo the account of journalist Julian Dibbell (2006: 149), who has described how the pleasures of making money on an American shard led to him losing interest in interacting directly with other players: 'as I invested myself more and more in the economy of UO players, I could feel myself drifting further and further from their community'.

In a world as large as Britannia, with so many users logging in and out erratically, and a rapid turnover of 'players' who might come to Britannia for a few weeks and then give up on *Ultima Online* altogether, long-term inhabitants often reported that their deepest and most profound sources of satisfaction did not come from their fleeting interactions with other users but rather from projects of self-formation inspired by a deep engagement with the possibilities opened up by being in the metaworld. Their claims also point to discontentment with the limitations of sociality in the actual world – a setting in which social interaction, but also practical opportunities for self-realization and individuation, are shackled by categories of class, gender, race, disability, or talent, political economic pressures, and the burdensome business of enduring social relations. In the actual world, as Allison (this collection) also reminds us, human agency can be fettered, and the dynamic matrix of relations in which people are placed may be less dynamic than they might like. It can feel, as Wilde ([1891] 1997: 1) remarked, 'sordid' to 'live for others'.

However, with only a few exceptions,[7] what users found special about being in *Ultima Online* was still directly linked to the 'massively multiplayer' nature of the metaworld, and its distinct brand of emergent sociality. While the software itself afforded the capacity to achieve on what was both a meritocratic and democratic basis – in that anybody with enough time, patience, and dedication could achieve a grandmaster status, and the resources required for this would be regularly replenished – the presence of others allowed forms of display and recognition that not only ratified users' accomplishments, but charged them with positive affect. Characters appeared to spontaneously take pleasure in each other's achievements – whether as customers or as interlocutors in the streets and fields of Britannia. The appearance of spontaneity is certainly relevant here – it suggests that people behave differently online compared to the more competitive and envious sociality of the actual world. Yet the fact that users can see conversations between all avatars on their screen, displayed as text above the avatars' heads, means that even these habits of congratulation could be seen as a learned protocol, an emergent virtual culture rather than a spontaneous expression of an intrinsically generous attitude. Nevertheless, this arrangement, as with the injunction to assist others by healing, fits closely with Wilde's vision of 'sympathy' as a sociality – that is to say a *way* of conducting relations – in which individual(ist)s allow other individuals to live however they might wish to, and take pleasure in each other's successes. Following from this, *Ultima Online*'s appeal can indeed be seen to stem from the way it has 'brought people together'. How this most typically occurs, however, is a distinct counterpoint to the development of 'tight-knit communities' and 'friendships' that the game's designers, developers, popular critics and even users have been so ready to imagine would be the case.[8] The language of 'meeting social needs' or of generating 'a community' in which one can really be oneself is thus not reflecting the communitarian utopia it first suggests so much as a more conservative laboratory of capitalist, acquisitive self-formation, which values the presence of others as witnesses to, and collaborators in, sympathetic individualism.

The Perils of Sociality

Yet some aspects of sociality in Britannia appeared – by Wilde's criteria – distinctly unsympathetic, the presence of others proving actively toxic to the projects with which users were preoccupied when online. Crowding out hunting grounds and 'kill-stealing' were relatively minor concerns; more serious were individuals whose online lives were hell-bent on spoiling the experiences of other users. Theft, trickery, and murder were threats that Britannians faced on a regular basis. Anyone venturing into Felucca, a 'facet' of the shard in which characters were allowed to attack each other (an appealing prospect for training, or to role-play duels or guild wars) faced the fearsome prospect of encountering a 'red' – a character whose name was written in scarlet above her avatar to indicate that she had killed other characters. Peter told me he was anxious about recruiting new members to his guild:

> We must be careful. There are some nasty so-and-sos out there. All guilds have to be wary and [our members] must be careful in who they recommend to join. There was, and might still be, a guild from Felucca that sent potential members out to destroy other guilds as a rite of passage. Such individuals can cause a lot of trouble.

Another regular threat was the 'scammer' who would offer to repair a piece of equipment, only to run off with it. Anubis, who regularly traded at forges around the country, had acquired a particularly bad reputation in this regard. When I met Anubis, I asked him why he 'scammed'. He was candid in his response. 'I guess I'm just mean by nature. I love tricking players out of everything they have, nothing beats that feeling. If I have a bad reputation, if I'm notorious – well, that means I'm doing it well.' This was his own form of in-game achievement.

Practices of this kind risked suffusing Britannia's brand of online sociality with mistrust and avoidance. The fraught interactions between a warrior named Nostradamus (himself a seasoned player killer) and a blacksmith named Derrick offer a case in point. Nostradamus had asked Derrick to repair his sword, adding 'but I really need this sword, please don't steal or something.' Derrick quickly fixed the weapon, and opened the window allowing him to transfer it to Nostradamus. He then closed this window without the sword having been exchanged. The words 'donation please sire *winks*' appeared above his avatar. Nostradamus immediately gave Derrick 150 gold pieces – far more than the repair was worth – and Derrick handed over the sword with a 'very generous sire, thank you.' Nostradamus was furious. 'You should have told me from the start that you want money,' he explained. 'I gave you money only because I was scared for my sword.' Derrick instantly tried to return the gold, protesting that he had used the 'wrong mouse button' but Nostradamus refused to accept the apology, saying Derrick's behaviour was 'not nice'. The fear of scammers pervaded and influenced their entire interaction.

Likewise, in an interview in 1999, before player-versus-player combat had been restricted to Felucca facet, *Ultima Online*'s producer, Starr Long, had said that the users could log on 'simply to enjoy interacting with other players' yet also warned that they should 'be careful when interacting with other players.... In fact, when travelling outside of towns, you shouldn't stop and talk to anyone you do not know.'[9] Such advice continues to apply for users whose avatars venture into Felucca, or Siege Perilous shard, an 'advanced' shard in which player-versus-player combat is permissible anywhere outside of towns. As Taxén (2002) notes, such antisocial behaviours drive some users away – though not as many as one might expect. For him, this is because their harms are outweighed by the programme's various pleasures. While I do not disagree with this analysis, what struck me during my own time in Britannia was that these antagonisms were often spoken of in enthusiastic terms – suggesting further dynamics may also be at work. While Nostradamus regularly boasted of his ability to kill grandmaster status characters, and the items he had thereby acquired, many users spoke in terms that went beyond the measure of individual accomplishment. John, for example, described the 'thrill' of forming a group of 'good, honest, villagers' in opposition to player-killers in the days before Trammel, and Anubis, as seen above, saw scamming as something that produces an unbeatable 'feeling'.

It seems highly relevant here that decisions to kill, trick or cheat other players are widely framed in terms of an individual's underlying 'nature'. When LadyGrey, a necromancer, decided she might enjoy trying to kill other characters, she posted on the Stratics message boards to ask whether her statistics and skill levels were high enough to prevent her from being massacred by her intended victims. Pilate replied that, in his view, 'the player makes the red, not the template'. Another respondent suggested that player-killing required 'hav[ing] whatever it is that makes anarchy thrive'. Anubis styled himself as 'a sociopath' and said he was 'just mean by nature'. By contrast, Titania emphasized that 'I don't kill other players, it just isn't my nature!' while Victoria lamented the difficulties she was having role-playing a character she had decided would be 'a bitch'. 'I haven't been able to make the transition very well,' she complained, 'that'd be totally against my own nature'. Zebedee explained that, in his view, 'our actions in the virtual world may more closely reveal our "true self", for good or ill, than in the real world … I have to wonder what the pleasure derived from contemptible acts reveals about a person'. Far from the experimental identities anticipated by some early Internet theorists (e.g., Stone 1995), being 'good' or 'mean' was seen here as something simultaneously freely chosen and innate, because only bad people would choose to be bad, and vice-versa.

How the enactment of the 'true self' can be conceived in Britannia is nevertheless tightly associated with the conditions of possibility engendered by the virtual setting. This includes the infrastructural parameters of the software, which allow for player killing, scamming, and so forth, but it also includes the broader narrative context within which *Ultima Online*, and its fantasy theme, is embedded – a host of games and literature explicitly organized around certain oppositions: 'good/evil', 'chaos/order', 'justice/injustice', and so on. These are not only presented as default positions between which one must choose, but also as being in a necessarily ongoing antagonism with each other. To be good involves encountering and defeating evil, and vice-versa. If, as Mackay (2000: 98) argues, the conventions and tropes of imaginary entertainment settings 'co-author' users' experiences, antagonistic cases of scamming and player killing are not necessarily 'unsympathetic' sociality, but can be an opportunity through which users shore up their own sense of being 'good' in opposition to characters they interpret as being 'mean' or 'evil'– not just at the level of the avatar, but also at the level of the self that is controlling it. Such a confluence of antagonists is not normally thought of as a desirable form of sociality. But the *Ultima Online* case underscores that visions of the good life need not be based on communitarianism and the erasure of difference and discord, but rather – in keeping with Wilde's argument – a utopian condition of self-realization achieved within and through a matrix of relations with others who are all striving towards their own distinct individualist ends.

Conclusion: Imagining Ethically

An ethnographic exploration of *Ultima Online* reveals some of the new directions sociality is taking through Europeans' and Americans' engagements with novel forms of communication technology – as well as how and why that sociality generates pleasure for software users. In keeping with Boellstorff's (2008) analysis of the 'creationism' evident in *Second Life*,[10] Britannians took pleasure from the fact that these fulfilled selves were something they had made through their own efforts and accomplishments – a distinctive possibility afforded by a virtual environment. A matrix of fleeting, sympathetic, and seemingly spontaneous relations through which they secured recognition of such projects of self-maximization proved intoxicating for many *Ultima Online* users – and it is possible that this pleasure in the company of others was what was being referenced by users' invocations of terms such as 'community', 'friendship' and 'camaraderie'. Certainly, that pleasure played a leading role in the ways users described their time in Britannia as surpassing their lives offline.

While anthropological (and other) investigations into utopias and utopian sociality have typically focused on contexts oriented to principles of commonality, equality and community, *Ultima Online* and its users' own empirical philosophies of the good show that the utopianism of self-realization might drive appetites for particular forms of sociality, even if they are described – or indeed designed by their creators – in terms redolent of longstanding communitarian traditions. Furthermore, when a communard at Twin Oaks, Virginia, an archetypal utopia based around 'community' and the rejection of private property, asks the documentary film-maker Kozeny (2002) 'who would have imagined that a guy like me, from one of the poorest neighbourhoods in New York, could become a shareholder in a million-dollar business?' it becomes clear that such a setting might also be viewed as an opportunity to realise individualist dreams of (capitalist) self-making. Yet as Kozeny's film reveals, communitarian ideologies continue to play a significant role in Twin Oaks; claims to establishing 'community' are not simply reducible to the pleasures of self-making. I would suggest this may also apply to *Ultima Online*, especially given that 'interacting with other players', and 'participating in a "virtual society"' are the principal reasons that Europa shard users give for why they renew their subscriptions – with skill mastery playing only a 'subordinate role' in their (self-declared) motivations (Kolo and Baur 2004: 13).

It is understandable that sociality might seem as if it ought to be the central appeal of participating in a virtual world. The idea suffuses marketing rhetoric surrounding these products, whilst academic cyberoptimist claims about social rejuvenation through the Internet have come to reach a wide audience both through 'human interest' media coverage and the publication of scholarly books aimed at the mass market (e.g., Stone 1995). The notion also taps into the broader interests in cultivating 'community' that characterize much turn-of-the-millennium social commentary, and which resonate with a genealogy of imagining the good life that stretches back for many centuries. Such tropes of utopian sociality can be seen as established 'cultural narratives', scaffolding through which people narrate and make sense of their own lives (Plummer 1995). They could therefore also serve, following Coleman (2010: 51–52) as a deeply felt 'condensation and re-enactment of a lifeworld', offering new avenues for experiencing life online, and contributing to the sense that one has experienced profound social betterment through participating in a 'virtual community', even as the affectivities and performativity of gameplay pulls users in different, and more isolated – if equally fulfilling – directions. That, I suggest, helps explain why WhiteKnight, an avowed powergamer of many years' vintage, found the prospect of new social interactions persuasive enough to keep his subscription. It is also why, despite all the player killing, and the scams, and the fact that they know most people play alone for most of the time, Electronic Arts' online marketing page still boasts the promise that participants can 'interact with an incredible player base and make new friends' in the very first line of their description of what new users can expect in-game.

So what could this add to a theory of human sociality? As Henrietta Moore and I have argued (this collection), human sociality is a dynamic relational matrix, the continually transforming form of which is shaped by humans' 'ethical imaginations': the contextually specific (but not contextually determined) 'forms and means ... through which individuals imagine relationships to themselves and to others' (Moore 2011: 16). Yet, following Moore (ibid.: 16), the ethical imagination is not limited to conscious thought and reflection, but incorporates affect, performance, the place and use of the body, unknowing, and incomprehensibility. The question this observation raises, though, is how these different elements of ethical imagining interact. Here the case of *Ultima Online* proves particularly suggestive. For what makes users value, enjoy, and drive forwards the sociality of Britannia is both the intensely felt pleasure of being a successful powergamer in a setting where others are disposed to be sympathetic – something that speaks to questions of affect and performance – and also the ability to represent the sociality of this online world to oneself and others in terms suffused with positive value in contemporary thought and commentary. Whereas the conventional utopia is seen as 'willed social change', conducted according to a 'shared blueprint' (Moore 1990), a formulation that foregrounds processes of conscious thought and reflection in a highly directed project of ethical imagination, *Ultima Online* suggests that conscious reflections on sociality might themselves be affective and performative processes: humans can desire to enact particular imaginations of themselves as ethical. Moreover, when ethical imaginations are pulled in competing directions by different templates of the good life, it might be precisely those settings that allow one to finesse those tensions – and so live a life that seems replete with both 'self-realization' *and* 'community' – that are experienced as utopian. As such, for all that the example of *Ultima Online* illustrates this collection's contention that sociality itself is continually emergent, dynamic and plastic, it also suggests that there can be analytically significant continuities and rigidities in how sociality is thought of in relation to the good life – and that this virtual world's capacity to uphold such established horizons amongst its users also plays its part in making Britannia a utopia, online.

Notes

1. All names are pseudonyms.
2. £9 in 2004 – excluding internet access costs, and the one-off purchase of the *Ultima Online* CD-Rom.
3. 85 per cent of users at the time were men. See <http://www.nickyee.com/daedalus/> (accessed 20 September 2011).
4. <http://www.uo.com/spot_19.html> (accessed 20 September 2011).
5. As in Boellstoff's (2008) study of *Second Life*, I studied *Ultima Online* from within the metaworld, taking it 'in its own terms' – of which commentary upon the incipient virtual world, and contrasts with the actual world, were prominent dimensions. See Williams (2007) for further discussion of online ethnographic methods.
6. Though some users had developed a separate expression, 'gfd' – the middle letters of the Qwerty keyboard run together – for use in circumstances so desperate that they were happy to let someone else destroy the creature that was aggressing them.
7. Notably animal tamers, who said that they had come to enjoy a companionship with their online pets that was unlike anything they had encountered in any other game.
8. Garriott himself decided to abandon his communitarian vision of a harmonious and ordered cyberlocale in favour of a more libertarian one after disputes began to arise in *Ultima Online*'s early days. However, that communitarian vision has remained a dominant trope of marketing and for users' narrativization of their experience.
9. <http://www.gamespot.com/features/uosg/dev3.html> (accessed 10 September 2011).
10. This is also an online metaworld, although unlike *Ultima Online* it does not require paid subscription, and is not fantasy role-play themed.

References

Aupers, S. 2007. 'Better Than the Real World'. On the Reality and Meaning of Online Computer Games. *Fabula* 48, no. 3–4: 250–269.

Boellstorff, T. 2008. *Coming of Age in Second Life: An Anthropologist Explores the Virtually Human*. Princeton: Princeton University Press.

Coleman, G. 2010. The Hacker Conference: A Ritual Condensation and Celebration of a Lifeworld. *Anthropological Quarterly* 83, no. 1: 47–72.

Dibbell, J. 2006. *Play Money: Or, How I Quit My Day Job and Made Millions Trading Virtual Loot.* New York: Basic Books.

Fishman, R. 1987. *Bourgeois Utopias: The Rise and Fall of Suburbia.* New York: Basic Books.

Foucault, M. 1986. Of Other Spaces. *Diacritics* 16, no. 1: 22–27.

King, B., and J. Borland. 2003. *Dungeons and Dreamers: The Rise of Computer Game Culture from Geek to Chic.* Emeryville: Osborne McGraw Hill.

Kolo, C. and T. Baur. 2004. Living a Virtual Life: Social Dyamics of Online Gaming. *Game Studies* 4, no. 1: <http://www.gamestudies.org/0401/kolo/> (accessed 25 July 2011).

Kozeny, G. (dir.) 2002. *Visions of Utopia: Experiments in Communal Living.* Fellowship for Intentional Community, Rutledge.

Levitas, R. [1990] 2010. *The Concept of Utopia* (Second Edition). Bern: Peter Lang.

Mackay, D. 2000. Toward a Phenomenology of the Role-Playing Game Experience. In *Phenomenological Approaches to Popular Culture* (eds.) M. T. Carroll and E. Tafoya, 97–111. Bowling Green: Bowling Green State University Popular Press.

Moore, H. L. 1990. Visions of the Good Life: Anthropology and the Study of Utopia. *Cambridge Anthropology* 14, no. 3: 13–33.

——— 2011. *Still Life: Hopes, Desires and Satisfactions.* Cambridge: Polity Press.

Plummer, K. 1995. *Telling Sexual Stories: Power, Change and Social Worlds.* London: Routledge.

Sargisson, L. 2010. Friends Have All Things in Common: Utopian Property Relations. *The British Journal of Politics and International Relations* 12, no. 1: 22–36.

Shaviro, S. 2008. Money for Nothing: Virtual Worlds and Virtual Economies. In *Virtual Worlds* (ed.) M. Ipe, 53–67. Hyderabad: The Icfai University Press.

Star, S. L. (ed.) 1995. *The Cultures of Computing.* Oxford: Blackwell.

Stone, A. R. 1995. *The War of Desire and Technology at the Close of the Mechanical Age.* Cambridge: MIT Press.

Taxén, G. 2002. *Guilds: Communities in Ultima Online.* Stockholm: Royal Institute of Technology.

Turkle, S. 1995. *Life on the Screen: Identity in the Age of the Internet.* London: Weidenfeld and Nicolson.

Wilde, O. [1891] 1997. *The Soul of Man under Socialism.* Salt Lake City: Project Gutenberg.

Williams, M. 2007. Avatar Watching: Participant Observation in Graphical Online Environments. *Qualitative Research* 7, no. 1: 5–24.

6

A Sociality of, and Beyond, 'My-home' in Post-corporate Japan

Anne Allison, Duke University

Rebuilding itself after the defeat of the Second World War, Japan became an economic superpower by the late 1970s. Its national lens radically changed from the militarism of empire building to the industrialism of domestic security. Citizens were now told to work hard – not to win a war but to increase prosperity at home. By toiling diligently at school, at home, and at jobs, Japanese subjects worked at once for the nation and for themselves. The country prospered and, with what was called its 'miracle economy', Japan gained the global prestige that had eluded it as a would-be imperial power. Meanwhile, the population enjoyed stable employment and the rise of consumer culture. Indeed, by the late 1980s, 90 per cent of Japanese identified as middle class.

Life became organized around a newly privatized notion of self. No longer subjects working for, and subjected to, the emperor, Japanese were now to work for themselves in the new 'enterprise society' (*kigyō shakai*). Geared to being the best one could be, technologies of self shaped the citizen as individual producer/consumer. Yet the individual was still attached to group(s): school for children, marriage for women, workplace for men. The home linked these two principles of individualization/affiliation. Not just the literal home or the traditional kinship system (*ie*) marking one's lineage but a new kind of home, at once modern and 'mine'. A dream home, encapsulating the Japanese dream of post-war prosperity, corporate capitalism, and nuclear family making. Referred to as '*mai homu shūgi*' (my-homeism), this is what people worked for and expected (at some point) to attain: a home, ideally located in a residential neighbourhood, stocked with the newest domestic electronics – washing machines, air conditioners, colour televisions, automobiles.

Not only a site for consumption, my-homeism centred on a social and productive unit as well. This was the grounding of the post-war nation-state: corporate capitalism that, nestling the family within, produced and reproduced through the gendered labours of a heteronormative family. A form of both sociality and capitalism, what has been called the 'family corporate system'

(Kimoto 2008) drove productivity. Hard-working men earned a family wage to support wife and kids at home, and the unpaid labours of mothers/wives freed men to devote all their energies to work while driving children to perform industriously at school. Companies also ran like a 'family' (Nakane 1967) in that core (male) workers attached to the workplace, and one another, like familial kin: lifelong bonds, company trips, late-night work followed by outings to drink (Allison 1994). *Sararīman* (salarymen) didn't work at Toyota, they belonged to Toyota. Meanwhile their wives ran the show at home: a family-corporate system that fuelled Japan's miracle economy as its hidden weapon (Silver 2003).

Home-based, family entwined, and productive of and for corporate capitalism: post-war Japan was a nation-state fed by the domestic and gendered labours of families. Such a politico-economic order embraces a principle of what Lee Edelman (2004) has called 'reproductive futurism': seeing one's future in the image of the child. At the heart of modernist politics, reproductive futurism is a belief in the progressive betterment of life that, staking progress on the next generation, attaches and delimits sociality to the heteronormative family and home. Speaking from a queer perspective, Edelman is critical of a polity that, so invested in this calculus of worth and futurity, consigns to social exclusion and 'no future' those unable or unwilling to reproduce.

Here, I take a different tack: looking at a nation-state and those citizens within it who, becoming increasingly unable to (re)produce, feel hopeless about the future, tied as this has been to the (re)productivity of the next generation. This is the case in Japan today where – with a falling birth rate (*shōshika*),[1] rising elderly population (*kōreika*), crippled economy, and, now, with leaking radiation and soaring reconstruction costs from the tsunami – the country is increasingly unable not only to reproduce new Japanese but to take care of those already existing. Edelman embraces the social 'death' sentence of those who fail to reproduce, but such a failure in Japan generates a deep sense of panic and unease. And the child, not moving (the country) forward, is the target of much of this concern. Due to shifts in labour and an economic recession brought on by the bursting of the bubble economy, an entire generation of youth has come of age with few or no prospects of viable employment. This 'lost generation'[2] has been crippled in their hopes for the future, including (for a large number of them) the ability to get married and have children themselves, something that over 90 per cent claim they desire. Often stranded at home or becoming homeless, Japanese youth – a category that is stretching later or becoming indeterminate – feel stuck. Mired in circumstances that show no signs of improving, young people are succumbing to a state that activist Karin Amamiya (2007) calls the 'precariat' – the precarious proletariat or working poor. One-third of all workers, but one-half of those between the ages of 15 and 24, excluding students, are irregularly employed (*hiseiki koyō*) which means no job security, no benefits, and wages that are static and low: 77 per cent of those irregularly employed earn less than 2,000,000 yen (£16,000) a year, putting them in the ranks of the working poor. Calculating poverty as less than half of the mean average income, Japan now has the second highest poverty rate of OECD countries, after the U.S. (Tachibanaki 2008) – and this despite the fact that its economy was, until just recently, the second strongest in the world.

The question I pose here is: what has become of sociality in an era when it is no longer organized so tightly by the family corporate system of post-war Japan, Inc.? That is, in these times of precarious employment (Kalleberg 2009),[3] what happens to the ontology of the social, particularly to and for youth, that demographic of the population around whom so much was once invested and staked? What does it mean that the country is confronting not only what is a much lamented crisis of an ageing low-birthrate population (*shōshikōreika*) but also a rise in poverty whose 'new face', as activist Makoto Yuasa (2008) has put it, is that not of the elderly or so-called lower class but of Japanese youth? A much publicized documentary on what it coined as 'net café refugees' (*net café nanmin*)[4] showed young people, usually working poor, who, essentially homeless, camp out in net cafes, otherwise known as places for fast-speed internet connection – young people who, from their teens to their forties, are struggling both physically and existentially to survive today. But of equal concern to Yuasa and Amamiya is the precarity[5] into which Japan as a whole has fallen. In their words, the country is undergoing refugeeization (*nanminka*) in this onset of the twenty-first century (Amamiya 2007). A startling thought. For if the nation-state is 'refugeed', what precisely is it a refuge from if not itself? From the secure home(land) it was once or is remembered to have been for its citizens.

Certainly the insecurity of jobs in what I have called post-corporate Japan is a major factor in all this. But are the shifts in Japan's economic landscape entirely to blame for what is a deep-seated sense of stasis, hopelessness, and unease amongst not only young people but the middle-aged and elderly? In a recent survey, 82 per cent of Japanese youth reported that they felt 'dark' about the future (Yamada 2003). And, in what has been an upsurge nationwide since 1998, suicide is the leading cause of death for young people between the ages of 18 and 24 and is rising fastest amongst the middle-aged of both genders.

The contemporary generation of Japanese youth is 'de-social', sociologist Michiko Miyamoto told me in an interview in 2008. This means not that they protest against society but, even worse in her mind, they withdraw from it. From her own research, Miyamoto reports that many young Tokyoites say they feel kindred with, if they are not literally themselves, *hikikomori*: those manifesting a condition of social withdrawal that, becoming newsworthy around 2000, is said to afflict about one million Japanese today. Officially defined by the government in 2003 as a 'person who, for a variety of causes, doesn't participate socially and doesn't spend time working or going to school outside of home,' *hikikomori* are a well-known social phenomenon: more males than females, usually starting at the age of fourteen or fifteen, and lasting as long as decades (Kaneko 2006). In that *hikikomori* are non (re)productive but still tend to remain at home (where mothers feed them and fathers pay their expenses), social withdrawal is a perversion of my-homeism. But this is not the only symptom of a changing, some say dissolving, landscape of sociality in post-corporate Japan. There is also a rise in the number of people who live and die alone; one-third of all Japanese live alone now and 32,000 die by themselves at home every year. Particularly for those with scarce resources, everyday getting along can be materially difficult and socially fraught. This leads to what has been variously labelled the 'relationless society' (*muen shakai*), a 'country of loneliness', and a citizenship becoming humanly poor.[6]

If youth were the centre and future of sociopolitics under the family corporate system of Japan, Inc., how does their place within the home and the 'liquid' economy (*ryūdōka*)[7] of the post-bubble signal the state of sociality today? And, as my-homeism retreats in fact, are new models of sociality, social belonging, and human value emerging in its place?

Belonging in a Deterritorialized World

Certainly, life in Japan, as everywhere around the globe today, has become increasingly deterritorialized. As the anthropologist Arjun Appadurai (1996) has argued, this is due, in part, to the increased movement of people, things, and information in ever more frenetic circuits of traffic and trade, and also to the mediatization of a world ever more prismed through media and digital technology. Life becomes more virtualized as well as schizophrenic in that people are continually jumping across time and space, bound but unbound to any one place, moment, or register. One might assume that this has an effect (and affect) on the social: what theorists from Karl Marx to Emile Durkheim have long claimed to be basic to humanity – the need to belong to some unit, endeavour, or community beyond the singular self, one that gives meaning to life and recognition or identity to the individual. Without a doubt, belonging was critically important and fastidiously tracked in post-war Japan. For the male, attachment was sutured to work. Where a man was employed, in what division, and what rank, defined identity: it was stamped on his *meishi* (business card) and constituted his primary allegiance (translating as breadwinner, often in absentia, at home).

Other group affiliations counted too: the schools one attended, the clubs one joined at university, the family one came from and married into. For a married woman, if and where she went to school mattered as well. But, more important, in terms of her own social identity and rank, was where her husband worked and in what position. Also, once she started having children, how they did in and beyond school became an important marker of her success as an 'education mama'. All of this was territorialized in the sense that, enduring over time and localizable in place, the attachments made to and by such social units rooted individual identity. Also, by becoming middle class – images and advertisements for which abounded in the rising pop and consumer culture – Japanese joined the imagined community of the post-war nation-state.

Such business practices as lifetime employment, wages based on seniority rather than merit, and the family corporate system were categorized under the rubric of 'Japanese-style management'. While these never pertained to the entire workforce (and benefited core workers in middle- to large-sized companies the most), an ideal and ideology of lifelong (if not lifetime) work became established for the male breadwinner. But starting in the 1980s, the economy shifted to more immaterial, flexible labour. And, aggravated by the bursting of the bubble economy in 1991, companies started to downsize, restructure, or shut down altogether. As lay-offs and unemployment rose, there was less hiring of so-called regular or core employees and more in the ranks of irregular labourers, who include part-time, temporary, contract, and day-labourers. This shift in labour practice and the delinking of what had been the nestling of family and corporation was officially promoted under the rubric of a 'new era in Japanese-style management' (*shinjidai no nihonteki keiei*). Applauding the flexibilization of the country's labour force, the government adopted other signature tendencies of neoliberalism: deregulation of labour policies, heightened reliance on the privatization of social services, and an ideological endorsement of the responsibility of the individual (*jiko sekinin*). Under this new regime of labour, what is productive of and for capitalism is less the family or the lifetime employment of corporate workers. Rather, it is the detached, flexibly adaptable and privatized individual – a deterritorialized, decentred, postmodern subject. And, in its 'new era of Japanese management style', this would appear to be the new face of Japan's post post-war national subject (Harvey 2007).

Writing about coming of age in Japan's 'new economy' of liquidization (*ryūdōka*), Karin Amamiya, born in 1965, describes her own generation. Children of baby-boomers who grew up under the Japan, Inc. model of hard work at school geared towards the adult roles of stable middle-class life, Amamiya's cohort entered the job market when times were bleak (the 'lost decade', also called the 'glacial age of hiring'). Finding that companies gave job priority to their older, veteran workers rather than young workers just starting out, many in her generation had also fallen into the trend of *furīta* – working freely, with no set duration or contract, in *arubaito* or part-time jobs. But what started off as a lifestyle option by a Recruit Company campaign in 1989 – urging youth to avoid a job-for-life in favour of come-and-go employment – *furīta* became more an economic fiat for young workers in post-bubble times. When Amamiya entered the labour force in 1993, it was as a *furīta*, a job and status she says was numbing for multiple reasons; she could be fired anytime, the pay was minimal, there was no promise of promotion, and the work could be done by anyone. As a worker, and as a human being, she was disposable. Certainly, the job status of a *furīta* (known more today by the blanket term *hisekikoyō* [irregular worker] which encapsulates contract, temporary, part-time and *haken* or dispatch workers) is precarious. Pay tends to be low and benefits non-existent. But Amamiya, who has emerged as something of the spokesperson for the irregularly employed, working poor, and lost generation of Japanese youth today, is careful to define the risk of precarity faced by young people in terms that are not just material. Employing the word *ikizurasa* (hardship of life), she defines it thus: '*ikizurasa* [hardship of life] is connected to poverty and labour issues. But, first, it's a problem of *ningenkankei* [human relationships]. And that's where I start – with an emotional sense of hardship' (Amamiya and Kayano 2008: x).

Honing in on human relationships, Amamiya describes the psychic turmoil of being a Japanese worker who lacks affiliation (*shozoku*). This is what companies once provided and still do for their *seishain* (regular workers): a steady salary, protection in crisis, and an identity. Irregular workers, by contrast, are on their own, struggling to make a living, and, in what has become a pervasive complaint, bereft of an *ibasho:* a whereabouts where one feels comfortable and at home (which, for workers, has tended to be the workplace). More than anything, according to Amamiya, it is the loss of a sense of belonging – recognition (*shōnin*) and acceptance by others – that troubles young precariat. Calling this *the* biggest issue facing young Japanese today, Amamiya portrays 'hardship of life' as an insecurity that is not only material but also ontological: a sense of existential emptiness and social negation (Amamiya and Kayano 2008). And, in an idiom that has gained much currency these days, she sees this as adhering particularly, if not exclusively, to those in the underclass of what is becoming a two-class, bipolarized, downturned society (Yuasa 2008). According to Masahiro Yamada in his much-cited *Kibō Kakusa Shakai* ('A Society of Differential Hope', Yamada 2003), Japan has moved from a society of an expansive middle class to one of class difference. What once was achievable by the majority of citizens – the my-homeism of a steady job, a family at home, and kids anticipating the same for their own futures – now divides the nation into 'winners' and 'losers'. And this division exists not only in reality but in the imagination as well – the capacity to see a different, and better, horizon of expectation beyond the present here and now. This is how 'hope' is commonly conceived. And, as Yamada notes about post-bubble Japan, hope (*kibō*) has turned into hopelessness for many in Japan today: those who can no longer access an 'ordinary life' (*hitonami no seikatsu*) (2003: 27).

'Ordinariness' (as many, including Yamada, define it) is a holdover from Fordist times, however. With its tokens of social citizenship, reproductive futurism eludes ever more Japanese today (the 'losers'), becoming a privilege of the dwindling elite ('winners'). Men with regular jobs, for example, are twice as likely to marry and have children as are men who are irregularly employed (Yamada 2003). Fewer people marry these days (the rate of those who will remain unmarried lifelong is 15.96% of men and 7.25% of women as of 2005) and those who do, marry later (the average age of marriage for women is 28.6 and for men, 30.4). And, for unmarried adults, a vast majority continue to live at home with their parents even into their thirties.

But as the reality of my-homeism fades, its cachet as a fantasy escalates. Longing to feel 'normal', people reinvest in the aspirational normalcy of the past (Berlant 2007: 281).

Hopes, Fantasies and Violence around Home

In a controversial article (*Kibōwa Sensō*, 'Hope is War') published in 2007, a 31-year-old, self-identified *furīta* argued that the hope of his generation was war. Still working a nightshift and living with his parents ten years after entering the labour force, Tomohiro Akagi described his conditions of life as 'unbearably humiliating'. With a monthly income of 100,000 yen (about £800, well below the poverty line), Akagi was finding it impossible to assume adulthood with a place of his own, a car to drive, children and wife. Living as if he were 'under house arrest', Akagi despaired of being forever stuck in the same dead-end job and in the life-stage of perpetual child. Describing this existence as not 'that of a human who can live having hope', Akagi felt betrayed. Having done everything he was supposed to – study hard at school, graduate from a good university, find and stick with a job – he had been denied what was promised him as an adult: a decent life and social citizenship. The corrective, he provocatively proposed, was for Japan to go to war to shake things up and spur social mobility as occurred after the Second World War. For today, despite the new flexibilization of the economy, the social order is not nearly flexible enough and those in the lower rungs (young precariat like himself) are crystallized in what is likely to be an underclass existence that is permanent. If war occurred, it would certainly be tragic, Akagi admitted. But everyone would suffer and, in this, there would be an equity grossly lacking today (Akagi 2007).

Strikingly, Akagi both identifies with, and feels dis-identified by, the Japanese nation-state here. For not only does he feel excluded from a national project that, in some sense at least, no longer exists (a middle-classness tied to the lifelong ties of the family corporate system), he wants to rekindle the latter and insert himself as a full-bodied citizen within it. As Ghassan Hage (2003) has written, the nation-state has three mechanisms it can (and should, in his mind) use for distributing hope to its citizens. These are: fostering a sense of belonging to the nation (national identification); cultivating investment in and expectations about a progressively better future (social mobility); and recognizing the importance of personal and collective dreams (social hope). When citizens feel plugged in – to a sense of a collective beyond themselves and a future beyond the here and now – they are more likely to feel hopeful. When not, there is a tendency towards what Hage calls 'paranoid nationalism': clinging to a sense of nation or community from which, feeling excluded , one attempts to exclude others as well.

Violence fuelled by an anxiety of incompleteness could be said to characterize the rampage of Tomohiro Katō, a young precariat who on 8 June 2007 drove a four-ton truck into a crowded intersection and then jumped out to stab seven people to death. Occurring in the electronics and *otaku* (fan) district of Akihabara in Tokyo, the act spurred what seemed a summer-long wave of indiscriminate attacks in public spaces – train stations, kiosks, shopping malls. In this case, Katō was a 25-year-old *haken* (temporary) worker who, having gone from job to job, thought he had been fired from his current one. Deeply troubled – as he admitted on the long trail of postings he left on a phone netsite – Katō wrote of his despair at being a *haken* worker with no firm attachments (to work, girlfriend, co-workers) to give him a home base (*ibasho*) anywhere. Devoid of the tokens of social status and connectedness, he had come to hate being alive and, as he posted the morning of the killing, 'I came to Akihabara because I wanted to kill people. I've come to hate society and am tired of life. Anyone is OK.' In the news reportage that followed, Katō was described as working poor, part of Japan's *suberidai shakai* – society where people slide ever downward – who was suffering from both loneliness (*kodoku*) and the failure to feel accepted (*shōnin*). And related to this was his estrangement from his parents: his mother, it was reported, had pushed the high-performing Katō academically then withdrawn her love when his grades declined in high school.[8]

Because of the (public, random, impersonal) nature of the violence, the attack was considered a terrorist act. But equally disturbing was the profile of the perpetrator, someone not so dissimilar from an increasing number of youth: irregularly employed, lonely and disconnected, socially estranged and existentially bereft. If the sociality of the new precariat was getting (dis) assembled like this, it was precarious not only for youth but for the population at large. In the commentary that ensued after the Akiba incident, there was much discussion of the conditions giving rise to a killer like Katō. In a round-table published in the journal *Rosujene* (Lost Generation), for example, the critic Toshihiko Kayano stated: 'if only we have hope and respect, we can live. But without a secure means of existence, many today have no place or sense of home at all (*ibasho*)' (*Rosujene* 2008: 34). Youth, as he noted, are driven to join right-wing associations for the promise of national belonging they offer, but are also driven into a despair that can spiral into violence either towards themselves (as in wrist-cutting and suicide, both of which are on the rise today) or towards others (as with Katō).

The very desire to be anchored in a social rubric at once familiar and materially secure is what seemingly drives teenage girls to answer, as 85 per cent did in a recent survey (Hakuhōdō 2005), that what they want to become in the future is a full-time housewife (*sengyōshūfu*). Safety (*antei*) is what appealed to them. In a study that also delved into the so-called human relationships (*ningenkankei*) of contemporary youth, the girls reported on the high degree of digital connectivity they have, especially with their peers. Virtually all of these girls owned their own mobile phones and many of these were continually switched on. But while this meant they were never – literally, digitally – alone, this also left them susceptible to a form of sociality dependent on what the two principal investigators of the study labelled 'instant communicative ability'. Those who could curry a high volume of phone transactions were considered most popular and those who couldn't felt lonely and friendless. The energy was speeded up, and many of the girls said they felt jumpy: their sense of connectedness as contingent and frail as it was multiple and dispersed.

In the kind of relationality emerging in this era of digitality and information capitalism, interpersonal connections are at once spread across a broader network and devolve upon superficial, if constant, contact. As a young woman in her twenties told me, her friends only share what is *tanoshī* (enjoyable) in their lives – favourite foods, television shows, celebrity gossip. But the hardships they keep to themselves: to not burden one's friends and to stay popular in an age when knowing how to read, and stay in sync with, the mood of the moment is everything – what is called *kūki o yomu* (nicknamed K.Y., as someone who can't read the scene, by youth). In the era of the mobile phone and internet, *ijime* (bullying) is said to be on the rise amongst school students as 'K.Y.' gets played digitally, becoming a game of sociality whose stakes have become ever more precarious and brutal (Amamiya and Kayano 2008).

As Amamiya (Amamiya and Kayano 2008) has related about her own years of being bullied, *ikizurasa* (hardship of life) often starts here when, designated a 'loser' by one's peers, the rejection and loneliness that ensues can last a lifetime. Pain is an all too common effect of the communication society for many youth, as Amamiya puts it. And, writing about the school system and the high rates of bullying today, the cultural critic Toru Honda has entitled a recent book, *Jisatsu suru nara, hikikomore* ('If You're Going to Commit Suicide, Withdraw') (Honda 2007). Here, 'withdraw' refers to the practice of social withdrawal mentioned earlier. Alongside of *hikikomori*, there is another category of youth, NEET (not in education, employment, or training), who, numbering as many as 2.5 million, are symptomatic of an era when youth have come to be seen as embodying less the productive and reproductive futurism of Japan, Inc. than the barren presentism of a Japan in decline.

From all I have come to understand about this condition of (de)sociality, it is extremely painful for the youth himself, for the family who cares for the shut-in usually inside their own home, and for a perceived 'society'. It also signals something rather different about the fabric of sociality that the *hikikomori* (and NEET) retreats from rather than clamours to be a part of, as in the case of Akagi, Katō, and the teenage girls craving to become housewives. The aspirational normativity of my-homeism has pressures and risks of its own: using the family/home to drive competitive performances (of men at work, women in mothering, children at school) that leaves little room for social or intimate relations of other kinds. 'I had no home at home', someone told me about growing up in a household where, by the age of five, he already knew that his academic failures made him a loser in the eyes of his mother (and everyone else). *Ningenkankei* (human relations) have become cold, another man said, giving as a reason the compulsion to compete that has driven, and individuated, Japanese since the end of the Second World War. A miracle economy that won accolades for 'Japan as Number One' may have been good for national growth, he continued. But it forced people into regimens of competition that have made us a 'lonely country' today. Speaking of his own family, and its incarnation of the Japanese dream – a father tied to an all-consuming job, a mother constantly goading her children to academically perform, and a home filled with consumer goods but emptied of warmth – he shouted out during our interview: 'The Japanese family should be nuclear bombed!'

Beyond My-Homeism: A Sociality for Precarious Times

Whether stranded from, or throttled by, the 'ordinariness' of a certain way of life – what I have been tracing here as the family corporate system of post-war my-homeism – Japanese today show signs of social precarity. Certainly, there are Japanese, including youth, who feel sanguine enough about their lives and not nearly as despondent or apocalyptic (even in the wake of March 2011) as my portrayal here may suggest. But a sense of hardship in everyday life and living together is also widespread, making for a sociality that more people feel excluded from or find to be precarious itself. And, on this, I make three points.

The first is that there is a care deficit in Japan that stems, in part, from the fact that the corporation and family were the *de facto* welfare institutions in post-war Japan. People were taken care of not so much by the state (that provided little welfare, as is still true today) but by those groups they laboured most intimately for: workplace and family. With the strains placed on both of these (with fewer workers getting regular jobs, and fewer Japanese marrying or being members of economically stable households), there has been a care deficit spiralling across the country that the government – prompted by its neoliberalization and reliance on individual responsibility – defers to privatized care givers. Those unable to pay for such commodified care are left stranded: stuck all alone in homes, or on the streets, where one hears of more and more deaths as well as suicides due to economic deprivation.

The second point is that there is a disparity in the way social citizenship gets calculated today. On the one hand, and as promoted by the government itself, flexible labour is heralded as the 'new era Japanese management style'. On the other hand, the falling birthrate and marital rate that accompany this economic shift are viewed as a social, even national, crisis. The government has taken a series of measures since the mid 1990s to promote, and assist, child rearing for married couples. It has also officially announced that the old gender pattern of men working and women staying at home to raise children is outdated, and that a new 'life–work balance' must be aimed for to help working parents. The message sent here is that having a family of one's own still matters and still constitutes the measure of social adulthood (Takeda 2008). And yet the low wages and precarious job security is a major obstacle in starting (or maintaining) a family for young, even older, workers. And, in this, the government is offering very little assistance to its newly heralded flexible labour force. As a result, it tends to be only those with regular jobs (the *seishain*) who can actually afford a family. If this is the measure of social citizenship, then no wonder so many Japanese feel excluded and exiled today.

My third point concerns the template for sociality that, even now and for so many, is nostalgically attached to the past. Not only is this past over and its familial model of sociality no longer in sync with current economic times, but the nestling of home with the capital relations of Japan, Inc. bore its own problems. The dominant power structures of profit production capitalized on the affective relations of home life. This meant that the home became a breeding ground for hyperproductivity in workaholic husbands, competitive students, and sacrificial mothers. Those who couldn't live up to the task often felt socially rejected, and rejected in the eyes of their family as well. Further, so sutured to productivity, families have become ill-equipped in what one young Japanese described to me as 'education of the heart'. Many Japanese feel lonely, she told me, and being at home – as we have seen – may not necessarily ease their sense of social disbelonging.

A reconstitution or shoring up of the family then, of the 'old' kind at least, is not necessarily a solution to the precarity of life and the fading, as some see it, of social humanity in Japan today. Rather, there needs to be something new. Something that, as Ernst Bloch wrote about hope (1986), comes from investing not in the past but in the future: a not-yet known future that bears the potential for new kinds of possibilities. Hope, in this sense, must not only capture the imagination but also drive the willingness to wage (socioeconomic) reform. This is what José Munoz (2009), borrowing Bloch's notion of hope (utopia), advocates. For queers, he argues, excluded from a heteronormative polity and assigned to 'no future', there is always the need to 'desire and imagine another time and place'. 'Queerness is utopian,' he states, 'and there is something queer about the utopian' (2009: 26). But he also goes further. To participate in utopia or hope in the Blochian sense 'is not to imagine an isolated future for the individual but instead to participate in a hermeneutic that wishes to describe a collective futurity, a notion of futurity that functions as a historical materialist critique' (2009: 26).

Forward-dawning, anticipatory illuminations of a there and then that, while not yet known, comes from the refusal to settle for a dissatisfying here and now – this is the notion of hope that makes more sense to me. Not as Masahiro Yamada (2004) defines it: as those Japanese who, dwindling in number these days, can still manage to realize the Fordist dream of secure job, material prosperity, marriage and kids. If only these so-called winners have hope today, then Japan, as a country, truly has become a land of refugees. But if the rubric of futurity and belonging can change – away from merely privatized (straight) families and corporate (capitalistic) affiliations to a notion of collectivity and a life at once more flexible and inclusive – might not hope blossom in new possibilities for an emergent sociality and, in Munoz's terms, a queer(er) Japan?

A reterritorialization of the social to the end not of national growth but of security of daily life for people – this is what political scientist Tarō Miyamoto (2010) has labelled *seikatsu hoshō* (life security): a new currency of life for a new 'we' of social citizenship. During fieldwork I conducted for three summers

(2008–2010) in Tokyo, Osaka, and Nīgata, I found signs of just such an emergent sociality.

Chīki no chanoma is a nationwide web of so-called regional living rooms funded by money coming from local governments, private donations, and also its own revenues.[9] The one I visited was in Nīgata-shi, which started, fittingly enough, out of an empty house. Its director, Keiko Kawada, also founded something called *Magokokoro Herupa* (heartful helper) in Nīgata in 1994: a volunteer care service that links up volunteers with persons requiring care of any kind such as assistance at home.[10] In 2003, she set up a *chīki no chanoma*, calling it *uchi no jikka* (our natal home), which is a form of drop-in centre. Open all day and even for overnight stays, it costs 300 yen (£2.40) for the day and 300 yen for lunch. Anyone can hang out here and the intention is to provide a welcoming place where everyone helps out – making the tea and passing around the chopsticks – to the best of their ability. The day I went twenty people were there: a Chinese migrant, a girl with Down's Syndrome, several elderly, and a number of middle-aged. One man told me that, after an accident a few years ago, everyone abandoned him: the doctors, the lawyers, his family. No longer able to work as a sake vendor, he came here and learned how to be human and feel part of a community again. In its printed materials, *uchi no jikka* calls itself 'a homey place where anyone can participate' (*daredemo sanka dekiru ibasho*).

Run by a *bansō sha* (a type of NGO), *Nutarri yori tokoro* is a multinoded community centre in the depressed neighbourhood of Nutarri in Nīgata-shi. The aim here is to tend to isolated and lonely residents: mainly the elderly (usually low-income) who dominate the neighbourhood and *hikikomori* from the neighbourhood (but also beyond). Due to quite different circumstances, both of these groups rarely meet other human beings at all. Here the hope is that, by putting them in touch with each other, the two will help one another out: the elderly – deficient in resources and company – and the *hikikomori* – deficient in human wherewithal. The premises are bright, with a work area in one corner for the group of *hikikomori* who spend their days on site being trained in various work and life skills. These young *hikikomori* (all male, between the ages of 18 and 35, the day I visited) also sell their labour (doing minor household and repair or construction work for 500 yen an hour) to local residents and merchants. In addition, they run a vegetable shop on the premises that stocks fresh and inexpensive produce.

Inspired by the popular if controversial reception given to Waturu Tsurumi's *Complete Suicide Manual* (*Kanzen Jisatsu Manyaru*) that sold over one million copies when it came out in 1993 (Tsurumi 1993), '*Stop Suicide*' talk events that reach out to those deemed to be suffering from depression and in danger of committing suicide started in the late 1990s. The one I attended in 2008 was held in what is known as the seedy sex district, Kabuki-chō section, of Shinjuku, in a house called Loft Plus One. Here five survivors of suicide attempts (including Karin Amamiya) were interviewed by a narrator who asked them to tell their stories: what led them to want to die, whether or not they ever felt like killing someone, how they had managed to survive and what their take-home message to the audience was. Four of the five also performed a form of spoken word. These events have become popular; I went to another in the summer of 2010 that was so crowded I barely got in. At the end of the first one I attended – which lasted three and a half hours – the participants (called *tōjisha*, or those with the experience) asked for questions from the floor. One in the audience got up to say that she was a *hikikomori* who hadn't left home for a year until tonight. Telling her how brave she was, Amamiya continued: 'Write me an email anytime. We're here for you. Stay alive!'

Started in 1993 and now spread across the country with 135 branch offices and 30,000 members, NALC. *Nippon (Japan) Active Life Club* is a 'time savings service' or 'time bank' (*jikan yotaku seido*) where one donates care labour and accumulates time in a bank book. One hour of care labour (whether of cleaning toilets or teaching a computer class) counts as one point, and deposited care time can be withdrawn either by oneself in the future or by a family member needing care now. While there are two categories of members (users and donors), the premise is that these two categories merge; one donates care in the present as insurance for one's own care reception in the future.[11] The currency here is not money but care, and users receive care not from family members but from strangers. In its promotional information, NALC labels itself a 'storehouse for the future' (*mirai no kura*). In that storehouses store valuables, what is being stockpiled here is care: something at once precious and scarce in Japan's ageing, 'relationless society'.

In all of the above we can see stirrings of new ways of being in the world and of being with one another. At once a politics and sociality of survival (Abélès 2009), these spaces/efforts/activities operate according to a different concept of belonging from those of corporations or family membership. And while appealing to people who are in need of help, they also operate on the premise of giving care and help to somebody else. They are social organizations built around precarity but also responsibility towards others: something the country has witnessed even more in the outpouring of volunteerism – much done for, and with, 'strangers' – seen in the aftermath of the earthquake/tsunami/nuclear reactor accident of March 2011. Nothing here would (yet) fully provide a livelihood – such as jobs and families have done in the past – for individuals. Yet, in the innovativeness with which they are designing a care for life, we can see the potental, in a precarious present, of a not-yet future for a new collective 'we'. Hope besides, and beyond, 'my-homeism' points to a sociality of a possibly different kind.

Notes

1. Ever since 1973 when it experienced its last baby boom, Japan has been struggling with a decrease in birthrate. As of 2011, it is 7.3 births per 1,000 population.

2. The first lost generation came of working age in the 1990s during the decade also referred to as the 'lost decade'. Though it has varied by year, the employment situation has basically not improved, producing further 'lost generations' of young workers in the twenty-first century.

3. I follow a number of scholars, including Arne Kalleberg, who define precarious work as 'employment that is uncertain, unpredictable, and risky from the point of view of the worker' (2009: 2). This is a worldwide phenomenon and has been far more the historical norm than the exception in most countries (Neilson and Rossiter 2008). But in the case of Japan – which, like a number of other developed industrialized countries, experienced a period of post-war Fordism that accorded many, if not all, workers regular jobs in the formal economy (guaranteeing stable wages, employment, and benefits) – the rise of irregular employment today registers as a loss or decline of an economic normalcy that was once taken as standard.

4. The documentary, *Netto kafue nanmin to hinkon Nippon* (Net Café Refugees and Poverty in Japan) aired in January 2007 on Japan Television. Mizushima (2007) has also written a book documenting the phenomenon of poverty and net café refugees by the same title.

5. 'Precarity' as a term was first picked up by European social and labour movements in the 1970s to activate against contingent, flexible, or irregular employment. In Italy and France (under the term *'precarité'*), a number of scholarly debates, movements, and practices emerged around the attempt to identify – and encourage – precarious workers as a new kind of political subject replete with new forms of political expression and collective sociality. I use the word 'precarity' here more as do certain activists in Japan (such as Karin Amamiya) as well as the theorist Judith Butler (2009) to index not merely the state or condition of precarious work, but also the existential and social condition of a life that feels risky, uncertain, and unstable. As Butler notes, precarity is differentially distributed; some are more vulnerable to it (for reasons of gender, class, ethnicity, citizenship). But what she calls 'precariousness' is the generalizable state of being human in which everyone is susceptible to risk – of disease, abandonment, injury, death. As with Butler and Amamiya, I am most interested here in the relationship between precarity and precariousness.

6. *'Muen shakai'* was coined by NHK, the national broadcasting system, in a television special on January 31, 2010. The phrase 'country of loneliness' (*kozoku no kuni*) is used in media coverage/commentary of current events (for example, *Asahi Shimbun*, 24 July 2011). The activist Makoto Yuasa (2008) speaks of poverty as not only material and economic, but also human and social.

7. There are many terms used to characterize the socioeconomic conditions of a Japan in which precarious employment (irregular employment which includes contract, part-time, temporary, and dispatch labour) has risen so substantially. *Ryūdōka* is one of the most common and it translates as fluid, mobile, flexible, or – as in Zygmunt Bauman's (2000) usage – 'liquid'.

8. For this account, and commentary, on what was called the *'Akihabara musabetsu tero jiken'* (Akihabara indiscriminate terrorist attack), I have relied primarily on a special issue of the journal *Rosujene* (Lost Generation), 2008.

9. *Chanoma* is the room in a traditional Japanese home where guests are served tea. *Chīki* or *Chiiki* refers to region or locale.

10. For more on Keiko Kawada, see the book written about her and her innovative care-giving (Yokokawa 2004).

11. Currently, only about 15 per cent of users are drawing on time they have banked themselves as donors. For those who have no points of care labour saved, NALC advises they can give 500 yen (£4) per hour for labour received. This is strictly optional, however, and is considered more a gift than a payment.

References

Abélès, M. 2009. *The Politics of Survival*. Durham: Duke University Press.
Akagi, T. 2007. *Kibōwa sensō*. *Ronza*, January.
Allison, A. 1994. *Nightwork: Sexuality, Pleasure, and Corporate Masculinity in a Tokyo Hostess Club*. Chicago: University of Chicago Press.
Amamiya, K. 2007. *Ikisasero! Nanminkasuru wakamonotachi*. Tokyo: Ōtashuppan.
Amamiya, K. and T. Kayano. 2008. *'Ikizurasa' nitsuite: hinkon, aidentitī, nashyonarizumu*. Tokyo: Kobunshashinsho.
Appadurai, A. 1996. *Modernity at Large: The Cultural Dimensions of Globalization*. Minneapolis: University of Minnesota Press.
——— 2006. *Fear of Small Numbers: An Essay on the Geography of Anger*. Durham: Duke University Press.
Asahi Shimbun (Morning Sun Newspaper). 2011. *Shinzai shiitamu miuchinashi: kozoku no kuni*. July 24: 1.
Bauman, Z. 2000. *Liquid Modernity*. Cambridge: Polity Press.
Berlant, L. 2007. Nearly Utopian, Nearly Normal: Post-Fordist Affect in *La Promesse* and *Rosetta*. *Public Culture* 19, no. 2: 273–301.
Bloch, E. 1986. *The Principle of Hope, Vol. One* (trans. N. Plaice, S. Plaice and P. Knight). Cambridge: MIT Press.
Butler, J. 2009. *Frames of War: When is Life Grievable?* New York: Verso.
Edelman, L. 2004. *No Future: Queer Theory and the Death Drive*. Durham: Duke University Press.
Hage, G. 2003. *Against Paranoid Nationalism: Searching for Hope in a Shrinking Society*. London: Merlin Press.
Hakuhōdō seikatsu sōgō. 2005. *10dai no zenbu*. Tokyo: Hakuhōdō seikatsu sōgō.
Harvey, D. 2007. *A Brief History of Neoliberalism*. New York: Oxford University Press.
Honda, T. 2007. *Jisatsusurunara, hikikomore: mondaidarake no gakkōkara mio mamoru hō*. Tokyo: Kobunsha shoten.
Kalleberg, A. L. 2009. Precarious Work, Insecure Workers: Employment Relations in Transition. *American Sociological Review* 74, no. 1: 1–22.
Kaneko, S. 2006. Japan's 'Socially Withdrawn Youths' and Time Constraints in Japanese Society. *Time & Society* 15, no. 2–3: 233–249.
Kimoto, K. 2008. Kazoku, Jenda. Kaisō. In *Koyōryūdōka no naka no kazoku* (ed.) K. Funabashi and M. Miyamoto, 33–54. Tokyo: Minerubua shoten.
Miyamoto, T. 2010. *Jiyū he no toi shakai hoshō*. Tokyo: Iwanami shoten.
Mizushima. 2007. *Netto kafue nanmin to hinkon Nippon*. Tokyo: Nihon terebi hōsō kabushiki kaisha.
Munoz, J. E. 2009. *Cruising Utopia: The Then and There of Queer Futurity*. Durham: Duke University Press.
Nakane, C. 1967. *Vertical Society*. Berkeley: University of California Press.
Neilson, B. and N. Rossiter. 2008. Precarity as a Political Concept, or, Fordism as Exception. *Theory, Culture & Society* 25, no. 7–8: 51–72.
Rosujene (Lost Generation). 2008. Special issue: *Akihabara musabetsuterojiken, 'teki'wa daredattanoka*.
Silver, B. J. 2003. *Forces of Labor: Workers' Movements and Globalization Since 1870*. Cambridge: Cambridge University Press.
Tachibanaki, T. 2008. *Intorodakushyon – kakusakara hinkonhe*. In *Kakusa to hinkon: 20 kō* (ed.) T. Makino and E. Murakami, 8–18. Tokyo: Akashi Shoten.

Takeda, H. 2008. Structural Reform of the Family and the Neoliberalisation of Everyday Life in Japan. *New Political Economy* 13, no. 2: 153–172.

Tsurumi, Wataru. 1993. *Kanzen jisatsu manyuaru.* Tokyo: Futa Shuppan.

Yamada, M. 2003. *Kibō kakusa shakai: 'makegumi' no zetsubōkanga nihono hikisaku.* Tokyo: Chikuma Shobō.

Yokokawa, K. 2004. *Sono tewa inochizuna: hitoride yaranai kaigō, hitoridemom ī rōgō.* Tokyo: Tarōjirōsha edītasu.

Yuasa, M. 2008. *Hanhinkon: 'Suberidaishakkai' kara no dasshutsu.* Tokyo: Iwanami shinsho.

7

Actants Amassing (AA)

Adam Yuet Chau, University of Cambridge

Bruno Latour has been launching a persistent attack on the Durkheimian fetishization of the social, which unnecessarily limits the scope of investigation and understanding and has misled the so-called 'social sciences' down a benighted path. This article is a response to Bruno Latour's call to deprivilege the Durkheimian social and to revive a Tardean understanding of 'society' as composed of not just humans as social agents but a multitude of monadic actants both human and non-human, sentient and non-sentient, organic and inorganic, material and non-material, representable and unrepresentable (Latour 2005, 2010). The core of the article is a multi-perspectival ethnography showing the convergence into one time-space of more than two hundred specially fattened pigs (the heaviest reaching more than 900 kilograms), a two-metre long crocodile, a few ostriches, hundreds of chicken and fish, tens of thousands of bowls of snacks, hundreds of thousands of other food items, thousands of bottles of liquor and soft drinks, thousands of packets of cigarettes, hundreds of packets of betel nuts, tens of thousands of people (including festival organizers and participants, vendors, craftsmen, truck drivers, ritual specialists, sing-dance girls, martial artists, government officials, policemen, school children, volunteers, and anthropologists and folklorists), hundreds of trucks, thousands of metres of electric wires, thousands of integrated circuits, tons of fireworks and firecrackers, millions of ghosts, deities, ancestors, heavenly soldiers, and more.

The time-space in question is the annual Righteous Martyrs Festival celebrated among a cluster of semi-rural Hakka communities in northern Taiwan,[1] at which households of a particular community responsible for that year's festival compete to raise the biggest (heaviest) pigs as offerings to the spirits of their 'forebears' who died defending their communities (such hosting responsibilities rotate among fifteen such communities, which are grouped together as village alliances). The biggest pigs are weighed and ranked and the winning households honoured. All the pigs are slaughtered, elaborately decorated, fitted onto trucks, paraded through the streets, presented to the spirits, and then eventually part-eaten at household-centred banquets (where anyone can sit down and eat without invitation) and part-distributed to friends, relatives and associates (as slabs of fatty pork) as tokens of the spirits' blessing. The day of the offering presentation at the Righteous Martyrs Temple (*yiminmiao*) and accompanying festivities draw tens of thousands of visitors, who come to see and pass judgements on the offerings, enjoy a wide variety of entertainments (which are also presented as offerings to the spirits) such as folk operas, instrumental music ensembles, fireworks, and singing and dancing (and often striptease) shows by scantily dressed young women on fancy mobile stages with elaborate lighting and sound systems.

I would like to designate the convergence and intense co-presence of above-mentioned diverse actants and all the associated activities, happenings and relationships with the expression 'actants amassing' (AA as a shorthand). The word 'amassing' suggests the active state of being in the process of forming a mass. In other words, I am using 'mass' as a verb; it definitely does not mean 'crowd', since the actants doing the massing are so many more than just human beings. I have pilfered the term from architecture – originally used to refer to the volume (massiveness) of built structures – in order to avoid using words with 'socio' as a root component. Even though I identify with Latour's de-Durkheimization project, I find his attempt to resignify words such as 'society' and 'the social' futile if not misguided. By now these concepts have become so entrenched not only in the disciplines of sociology and anthropology but also in common discourse, therefore it would be more advisable to invent new words and expressions or to invest theoretical value in existing words (e.g., massing) that do not carry any heavy baggage of received meanings. I have the same reservations about attempts to streamline and standardize the conceptual referents of 'sociality', the main operating concept of this volume. Latour's more recent invocation of the concept of 'composition' is potentially more appealing, though it has the unfortunate connotation of a little too much human agency (though such associations might have been intended) (see Latour 2010). Deleuze and Guattari's concept of 'assemblage' comes closest to what I have in mind. So AA (actants amassing) has genealogical affinities with both Latour's ANT (actor-network theory) and Deleuze and Guattari's ruminations on 'assemblages', 'rhizomes', 'lines of flight', 'desiring-machines', and 'chaosmosis' (Deleuze and Guattari 1987; Guattari 1995).

Apparatuses of Capture

ANT sees various actants as being connected in a dynamic and fragile web of suspension (with associations of various degrees of strength and durability), forever jumping over the time lags between t (temporal coordinate, i.e., a particular point in time) and t + 1 (i.e., the moment immediately following the aforementioned moment) in a permanent state of volatile heterogeneity. For

Latour, institutions (such as universities, states, laboratories, companies, technological marvels, and so on) are only as real and enduring as the illusory moving images we see in a magical lantern. With this much I concur. But what forces compel these institutions and other seemingly real things to pull themselves over the existential gaps from t to t+1? What forces propel elements of these institutions and other seemingly real things to fall off and join other entities/assemblages, thus contributing to their form-shifting and even eventual disappearance (and, of course, in reality they are always shifting forms and always disappearing)? Latour has demonstrated some of these forces in his case studies (e.g., on the conceptualization and eventual non-realization of the guided-transport system Aramis, Agencement en Rames Automatisées de Modules Indépendants dans les Stations, in Paris in the 1970s and 1980s), although I think more conceptualization is needed to get at the mechanisms of 'composition' and what might be called the various compositions' inter-actantal *mises-en-cohérence*, conceptually and spatiotemporally.

A useful concept that will help us in this endeavour is 'apparatuses of capture', which is introduced by Deleuze and Guattari (1987) and re-worked by Kenneth Dean, the ritual studies scholar, in the context of analysing the complex ritual networks and 'ritual machines' in southeastern coastal China (Dean 1998: 45; also Dean and Zheng 2010). In explicating the exuberance of ritual performances on the Fujian coast (across the Taiwan Strait from Taiwan), Dean defines 'apparatuses of capture' as 'the capture and temporary consolidation of social, economic, political, and libidinal forces by cultural forms' (Dean 1998: 45). We can expand the range of items and forces to be captured and consolidated beyond the 'social, economic, political and libidinal' and the formal agency as broader than merely 'cultural'. I see my task as explicating how certain 'compositional assemblages' – here I am combining Latour's notion of 'composition' (Latour 2010) with Deleuze and Guattari's notion of 'assemblage' (Deleuze and Guattari 1987) – came about and have seemingly attained staying power. What are the compositional equivalents of the configuration of gravitational and other forces that keeps the planets in their tracks? The answers are necessarily fluid as they depend on at what level of complexity and along which plane and axis the analysis enters. But as an anthropologist, I prefer to enter the thicket via 'compositional forms' that can seem to be more or less put together by humans, while doing my best to foreground the agency (not necessarily relating to consciousness or agentive desire) of non-human actants.

I will be presenting fragments of the 2009 festival from the 'perspectives' of various actants (though still a very tiny percentage of all the actants captured) that 'massed' on those hot and humid Taiwanese late summer days.[2]

Figure 7.1 The display of decorated giant pig offerings in the temple square in front of the Righteous Martyrs Temple in Xinpu, Xinzhu County, Taiwan. Only the top thirty ranked giant pigs have the honour of being displayed in front of the temple (though altogether there are thirty seven giant pigs on display because of many tied ranks among some of the pigs).

The Giant Pig

I am a pig. A giant pig. I now weigh 1,531 Taiwanese *jin* [about 918 kilograms; 1 Taiwanese *jin* equals 0.6 kilograms]. I have just been weighed this morning by the organizers of the giant pig offering competition – and may I say that I actually also *feel* my own weight? Have you ever felt the tensile tug of weighty matter inside yourself?

I don't have a name. I am not a pet. I belong to the category of giant pigs intended to be slaughtered and offered to the righteous martyrs' spirits at the temple festival tomorrow. I am about three years old. I was born and raised in a professional pig farm not too far from this village. When I was two my present owners Mr and Mrs Zhang came to the farm and identified me as a potential prize-winning pig and signed a contract with the pig farmer who raised me, specifying how he would be compensated if I could manage to win one of the top prizes.

About two hundred households in the village-alliance community responsible for hosting the temple festival have contracted a giant pig or raised their own, and about sixty households with the biggest pigs entered the competition. I came out ranking third in the competition! Mr and Mrs Zhang are very pleased. They will have certain knowledge that the righteous martyrs will bless and protect them for years to come. My pig farmer owner will get a huge bonus for helping them to achieve this feat (on top of the agreed payment by the kilogram). I am obviously very proud of this achievement, as I spent three years eating and eating and eating so as to grow fatter and heavier and to beat the other competition pigs, some of whom were being raised side by side with me in the same farm. I drank milk from my mother's teats, fighting like crazy with the other dozen or so baby piglets. But soon my pig farmer owner began feeding me all kinds of delicious food, including lots of small fish called *qiudaoyu* (literally 'autumn knife fish' [*Cololabis saira*]) caught in the South China Sea and Japan Sea. I also drank a lot of milk and beer. I ate a lot of good food but I can't say my life was good since, as soon as I was chosen as a potential prize pig, I was confined in a tight enclosure so I couldn't move around; that way I could concentrate on growing fat and not waste any precious energy. I eventually grew so big that I could hardly stand. Towards the last year or so of my life I was feeding lying down. And instead of feeding on my own, the pig farmer twice daily manually fed me liquidy, highly nutritious feed down my throat using a tube – up to 40 kilograms a day! (Some pig farmers even resort to really deviant means to make the competition pigs heavier, like force-feeding it with iron sand right before the weigh-in!) Some animal rights activists have condemned this inhumane treatment of us competition pigs. But I say somebody has got to sacrifice a little in order to become a sacrifice!

I was transported by truck from the pig farm to the Zhang residence a few days ago. Because of my size and weight, lifting me onto and down the truck proved to be a difficult operation (like the weighing operation, which was done by dragging me onto a flatbed scale). Many a prize pig gets injured this way, and an injured pig does not make a good offering, does it? The Zhangs prepared a temporary sty in front of their house under the awning, made of sandbags and fine black sand. I settled in nicely, enjoying the best food of my life for a few days, hand fed to me by Mrs Zhang. There were cabbages, corn, fish, cuttlefish, rice gruel, beer, milk, and more industrial pig feed (laced with growth hormones?) given by the pig farmer. Feeding me at this late stage is important because I could still manage to grow quite a few kilograms, and to compensate for the kilograms lost due to the stress and moving during the transit. I have forgotten to mention how hot it is. The highest temperature today was 38 degrees Celsius. To help me keep cool the Zhangs installed two fans and two mist sprayers around me. As all the other giant pigs, I was put outside to be viewed by as many people as possible, a proud display of the efforts of the household. As the Zhang residence is by the road, many passers-by stopped to take a look at me and make comments and chat with the family members. Before the weigh-in and the announcement of the prizes a lot of people were visiting many of the households with competition pigs and guessing which ones would be ranked the highest. I heard there were bookies who set up betting parties for people to bet on the ranking order of the three top-ranking pigs.

I don't know the Zhangs very well since they didn't raise me for long themselves. In the past all households raised their own pigs, including (and especially) competition pigs. The competition was really meant to demonstrate how committed the households were in raising the biggest pigs and making the heaviest offerings. But the economic transition in Taiwan in the 1980s and 1990s meant that very few households remained farmers, so it didn't make sense any more to raise your own pigs; raising a pig takes a lot of work and attention, so when members of the households are busy making money in all sorts of ways (factory work, trade, business, home factories, etc.) there is no one left to feed the pig, especially when the adult women of the household are all otherwise preoccupied because they are often the backbone of household businesses. Meanwhile professional pig farming in Taiwan had become very sophisticated, thanks to decades of efforts to industrialize pig farming (thanks to the agroindustrial policies and developments of both the Japanese colonial government [1895–1945] and the Nationalist government after 1949). So it was only natural that festival households began contracting pig raising to professional farmers, and that a system of correspondence between prize ranking and compensation and bonus evolved and eventually became standardized. There are even standardized prize pig contract forms for both parties to complete and sign. Taiwan used to export a lot of pork, especially to Japan, but foot-and-mouth disease broke out in 1997 and hit the pig farming industry really hard. The export of pork ground to a halt almost overnight and never resumed. So this gave professional pig farmers in the areas with giant pig competitions even more incentive to engage in competition pig raising so as to earn extra cash.

Now it's past 11pm, and the auspicious moment for my slaughter has come. This has been calculated by ritual specialists and announced beforehand to all households with competition pigs to slaughter. About sixty people surround me: members of the Zhang household, the butcher and his team mates, curious passers-by (including many children), reporters and an anthropologist and his assistant. About seven or eight people are in the butcher's team. A lot of preparation has gone into the slaughter: knives, buckets, a boiler with a big tank of boiling water that's refilled constantly, rice wine and salt (to be sprayed and spread on me later), and a metal frame for holding my skin up later for decoration.

The butcher takes out a big knife at least two feet long. I am flipped over by his helpers so I am lying on my back with my feet held up. I struggle of course, but not too rigorously. The knife goes in by my neck straight into my heart, so deep that only the handle of the knife is visible from outside. Then the knife is pulled out and hot blood gushes out onto the dirt ground. Though the air temperature is over 30 degrees Celsius you can still see the steam coming out of the blood. The butcher's helpers wash the blood away with buckets of hot water. I let out my last, hot breath.

Figure 7.2 The mounting of the giant pig 'sur/face' onto the metal frame. Note the dead crocodile in the background.

Figure 7.3 The decoration of the giant pig offering. The man in yellow polo shirt in the foreground is Mr Zhang. The mouth of the young man with the kettle of boiling water on top of the giant pig has been stained red by betel nut juice.

Figure 7.4 The giant pig, elaborately decorated and mounted on the back of a special truck. Note the framed prize certificate issued by the county government, the framed picture of the owners of the pig with the pig before it was slaughtered, the incense stick and other offerings in front of the pig (including the pink-coloured buns in the shape of towers, cases of Taiwan beer, a duck, a chicken, and some cooked internal organs of the pig).

The butcher and his helpers will then cut me open, take out all my innards, remove the entire skeletal frame, cut out most of the meat (which is cut into long strips waiting to be cooked for tomorrow's banquet), and leave only the outer surface intact (i.e., my skin and an inch or so thick of subcutaneous fat). They then will wipe rice wine and salt all over my remaining carcass to prevent it from going bad too quickly. Then they will take a break from me to slaughter the crocodile (see below), which is the Zhang's companion offering to the spirits. After they are done with killing the crocodile they will spend the rest of the night (the next five to six hours until dawn) decorating me. By about seven in the morning the next day I will have been mounted onto the specially decorated truck and moved to the temple square of the Righteous Martyrs Temple together with the other thirty-six prize-winning giant pigs. While my 'skin' is being displayed at the temple, the Zhangs' helpers will be busy cooking my meat, together with the edible innards, in preparation for the banquet that the Zhangs will host in the evening. My 'skin' will return to the Zhang residence after about six hours (after the spirits have consumed the offerings), and at the right moment close to midnight, after the hungry ghosts have also consumed their meals, the butcher and his helpers will carve my skin into long strips of fatty slabs so that the Zhangs can distribute them to friends, relatives and business associates. Because I am a blessed giant pig, receiving a piece of me will bring good fortune to the recipients. However, in recent years more and more people are reluctant to receive such a large slab of fatty pork as they don't know what to do with it – the days of cooking with home-prepared lard are almost completely gone.

The Crocodile

I am a crocodile. I am now tied up by one of my hind legs to a post by the Zhangs' house, my mouth bound shut by industrial-strength adhesive tape. I am four years old and am pretty big already (about two metres long from nose to tail-tip), though certainly not as big as the pig, whose slaughter I have just witnessed merely a few feet away from my nose. I was born and raised in a crocodile farm in southern Taiwan. In recent years, a few crocodile farms have sprung up in southern Taiwan to cater for the Taiwanese taste for exotic meat (and our skin can also be harvested for making bags and other accessories). I grew up together with hundreds of other crocs. Most do not live to more than two years old since they would be slaughtered for meat and skin, although some have been allowed to live longer and grow bigger for pseudo 'nature tourism' purposes – as some of these crocodile farms are open to tourists, who love to take pictures with big, bad crocs – and occasionally, unfortunately for me (and despite the honour!), to be bought to serve as offerings at temple festivals. Crocodiles have not been offerings at the Martyrs' Festival until now. In a way I should feel honoured and proud to be the first croc offering to the righteous martyrs. Mr and Mrs Zhang are certainly proud of the fact they have pulled off a major innovation – not only are they the *first* household to introduce crocs as offerings but they are the *only* one that is doing it (there is always additional cachet for being the one and only). It is traditional practice at the Righteous Martyrs Festival to have a companion offering piece to go with the giant pig offering. The traditional companion piece is a goat. In fact there is a competition to see which household's goat has the widest horn span (usually there are a dozen or so households that include a goat in their repertoire of offerings). Some households have innovated recently, using ostriches as the companion offering (there are two ostriches this year). So the Zhangs' innovation is merely a variation on this.

The butcher commands his helpers to tie me up on a wooden board with my belly facing out. Then the board is propped against the wall of the Zhang residence. My moment has come. The butcher doesn't wait too long before slaughtering me because a lot of the onlookers are eager to see how he would do it (most of them have never seen a croc in real life, let alone seeing one killed).

The butcher claims that he has slaughtered crocs before. Maybe he's bluffing. He takes out a smallish knife and tried to poke it into the middle of my chest. It won't go in! Then he tries harder, using his fist to hammer on the butt of the knife. The knife still won't go in! People begin to laugh, and the butcher risks losing face big time. Then he takes out a hammer to hammer the knife in. It finally pierces through my hard belly plaque. He then proceeds to use a pair of scissors to cut through the belly plaque. A one-foot long vertical slit opens up in the middle of my belly. Unlike the slaughter of the pig, there isn't any blood gushing. Now it's the big moment. The butcher pokes his hand inside me and pulls out my heart! He gives it to one of his young helpers, who puts it in his palm and parades around excitedly to show the curious crowd. My heart, no bigger than a prune, beats rhythmically in his hand. The crowd breaks into an excited wave of exclamations and commentaries, and many take out their cameras and mobile phones to take a picture of my heart. Then I am gutted. Tomorrow I will be decorated and displayed in a mini-aquarium next to the giant pig offering as a companion piece. The mini-aquarium is basically a shallow basin with water and water lilies and I am made to perch on top of a rock looking ferociously alive. Many visitors get a fright upon first seeing me.

A Betel Nut

I am a de-shelled fresh betel nut. I have been cut along my length, laced with lime (calcium hydroxide paste), and wrapped in a single betel leaf. People chew me as a stimulant, similar to smoking and chewing tobacco, or chewing *khat/qat* in some Middle Eastern and African countries, or, for that matter, drinking coffee or tea. People would chew me for a few minutes, mixing their saliva together with the lime and chewed-down leaf and nut into a bloody red wad (due to a chemical reaction), and after they have sucked all the taste and potency out of the mixture they would spit it out onto the ground. That's why many pavements and streets in Taiwan are stained with splatters of bloody red betel juice in varying degrees of decomposition, from the freshly spat wet and bright-red ones to the sun-scorched greyish outlines of those of older vintage. Legend has it that some foreign visitors to Taiwan who had not heard of this practice, upon seeing these bloody splotches, thought that the Taiwanese were working so hard that they were vomiting blood!

Regular chewers would chew a few dozens of nuts each day. I am in a box of thirty other similar betel nuts (all neatly lined up), bought by the butcher (the man who slaughtered the giant pig). The butcher and his team mates could have bought betel nuts from those scantily-dressed 'betel-nut beauties' selling betel nuts from their brightly lit and fancily decorated small glass booths along the roads, but they prefer buying larger quantities from professional betel nut preparers. Some of the men amongst you get a kick out of buying betel nuts from the hot girls because they bring the nuts to your car and you can gawk at their much exposed tits and legs (you are supposed to gawk at them because they might get offended if you don't!) and engage in brief 'spicy', flirty chit-chat, but their betel nuts are more expensive – in smaller packets – and not as good as those prepared by professionals. The professional betel nut preparers and vendors tend to be family businesses that sell betel nuts in regular shops in towns and cities, also along major roads because a lot of the customers are drivers; no hot girls there.

I should be consumed within a few hours; otherwise I will go bad, given how hot the weather is in the summer here. I will last longer if you put me in the fridge, but most betel nut chewers prefer to buy packets of freshly prepared betel nuts. So a regular chewer's daily life is punctuated by small trips to, or stops at, betel nut vendors. Don't look down on a small nut like me. According to some sources,[3] every year the Taiwanese spend more than 100,000,000,000 Taiwan dollars (about £2 billion) on buying betel nuts. About seventy thousand farming households are engaged in cultivating and harvesting betel nuts in Taiwan, and many hundreds of thousands of individuals' livelihoods depend on the betel nut trade (farmers, transporters, wholesalers, preparers and vendors, merchants who import more betel nuts from Thailand and other Southeast Asian countries when the Taiwanese betel nut trees are not in season, and the 'betel nut beauties'). This is why the government cannot push too hard in eradicating this supposedly 'pre-modern', 'low-class' and surely carcinogenic practice (mostly contributing to higher instances of oral cancer).

The Giant Iron Frame

I am a giant alloy iron (*baitie*) contraption especially made to hold and frame the giant pig offerings. In the past the pig offerings were put on a simple vaulted wooden frame so the pigs would lie horizontally, looking as they did when alive. People used to take the increasingly large pig offerings to the Righteous Martyrs Temple over many miles of rugged terrain. Then the roads were built and people began to use tractor trucks to bring the giant pigs. The decorations on the giant pig offerings used to be relatively simple. People piled on more and more elaborate decorations onto the pigs, until professional giant pig decorators came onto the scene. These professionals would provide the large trucks and fit increasingly fancy 'bling' around the pigs (complete with modular 'gothic' towers and blinking neon lights). And in order to exaggerate the size of the giant pigs some genius in the 1970s invented me, a metal frame with a curved front so that the entire pig's surface can be draped over the front with the head at the bottom and tail at the top and spread taut across the curved surface of the front like a large round sail or canvas. Then the whole thing is mounted onto the back of the truck facing the back, so an unsuspecting spectator might mistake the size of the truck as the size of the giant pig! This invention was so successful that the design quickly spread to all the communities where there were giant pig competitions. And because of the combined weight of the giant pig and the metal frame people now have to use forklifts to mount the pigs onto the trucks.

The Hungry Ghost

I am a hungry ghost. When I was alive I was a fisherman off the coast of northern Taiwan. During a very bad storm our fishing boat capsized and I and all my mates on the boat drowned. I never married and had no descendants, so I couldn't become an ancestor and receive regular offerings from my descendants. My spirit thus became a ghost. For more than two hundred years now I have been roaming around hell, trying to grab whatever food I can lay my hands on, like those offerings laid out for other people's ancestors. There are countless 'hungry ghosts' like me fighting amongst ourselves for these leftovers. A lot of us are in a kind of hell that's called 'flaming mouth', which means that whatever we put in our mouths immediately turns into a ball of flame. Even if we can grab onto some scraps of food, we are still always hungry – hence our name. The merciful Buddha has designed a ritual to relieve us from this so that we can actually eat the offerings, but this ritual is conducted too sporadically to benefit most of us.

We hungry ghosts are released from hell for the entire seventh lunar month each year so that we can roam around the human world. This is when the humans feed us with all kinds of offerings so that we don't bother them and cause them trouble. During this month households and businesses put out tables of offerings for us to feed on. There are ducks, chicken, pork, beef jerky, instant noodles, crisps, candies, biscuits, and cakes. Well, we can only feed on the 'spiritual aspects' of the offerings, so after we are done feasting the humans take the food items back and eat them (while we gulp up everything in a flash they can take their time to eat these in the next days and weeks). Because people buy so many food items during this month, the supermarkets in Taiwan during this time of the year all have 'ghost month' sales to compete for customers. Often members of the household or business would choose their favourite food items to use as offerings. We hungry ghosts don't care that much what kinds of food are put out; we are grateful that people put out any offering at all! But it's true that we might cause trouble if they don't feed us anything; this is why the Taiwanese call us 'good brothers' (*haoxiongdi*) and treat us nicely to make sure that we leave them alone.

I have mentioned the offering tables households and businesses put out for us, but these are small meals compared to the giant feasts that communities put out collectively for us. On the fifteenth day of the seventh lunar month it is the Middle Prime (*zhongyuan*) Festival, which is when communities stage collective offerings to us, with rows and rows of food offerings and dazzling shows such as folk operas and fireworks. The best part is the rituals conducted by Buddhist monks or Daoist priests (they are hired by the communities), which lasts for days, culminating in the final 'feeding the hungry ghosts' segment on the night of the grand offering. In the case of the Righteous Martyrs Festival, it's the day when the giant pigs are displayed, when all the offerings are to be miraculously multiplied a million-fold through ritual magic. A feast it is indeed! But the price we pay by feasting on this banquet is that after the banquet we have to go back to hell. We will suffer another year of ordeal before the next round of feasts. Such is life for us hungry ghosts.

The Righteous Martyrs

We are the so-called righteous martyrs (*yimin*). We were young men who died defending our communities against other groups (especially in the many battles between us Hakka people and the aboriginals and Hokkien people) or who died fighting alongside Qing government troops against rebels. These battles and fights happened in the eighteenth and nineteenth centuries, and thousands of us died without even having got married and produced heirs, which means that we had no descendants to burn incense for us or feed and clothe us on a regular basis. So we were not that different from the hungry ghosts mentioned above. But thanks to the initiatives of some Hakka community leaders in the past our bones were gathered and buried together and a temple was built to honour us, thus ensuring that we would receive offerings and not go hungry like the hungry ghosts. The annual Righteous Martyrs Festival's purpose is to commemorate our bravery and contribution to our communities and to make offerings to us (the giant pigs and the rest of it).

The Xinpu Righteous Martyrs Temple has served as the centre of the cult of righteous martyrs. In the past hundred years or so the temple has spawned dozens of branch temples through the practice of 'incense division', where a new community wishing to establish their own temple would bring the fire and incense ashes from an older temple to their new temple. This is why during the annual festival in our honour a lot of branch temples send representatives to their 'ancestral temple' to pay respects. And these branch righteous martyrs temples have their own festivals and rotational hosting communities. Scholars studying the cult of righteous martyrs have mostly treated us as a sub-genre of ghosts, but in recent years many Hakka community activists are contesting this view, saying that we are more like deities. Of course, in Chinese religious history there have been many deities who were ghosts first, so we are in the process of being upgraded to deity status. Meanwhile, in order to appeal to younger people, some Hakka cultural workers have been engaging in efforts to 'cute-ify' us, even making smiley righteous martyr dolls!

Mrs Zhang

I am forty years old. My husband and I are in the funerary business. He specializes in conducting funeral rituals whereas I take care of all the other related matters such as bookings, commissioning invitation cards and wreaths, etc. I am originally from another township not very far from here (half an hour's drive away). Our household has six members: my husband, his elderly mother, myself, our three children (all at school-age). My father-in-law died a few years ago, so my husband is the head of the family. But he is a rather shy man and focuses on the technical aspects of the business while I, more gregarious, deal with customers and relations with other businesses (including our suppliers). When it was our community's turn to host the Righteous Martyrs' festival, our household would always raise a pig. Of course we would! You only get to do it every fifteen years. There are still some households that don't do it – either they don't have the money or they are not that committed to the custom. Anyway, we were going to contract the raising of a competition pig to a pig farmer, as most people do nowadays, and went to choose a potential prize pig. We decided this time that we really wanted to spend however much was necessary to win this giant pig competition. My mother-in-law's health hasn't been very good and we hoped that raising a prize-winning pig would bring blessings from the righteous martyrs and the deities and my mother-in-law would feel better.

Seeing that our chosen pig wasn't making enough progress to fatten itself, we scouted around and found a different pig farmer and chose a much bigger pig (the present pig), which turned out not to disappoint us at all. We are very happy that we won third place. We are spending a lot of money but it's all worth it. Look how many people have come to look at our pig! And many more people will come to the banquet tomorrow evening because of the reputation of our pig. We are also hiring the butcher and his team of helpers. We won't tell people where we found them or how much we are paying them but it's all money well spent. Look how efficient they are at slaughtering the pig and how beautifully it's getting decorated.

A Sing-Dance Girl

I am a sing-dance girl, performing on mobile stages, the so-called 'electronic flower trucks' (*dianzi huache*). The electronic flower truck with sing-dance girls seems to be a genuine Taiwanese invention. These trucks are fitted with sophisticated sound and lighting systems (hence 'electronic') and are elaborately decorated (hence 'flower'). In the past ten years or so, newer and much more elaborate 'electronic flower trucks' have developed. These trucks can open up and form a complete stage, with fancy lighting and sound systems, and sometimes a steel pole so that we can do some pole dancing. We are often the major attractions at any festival occasion, with people young and old watching

Figure 7.5 The 'electronic flower trucks' with scantily dressed young women dancing and singing by the side of the giant pig offerings. Note that far more people are watching the sing-dance girls' performance than the giant pig offering to its side.

us perform. At the Righteous Martyrs Festival, some of the winners of the giant pig competition hired electronic flower trucks to be side offerings to the spirits, and of course to add to the 'hot and noisy atmosphere' (*lau-jiat*).[4] They say that the righteous martyrs will appreciate us sing-dance girls in particular because they died as young men without ever having slept with women.

People usually call us 'spicy girls' (*lamei*) because of our sexiness. I am twenty years old and I have been a sing-dance girl for two years now. We basically follow the rhythm of the communal festivals in northern Taiwan – different regions of Taiwan have their own supply of sing-dance girls and we rarely cross into others' territories. When there aren't any temple and communal festivals we perform at funerals or night clubs. I am self-employed, though I have my 'protector' (head of a local gang) to whom I pay a fee. We will get bullied if we don't have a protector. The owners of the flower trucks are the nodal points of our activities. For example, when one of them gets a job for a funeral, he calls up a few of us to come along. He will get paid by the client and then he pays us according to how many 'numbers' each of us does. For a large communal festival like the Righteous Martyrs Festival, there will be many electronic flower trucks hired by different households but appearing at the same time, so a large number of us sing-dance girls will come and we rotate from truck to truck to add variety

Figure 7.6 Sing-dance girls perform on an electronic flower truck's fold-out stage next to the giant pig display in the evening of the Righteous Martyrs Festival back in the communities of the hosting households.

to each stage and to make more money. If we work really hard the clients will tip us on the side. Most of us do striptease upon request to make more money. Some even perform very 'not-suitable-for-children' acts on stage (like sexual acrobatics and even live sex acts) – but they only do these really late at night after the kids have been sent to bed. But we can't do this kind of thing at the festival this year because the local police station has sent dozens of officers to keep an eye on us, so that nobody does anything indecent. A lot of them even film us with video cameras the whole time we perform, apparently for their records. I am sure they are just filming us so they can watch us for fun afterwards. They are wearing uniforms so we know which ones are the cops, and we tease them a lot while performing.

The Buddhist Priest

I am a professional Buddhist priest (see Wang 2009). I am not a monk. I have a wife and three children. I have inherited my trade from my father and will pass the skills on to my sons (or at least one of the two sons). Because I don't live in a monastery or temple but live amongst regular people, you might want to call me a 'householder ritual service provider' (see Chau 2006b). Yes, I make my living by providing ritual services at funerals and communal festivals. At funerals and commemorative rituals my job is to smooth the transition of the deceased from the world of the living to the world of the dead and to accumulate karmic merits for the deceased and their family members. At communal festivals such as the Righteous Martyrs Festival my job is to ritually transfer the offerings to the deities, righteous martyrs and hungry ghosts. I also use the ritual manual to determine the auspicious timing of various segments of the festival, e.g., when to slaughter the giant pigs, when to release the water lamps, when to conduct the 'offering to the Jade Emperor' and 'feeding the hungry ghost' rituals, etc.

We always work as a team because our rituals are complicated, involving a lot of paraphernalia and various ritual components. For smaller rituals three of us would suffice, but for larger communal rituals we would need at least five ritualists as well as a team of ritual musicians. A client (be it a household or a community) would call me at my shop to arrange the ritual service, and depending on the scale of the job I might need to sub-contract segments of it to my buddies who are ritual service providers in neighbouring communities. My whole family is involved in ritual work. Those who are not doing the rituals directly (like my wife, younger son and daughter) would help make the papier-mâché ritual paraphernalia, all destined to be burnt at the end of the rituals (see Scott 2007). Burning these papier-mâché offerings sends them to the spirits. Every year the Taiwanese burn a huge amount of paper offerings to the spirits, including tons and tons of paper money. The mountains of ashes left behind (and particles flying in the air) create pollution problems. Because of increasing environmental consciousness, more and more temples are fitting smoke processing vents on top of the paper offering burning furnaces and prohibiting the burning of incense inside the temple halls – a few even go so far as implementing virtual burning of incense and paper money on the internet! The environmental protection bureau of the local government also sends officers around during religious festivals to persuade people to not burn as many paper offerings. This is a difficult issue. The advocates of environmentally conscious worship say that what matters is 'one's sincere heart', not how many offerings one burns or how much money one spends. But Chinese religion just wouldn't be the same without the burning of paper offerings.

The Local Politician

I am a politician running for the mayoral office of Xinzhu County. The election is scheduled for later this year. I am running on the Nationalist Party ticket, against the Democratic Progressive Party candidate. The campaign to win more votes has entered a feverish pitch. Because of the tens of thousands of people showing up at the Righteous Martyrs Festival, it is a perfect occasion for me to show my face and for my team to drum up people's support for me and for our party. We have mobilized dozens of campaign workers and volunteers to come to the festival to broadcast our political platform and messages using our campaign vans, distribute pamphlets and other media with my face and slogans printed on them. We give out free packets of tissue paper and fans so that when people use these items during the festival, they will hopefully read and respond to our messages printed on them. Those people working for my campaign are all easily recognizable because they all wear our specially designed campaign T-shirt. Our rivals are busy doing the same thing.

The incumbent mayor has just come to the temple to pay respect to the righteous martyrs, and of course with a big supporting cast in tow. You see, politicians nowadays have to come to the people to 'stage a show' (*zuoxiu*) to demonstrate that we support grassroots religious activities even if some of us think all these are silly superstitions. In the past, before Taiwan became democratized and when the Nationalist Party ruled the island as a one-party state, there were no elections, so politicians only needed to curry favour with their superiors. But now it's the votes that make the career of a politician, from the lowest of township representatives up to the president! This is why, because the Righteous Martyrs Temple is one of the most famous temples in Taiwan and *the* most important temple for the Hakka, even the presidential candidates from both parties come to the temple to pay respect to the righteous martyrs and ask for their blessings, and it's also politically necessary for the elected president to visit the temple again to thank the righteous martyrs for having helped him get elected. On this occasion, he presents to the temple a large, fancily carved plaque with laudatory inscriptions to be hung inside the temple, thus demonstrating the connection he has with the temple, the righteous martyrs, and the people. The rafters of the temple hall are crowded with these plaques hanging all over the place (those from presidents, mayors, other kinds of politicians and important people). The incumbent mayor not only has to present offerings to the righteous martyrs and bow to their tablets multiple times, he and his wife have to sit through an elaborate ceremony inside the temple to give gravitas to the Righteous Martyrs Festival. And they have to present award certificates (in the name of the county government) to the households with the top thirty ranked giant pigs and have their pictures taken together with the prize winners. There are about thirty to forty journalists with cameras, video cameras, sound guns, tripods and microphones. So tomorrow all the major as well as Xinzhu local news media (newspapers, TV, online news, and even blogs) will have coverage of this event, and as a result the mayor gets maximum exposure. This is why we call this 'staging a show'. The giants pigs are for show, we politicians are for show, we are all for show. The giant pigs win prizes, we politicians win elections. Haha.

Conclusion: A Matter of Coherence?

These fragments of narratives show better the various 'apparatuses of capture' and elements (and processes and mechanisms) of convergence than demonstrate how they cohere. Why do so many human and non-human actants 'mass' in this particular time-space every year? There would not be any Righteous Martyrs Festival if these actants suddenly stopped 'massing'. So something is compelling them to converge thus year after year. The composition sticks. Here is where Alfred Gell comes in. In *Art and Agency* (Gell 1998), Gell explicates the generative potential of artistic forms, suggesting that artistic forms as a whole within a particular cultural setting, or works within the overall oeuvre of a particular artist, are transformations of one another; in other words, they somehow cohere. A 'compositional' principle, once invented and tried and found useful (for all kinds of reasons, and not all conscious), will persist in time, and various elements get captured and consolidated and the web thickens and becomes increasingly sticky (so actually more elements want to 'get captured' instead of falling off). The composition asserts substantial 'gravitational pull'.

One primary compositional form informs the Righteous Martyrs Festival (though it is widely found in many other festival contexts in Taiwan and other Chinese worlds): hosting (see Chau 2006a). Hosting is one of the most important and fundamental idioms in Chinese social life. It refers to the practice (or ensemble of practices) of inviting, feasting and sending off of guests on important occasions. These guests can be humans, deities, ancestors or ghosts. It is through reciprocal hosting that a household asserts its place in the social universe. But hosting is not simply or primarily about exchanges and social interactions, though these are important elements. Rather, we might say that hosting provides the setting for 'massing'. In the Chinese context, hosting is an idiom to produce and consume 'social heat' (*honghuo* or *re'nao*) due to a long-established 'festive regime' (see Chau 2006a and Chau 2008). I have called hosting occasions instances of 'rites of convergence' (as opposed to van Gennep's and Victor Turner's 'rite of passage'; see Chau 2006a), where heterogeneous elements are thrown into one compositional assemblage over a specific duration.

The idiom of hosting is re-enacted again and again at the Righteous Martyrs Festival: at the households that raised the giant pigs; at the Righteous Martyrs Temple; at the river bank (where water lamps symbolizing offerings are sent downstream); by the households whose turn it is to host and organize the festival; by the hosting community collectively; by the Buddhist priests; by the politicians; by the local government; through food and drink as well as magical formulae. And the guests include deities (the entire hierarchy from the highest of the high, the Jade Emperor and the Buddha, down to the lowest of the low, the heavenly soldiers), ghosts, ancestors and pseudo-ancestors (or half-ancestor and half-ghost, i.e., the righteous martyrs), and humans.

But two other important compositional forms accompany and have been integrated into the hosting idiom: competition and rotation. The hosting households compete amongst themselves to see who can raise the biggest pig (and thus who are or to be more blessed by the deities and spirits), who can present the giant pig offerings in the most elaborate and beautiful way, who will host the biggest banquet, and who have the largest networks of friends and associates to whom to give the pork slabs; the fifteen rotating hosting communities compete (in a serial manner over the course of cycles of fifteen years) to see which communities can put together the best and most 'red-hot' temple festival; and the politicians (admittedly a much more recent addition, or captured element, to the festival scene) compete to see who can stage the most sincere and elaborate 'show' to garner the blessings of the spirits and to attract votes, etc.

Rotation is a pervasive cultural form (or compositional principle) in the religious landscape in Taiwan and other parts of the Chinese world (see Sangren 1987: 96–101). In the case of the Righteous Martyrs Festival, we find a classic example of nested and fractalized (see Gell 1998) rotational arrangement: the main annual festival organizers and hosts are rotated amongst fifteen communities (territorially defined clusters of villages); within each annual on-duty (*zhinian*) community, the main organizing and hosting responsibility is rotated amongst all the member villages; and within the chief hosting village, the leading hosts (especially the chief and deputy incense-pot hosts, *luzhu*) are rotated amongst the most respected members of the village.[5]

There are, of course, many, many more compositional forms operating at the Righteous Martyrs Festival than space will allow me to explore in this article. I hope I have adequately demonstrated how 'actants amassing' (AA) can serve as a good entry point not simply for dismantling the Durkheimian fetishization of the social but as a productive way of revealing previously hidden or understudied connections and coherences (not just adherences) amongst various actants as well as the 'apparatuses of capture' and 'compositional forms' that bring them together and tumble forward along with them. I will not, like Latour, advocate any utopian compositionism (Latour 2010). Instead, I merely offer the giant pig display and the Righteous Martyrs Festival as a compositional assemblage, folding and unfolding, folding and unfolding, folding and unfolding (see Deleuze 1993).

Acknowledgements

I thank Henrietta Moore and Nick Long for their kind invitation to present a paper in the Department of Social Anthropology Senior Seminar Series at Cambridge in Michaelmas Term, 2009, and the subsequent invitation to contribute to the volume on rethinking sociality. I have presented related materials at a few other venues over the years: an American Anthropological Association annual meeting panel in 2005 on Chinese religious practices; a departmental seminar in the Department of Social Anthropology at the London School of Economics in 2006 at the invitation of Charles Stafford; an informal gathering with young Hakka cultural workers and researchers at the Hakka Cultural Centre in Xinzhu (Hsinchu) in the summer of 2009 at the invitation of Ye Jih-jia; a seminar at the Department of Archaeology and Anthropology, the

University of Taiwan in the summer of 2009, at the invitation of Lin Wei-ping; in May 2011 at an international conference on ritual and technology at the Max Planck Institute for the History of Science, Berlin, Germany, organized by Grace Shen and Dagmar Schäfer; and in July 2011 at an international conference commemorating the centenary of the publication of Emile Durkheim's *Elementary Forms of Religious Life*, at the invitation of David Gellner. I benefited immensely from the inputs from the audience members on all of these occasions, though the present article has departed quite a bit from these earlier versions, which focussed more on 'technologies of exuberance' especially the decoration ('bling-ification') of the giant pigs. The central arguments presented at these seminars will form the core of other articles (see Chau, in preparation). I also want to thank Nick Long for his very helpful comments and suggestions on earlier drafts.

I want to thank the people at the Righteous Martyrs Festival in Xinpu (Hsinpu), Xinzhu (Hsinchu), Taiwan for contributing to my study (especially the organizers of the festival in the summer of 2009 and members of the prize pig households I have spoken with). I want to thank especially Ye Jih-jia and Yen Ping-jing for assisting with my fieldwork during the festival. I am grateful for the insights and help I have received from Taiwanese scholars Chiu Yen-kuei, Julia Huang, Lin Wei-ping and others. Many of the conceptual inspirations have come from Giles Deleuze and Félix Guattari, Bruno Latour, Kenneth Dean, Brian Massumi (Massumi 2002) and Alfred Gell.

Notes

1. Drawing here on fieldwork conducted by the author in the summer of 2009. For earlier anthropological studies on giant pig festivals in Taiwan see Ahern (1981) and Weller (1987). For studies on the Hsinpu Righteous Martyrs Festival see Chiu (2000) and Lai (2001).

2. A kind of representational conceit is inevitable as I try to make pigs, a crocodile, a betel nut, a giant alloy iron frame, a hungry ghost, righteous martyrs and even people 'speak' (or narrate) the way they do here – what Bruno Latour calls 'the privileges of prosopopoeia' (Latour 1996: x). This is partly inspired by how Latour (1996) makes Aramis speak its mind, even when it only existed as an idea, a project. Non-human actants usually don't 'speak' like this, but at least I have given them some kind of 'voice'. Having them 'speak' allows the forces of capture to emerge more clearly and 'naturalistically', however deceptively. To the extent that actants do not need to have any material reality – for example, Latour's Aramis is merely a conception and prototype rather than a real train system – apparently immaterial 'things' such as ghosts and spirits can also be conceived of as actants. I need to insert a caveat here about 'putting words in the mouths' of real people. The narratives below given by real people are not recorded speech; they should be treated in the same way as the 'speech bubbles' created by cartoonists and magazine editors to 'give voice' to politicians and celebrities; in other words, they are 'composed' by the anthropologist (but based on research as well as imagination informed by research and ethnographic understanding).

3. See Chinese wiki entry on betel nuts in Taiwan at <http://zh.wikipedia.org/wiki/%E6%AA%B3%E6%A6%94> (last accessed on 14 May 2012).

4. *Lau-jiat* is the Southern Fujianese (Taiwanese) equivalent of the Mandarin word *re'nao* or *honghuo*, which I have glossed as red-hot sociality or social heat (see Weller 1994: 113–28; Chau 2006a: 147–68; Chau 2008).
5. Although selected by divination, this arrangement is still rotational in essence as households that have served as leading hosts one year cannot put forward their candidacies in future rounds until all the prominent households have served in these roles.

References

Ahern, E.M. 1981. The Thai Ti Kong Festival. In *The Anthropology of Taiwanese Society* (eds.) E.M. Ahern and H. Gates, 397–425. Stanford: Stanford University Press.
Chau, A.Y. 2006a. *Miraculous Response: Doing Popular Religion in Contemporary China*. Stanford: Stanford University Press.
——— 2006b. Superstition Specialist Households?: The Household Idiom in Chinese Religious Practices. *Minsu quyi* [The Journal of Chinese Ritual, Theatre, and Folklore] 153: 157–202.
——— 2008. Social Heat: The Sensorial Production of the Social. *Ethnos* 73, no. 4: 485–504.
——— 2011. Modalities of Doing Religion. In *Chinese Religious Life* (eds.) D.A. Palmer, G. Shive and P. Wickeri, 67–84. Oxford: Oxford University Press.
——— Forthcoming. Guanxi/laiwang de zuozongjiao muoshi: yi Taiwan Mazu raojing jinxiang wei li. In *Mazu yu minjian xinyang xueshu lunwen ji* (ed.) Wang Jianchuan (Wang Chien-chuan)..
——— in preparation. Technologies of Exuberance. In *Ritual as Technology and Technology as Ritual* (ed.) Grace Shen and Dagmar Schäfer. Publisher to be determined.
Chiu Yen-kuei (Qiu Yangui) 2000. Cong jidian yishi kan bei Taiwan yimin xinyang: yi Fangliao baozhongci dingchounian Hukou lianzhuang zhinian zhongyuan wei li. In *Di si jie guoji kejiaxue yantaohui lunwenji: zongjiao yuyan yu yinyue ce*, 1–47. Taipei: Institute of Ethnology, Academia Sinica.
Dean, K. 1998. *Lord of the Three in One: The Spread of a Cult in Southeast China*. Princeton: Princeton University Press.
Dean, K. and Zheng Zhenman 2010. *Ritual Alliances of the Putian Plain. Volume One: Historical Introduction to the Return of the Gods*. Leiden: Brill.
Deleuze, G. 1993. *The Fold: Leibniz and the Baroque* (trans. T. Conley). Minneapolis: University of Minnesota Press.
Deleuze, G. and F. Guattari 1987. *A Thousand Plateaus: Capitalism and Schizophrenia* (trans. B. Massumi). Minneapolis: University of Minnesota Press.
Gell, A. 1998. *Art and Agency: An Anthropological Theory*. Oxford: Clarendon Press.
Guattari, F. 1995. *Chaosmosis: An Ethico-Aesthetic Paradigm*. Translated by P. Bains and J. Pefanis. Bloomington: Indiana University Press.
Lai Yu-Ling 2001. Xinpu Fangliao yiminye xinyang yu difang shehui de fazhan: yi Yangmei diqu wei li. Master's Thesis, Department Graduate Institute of History, National Chung-yang University, Taiwan.
Latour, B. 1996. *Aramis, or the Love of Technology* (trans. C. Porter). Cambridge: Harvard University Press.
——— 2005. *Reassembling the Social: An Introduction to Actor-Network Theory*. Oxford: Oxford University Press.

——— 2010. An Attempt at a 'Compositionist Manifesto', *New Literary History* 41, no. 3: 471–490.

Massumi, B. 2002. *Parables for the Virtual: Movement, Affect, Sensation.* Durham: Duke University Press.

Sangren, S. 1987. *History and Magical Power in a Chinese Community.* Stanford: Stanford University Press.

Scott, J.L. 2007. *For Gods, Ghosts and Ancestors: The Chinese Tradition of Paper Offerings.* Seattle: University of Washington Press.

Wang Kui 2009. *Fojiao xianghua: lishi bianqian zhong de zongjiao yishu yu difang shehui.* Shanghai: Xuelin chubanshe.

Weller, R.P. 1987. The Politics of Ritual Disguise: Repression and Response in Taiwanese Popular Religion. *Modern China* 13, no. 1: 17–39.

——— 1994. *Resistance, Chaos and Control in China: Taiping Rebels, Taiwanese Ghosts and Tiananmen.* Seattle: University of Washington Press.

8

Doing, Being and Becoming
The Sociality of Children with Autism in Activities with Therapy Dogs and Other People

Olga Solomon, University of Southern California

A teenage girl walking a dog down a suburban Southern California street is an ordinary sight but the pair that can be seen every day in the neighbourhood where I live is not quite ordinary. Over the past ten years I have watched this girl walk this dog in the purposeful, hurried stride of a person who has things to do. During these years the dog has turned from a lanky puppy into a dignified Golden Retriever, and the girl has turned from a slightly overweight child with a developmental disability into a confident-looking, athletic teenager. She and I have always exchanged greetings but recently I lingered after saying hello and asked her what her dog's name was. 'Sunshine,' she said, and added that the dog is now ten years old, that she got the dog right after September 11th, 2001, and that she works to pay for dog food and veterinary bills. 'There is even some money left for myself,' she said with a smile, but this did not come across as ironic. I looked at the girl's smiling face and wondered how much of this conversation was made possible by the dog sitting at her feet.

Such observations of children's sociality in interactions involving dogs were not new to me. But it was a single experience that moved me to pursue research in this area: at a park in a Southern California town, my own dog, a female border collie, carefully placed a Frisbee at the feet of a girl who was standing nearby with her father, inviting her to play. The dog then assumed an anticipatory position in preparation for what she expected to happen next: that the girl would pick up the Frisbee and throw it. Without hesitation, the girl, who appeared to be about five years old, picked up the Frisbee and threw it. The two began to play with one another, the girl threw the Frisbee; the dog caught it and placed it at her feet, again and again. In these moments, the girl and the dog chose each other through their engagement in this activity, creating a world in which this child and this dog were doing, being and becoming 'with' each other in ways that were seemingly ordinary but, as it turned out, were transformative and significant. The girl was being a child who was good at playing with dogs, as children often are. The six-year-old dog, barely two weeks before adopted from an animal shelter, was being a dog that was good at playing with children, as dogs often are. The doing, the being and the becoming were mutually constitutive as both the child and the dog were being and becoming 'ordinary' (Sacks 1984), playing with each other.

The girl's father and I silently watched this game until he broke the silence: he asked me with tears in his eyes if I would sell him the dog for any sum because his daughter had autism and had never played with anyone before. I gently declined, taken aback by the urgency of his request, but this memory troubled me for years. Years later, I conducted a study on how children with autism interact with therapy dogs because I wanted to see if it was possible for more children with ASD and their families to have such experiences.

To this end, in this chapter I draw upon a digital video data corpus of approximately sixty hours of interactions involving five children (four boys and one girl, ages four to fourteen), all diagnosed with ASD, their parents, siblings and peers, and six specially trained therapy dogs and their trainer.[1] Analysing the data, I explore from an occupational science and occupational therapy perspective how theories of human sociality inform our understanding of the ways in which a child's social engagement is supported during child–dog interactions; and how analysis of the data, in turn, might inform these theories.

'Doing, being and becoming' in the title of this paper signify the three components of occupation (Wilcock 1999), a key concept of the occupational science and occupational therapy perspective, which illuminates the interrelatedness between what people do (*doing*), who they are (*being*) and the kind of people they are developing into (*becoming*). This perspective contributes a theoretically rich, interdisciplinary framework to the broader discussion of sociality through a nuanced, theory- and practice-based understanding of the multidimensional relationships between behaviour, health and well-being across contexts and temporal frames (Glass and McAtee 2006). The primary concern of this field is with the engagement in occupations that support health, well-being and participation, with an eye for understanding how human social actors are engaged in activities in particular contexts of their lives (Clark and Lawlor 2009; Clark et al. 1991). The conceptual foundations of occupational therapy practice include, for example, using environmental modifications and specialized equipment to augment and maximize ways in which a person with limited ability engages and carries out activities during therapy; as well as creating environments where individuals can develop new skills (Kielhofner 2009: 5–6). Sociality is thus viewed as a constitutive process that supports engagement, relatedness and participation in everyday activities with other people. Children's engagement in occupations with others is an important area of occupational science and occupational therapy. Lawlor (2003), for example, argues that the study of childhood occupations should be reframed as a study of children as 'socially occupied beings doing something with someone else that matters' with the analytic focus on childhood experiences that are socially constructed through adult and child co-created action sequences (Lawlor 2003: 424).

Based upon this framework, the study focuses on the forms of sociality that are enacted through embodied, coordinated actions with communicative partners, both human and canine. This contributes to existing theories of sociality by expanding the analytic horizon to include, as Weil (2006) suggests, 'ways of knowing that appear to work outside those processes of logocentric, rational thinking that have defined what is proper to the human, as opposed to the nonhuman animal' (ibid.: 87). A recent 'counter-linguistic turn' in disability studies and animal studies has focused on 'forms of subjectivity that are not language-based' (ibid.). Berger (2005) reminds us that the 'counter-linguistic turn' does not reject the 'linguistic turn'; rather, it proposes that 'there *is* an other of language, whether or not this other can be conceptualised' (ibid.: 344, italics in the original). Occupational science and occupational therapy perspectives share a concern with the experiences of people whose conditions impact linguistic ability, such as ASD. It contributes an understanding of the meaning of daily activities for individuals with ASD 'despite developmental, linguistic, and perceptual differences' (Spitzer 2003: 68, see also Park 2008, Miller, Kuhanek and Watling 2010).

This chapter examines ways in which therapy dogs mediate the sociality of children with ASD to illustrate that sociality is better conceptualized as a mediated property of the sociocultural environment rather than an individual characteristic. In doing so, I aim to problematize key approaches to sociality through illuminating aspects of normative social behaviour that for the most part are analytically invisible in these approaches. The point of theoretical departure is an examination of how human sociality has been conceptualized in social science; this is followed by a consideration of dogs as co-participants in social interaction. The chapter concludes with an analysis of two examples of video-recorded interactions among children with ASD, other people in the children's lifeworlds, and therapy dogs.

Autism and Sociality

ASD (Autistic Disorder, Asperger's Disorder, and Pervasive Developmental Disorder Not Otherwise Specified: APA 2000) manifests in early childhood as delayed or atypical sociocommunicative development and restrictive or repetitive behaviours and interests. Impaired social reciprocity is the central, defining clinical characteristic of autism (Carter et al. 2005). A toddler who does not look at her parents for social referencing, a teenager who interjects in a conversation to talk about a special interest, or an adult who does not respond to another's complaint about having a terrible day – all manifest an impairment in social reciprocity (Gotham, Bishop and Lord 2011).

In a commentary entitled 'On Being Autistic, and Social', Richard Grinker (2010), a cultural anthropologist who has an autistic daughter, writes that 'we need to focus attention on the anthropological study of a form of difference that has previously been conceived of as lying outside the realm of the social. The concept of "diversity", with all its positive connotations of acceptance and celebration of difference, need not refer only to gender, race, ethnicity, and religion. We can also begin to celebrate a diversity of minds.' (ibid.: 182). Autism and sociality are thus no longer considered incompatible. Yet for decades autism was thought to be the antithesis of sociality, and it still challenges its current conceptualizations. Autism foregrounds the embodied, actional and experiential dimensions that are often overlooked in linguistic and cognitive approaches to sociality. The example of autism strongly suggests that sociality may be less a property of an individual to be 'social' and more a mediated property of sociocultural environments in which the individual is expected to act in socially normative ways.

Ochs and Solomon (2010) stress that 'autistic sociality' 'is not an oxymoron but, rather, ... a reality that reveals foundational properties of sociality along with the sociocultural ecologies that demonstrably promote or impede its development' (2010: 69). Sociocultural ecologies that support the sociality of individuals with autism across the autism spectrum, from the most severely affected to the most high-functioning, are often those environments where social interaction is *mediated* – by technological or other means. Examples of such environments include computer-mediated, literacy-based interactions that may include voice-output assistive devices (Gillette et al. 2007); socially assistive robots (Feil-Seifer and Mataric 2008) and virtual reality technologies (Strickland et al. 1996).

Environments that include companion animals (i.e., pets), or therapy- or service-animals is a subset of mediated environments that support the sociality of those with ASD. Some children, youth and adults with ASD seem to have a special proclivity for interacting with animals, and, in the company of animals, with other people. Even animals at the zoo that are not directly engaged in interaction with children with autism may facilitate sociality (e.g., Sams et al. 2006). Interactions with animals, however, are not a panacea for ASD. It is still unclear whether an affinity towards animals is shared by many individuals with autism, but for those who do share this affinity, it presents an opportunity to actively restructure their social world in a way that supports their sociality (Solomon 2010).

Key Approaches to Sociality:
The Problem of 'What is Human in Humans'

The idea that human beings share a fundamentally social 'human nature' has a long philosophical tradition. The enduring theme in Western social theory is the relationship between an individual and others, primarily whether an individual's interests stand in conflict or in harmony with the interests of other people in a social group. Reconciling cultural differences with universally human aspects of social behaviour has, however, been a challenge. Fiske (1992), for example, has proposed that human sociality across cultures is constituted through a combination of four elementary forms: communal sharing, authority ranking, equality marking and market pricing. These forms, Fiske claims, are 'endogenous products of the human mind, generated by universally shared models of and for social relations' (1992: 690). Economist Herbert Gintis (2000) attempted to account for the maintenance of high levels of sociality in human groups despite low levels of relatedness by contrasting self-interested individuals' behaviour with that of 'strong reciprocators' who voluntarily and sometimes anonymously contribute to the common good of their group.

Such approaches exemplify Richard Rorty's contentions that 'much of the rhetoric of contemporary intellectual life takes for granted that the goal of scientific inquiry into man is to understand "underlying structures", or "culturally invariant factors", or "biologically determined patterns"'. The goal, Rorty asserts, is to 'construct an epistemology which has room for a kind of justification that is not merely social but natural, springing from human nature itself, and made possible by a link between that part of nature and the rest of nature' (2002: 423–424).

There is considerable concern in theories of human sociality with the distinction between the human and the non-human, and with how human nature relates to 'the rest of nature', the non-human worlds. Most of this distinction has to do with the 'uniquely human' capacity for language (see Jackendorf and Pinker 2005). Latour (2004) draws 'the line in the sand' between speaking humans, especially of the (social) science denomination that he somewhat derogatorily calls 'lab coats', and what he calls 'nature' comprised of non-humans that encompass any entity 'apart from ourselves' (Latour 2004: 33) from planets, galaxies to stones, trees and animals on whose behalf the 'lab coats' speak. For Latour, there appears to be a tension in the ontological hegemony of humans who deem non-humans 'mute' and usurp the communicative capacity and meaning-making through speaking about them to other humans in human language, often with dreadful consequences (see, e.g., Hearne 1986, 1994; Goodall and Bekoff 2002). Arguing for an even stronger ontological divide between 'the human' and the rest of the physical world, Searle (2010: ix) asks: how can we 'give account of ourselves, with our particular human traits – as mindful, rational, speech act-performing, free-will having, social, political human beings – in a world that we know independently consists of mindless, meaningless, physical particles? ... In answering that question, we have to avoid postulating different ontological realms, a mental and a physical one, or worse yet, a mental, a physical and a social'. Searle gives an account of human sociality, and of collective and individual intentionality, as a social ontology based upon a theory of speech acts and the 'exact role of language in the creation, constitution, and maintenance of social reality' (Searle 2010: ix).

The fields of cognitive, linguistic and social anthropology have all played an important role in the conceptual development of the term 'sociality'. As Enfield and Levinson argue:

> At the heart of the uniquely human way of life ... is our peculiarly intense, mentally mediated, and highly structured way of interacting with one another. This rests on participation in a common mental world, a world in which we have detailed expectations about each other's behaviour, beliefs about what we share and do not share in the way of knowledge, intentions, and motivations. This itself relies both on communication (linguistic and otherwise) and on a level of cooperation unique in the animal world. This mode of cooperative, mentally mediated interaction enables the accumulation of cultural capital and historical emergence of cultures. (2006: 1)

Framed within this ontological divide between the 'uniquely human' and the 'non-human', it is significant that what counts as 'human sociality' is inextricably and powerfully linked to certain kinds of language and speech as media for the production of meaning, as well as to certain kinds of mind, perception, intersubjectivity, sources of knowledge and reasons for moral conduct. By the end of the twentieth century and at the beginning of the twenty-first, 'human sociality', so conceived, has become a central concept in social science concerned with human development and human nature, and is now a cornerstone of ontological understandings of human cognition, society and culture, and of 'what is human in humans' (Stengers 2005: 995).

The field of biosemiotics, i.e., the study of forms of communication and signification observable both within and among living systems (e.g., Favareau 2002, 2008) theoretically bypasses this ontological divide by extending its reach to non-human social phenomena and by stressing the reciprocally enacted, context-generating sequential organization of action-in-interaction. Haraway (2008: 235) takes the discussion further, arguing that 'it is no longer possible scientifically to compare something like "consciousness" or "language" among human and non-human animals as if there were a singular axis of calibration'. Rather, humans find themselves 'in rich, largely uncharted, material-semiotic, flesh-to-flesh, and face-to-face connection with a host of significant others'.

The question that remains, however, is where the phenomenon we call 'sociality' is located? Is it *in the mind* of each person, as Searle believes, or *in the structures of social actions* that have potentialities to create 'contexts of relevancy, constraint and possibility for each other's immediate next' action, as is argued by Favareau (2008) – or perhaps both? Another related question that is critical to consider: what is the composition of the 'assemblages of nature' (Latour 2005: 2), i.e., what kinds of participants are assembled and in what configurations, or figures (Haraway 2008)? Of great importance here is the phenomenological difference *between* configurations called 'family', 'community' or 'society', as well as the interaction *among* these entities, and across the divide between human and animal, e.g., among children with ASD and therapy dogs.

In summary, three taken-for-granted characteristics of sociality are especially noteworthy because they both shape and delimit how sociality is conceptualized. *Firstly*, there is an expectation of a strong association between sociality and language, specifically that sociality (whether Latour's, Searle's, or Enfield and Levinson's) is realized – from mostly to exclusively – through language, a theoretical tradition that originates in the structuralisms of Saussure, Lévi-Strauss and Lacan. Human–animal interactions, especially when the humans in question have an impairment in linguistic communication, present opportunities to examine whether this assumption holds under scrutiny. *Secondly*, there is an assumption that sociality is achieved through intrapersonal mental processes such as attributions of mental states, beliefs and intentions of other humans that are used to interpret their actions, together called 'Theory of Mind' (e.g., Baron-Cohen et al. 1985). Because autism has been considered primarily as a disorder of Theory of Mind (ibid.), an examination of sociality of those affected by ASD puts this assumption to the test. *Thirdly*, it is assumed that sociality so conceived is a uniquely human way of being with other humans. An analysis of social interactions of children with ASD and therapy dogs challenges this assertion. It demonstrates that sociality is a process mediated by canine communicative partners and thus constitutes an interspecies phenomenon.

Perspectives on the Sociality of Children with ASD: Being at Home in the World

Mary Reilly (1962: 2), one of the early theoreticians of occupational science and occupational therapy, argued that 'man, through the use of his hands, can creatively deploy his thinking, feeling and purposes to make himself at home in the world and to make the world his home' (1962: 2). The notion of 'making yourself at home in the world and making the world your home' reverberates with the recent scholarship on 'worlding', and an occupational science and occupational therapy perspective thus stands to both inform, and gain from, recent theoretical developments in this area.

The concept of 'worlding' has been discussed, among others, by Haraway (2008) and Stengers (2005), who posited that 'the world' is a possible unknown constructed together by multiple, diverse entities. These entities enter into each other's presence and are 'response-able' to and for each other, i.e., are engaged 'in relationships of response' (Haraway 2008: 82) and are willing to take ontological risks by responding to each other in an act of 'response-ability' (Stengers 2005). The response is an act that draws ontological entities into *figures*, 'material-semiotics nodes or knots in which diverse bodies and meanings co-shape each other' (Haraway 2008: 5). The *figure* is a co-shaping, a 'becoming with', that for Haraway is also a 'becoming worldly' in a practice of inhabiting a certain kind of world where the humans grapple with retying the knots of multispecies response-ability (ibid.: 3). The process and practice of 'worlding' is useful to think with because it is intensely relational, actional and social, yet it does not assume that the entities in the presence of each other are all necessarily human. In my earlier example of my dog inviting a girl to engage in the game of Frisbee, the girl and the dog drew each other into a child–dog *figure*. The *figure* generated a possible world in which the girl could do and be what she has not yet done or been before, i.e., a social, relational, joyful five-year-old who plays, albeit not yet with people. The possibility of playing with people as well as with dogs has been subjunctively cast, promised by the child–dog engagement.

In a related discussion, Holland et al. (1998) combine the notions of *figure* and *world* and develop a concept of 'figured world' that captures the subjunctive quality of becoming. A 'figured world' is 'a socially and culturally constructed realm of interpretation where particular characters and actors are recognised, significance is assigned to certain acts, and particular outcomes are valued over others' (Holland et al. 1998: 52). Rather like Haraway and Stengers, Holland et al. (ibid.) see human beings as drawn to and recruited into the figured worlds where their identities and agencies are formed dialectically through co-participation in activities, performances, and discourses. Important to this discussion is an observation made over forty years ago by Boris Levinson, a child psychiatrist and the founder of animal-assisted therapy who worked extensively with children with ASD:

> When the child plays with the dog, he establishes his own world, the boundaries of which he himself prescribes. The therapist, therefore, participates in a common adventure by entering into a corner of the child's world where the child feels secure. This is where the therapist and the child find an equal footing; this is where the doors of communication are likely to open between child and therapist. (Levinson 1969: 67–68)

Such conceptualizations of 'world', 'worlding' and 'figured world' that draw together children with ASD and dogs may be a relevant response to Latour's pondering about the 'assemblages of nature' (2005) and Searle's (2010) questioning about what to do about the 'non-human matter' (a category that includes both rocks and animals) that surrounds 'mindful, rational, speech act-performing, free-will having, social, political, speech-act producing humans' (2010: ix).

In the study of children with ASD interacting with therapy dogs, the relational aspect of 'worlding' has been paramount in the sense that the families, besides changing their schedules to accommodate an hour or longer visits of the dogs, the trainer and the researcher, were also willing to engage in the imaginative practice of creating another kind of space, 'the open', i.e., 'the space of what is not yet and may or may not ever be; … a making available to events' (Haraway 2008: 34; see also Agamben 2003). It is both a space and a potential world (Abram 2010) where the children may have experiences and opportunities of practical mastery that they may not be able to have otherwise. Coming to and being in 'the open' is constituted by the willingness of the parents to both hold on to and to suspend the sense of 'what is at stake', not putting any pressure on the child or the trainer in regards to what they should do relative to what the parents wish to happen, and yet to watch closely for the signs of enjoyment, competence and engagement, all indicating the possibility of development and change.

Against this theoretical landscape I now examine interactions that include two kinds of participants, each differently endowed in terms of their communicative potentialities: children with ASD, a condition that hinders communication, and 'therapy dogs' – predictable and attentive, albeit non-speaking, communicative partners.

Child Meets Dog: The 'We' of Child–Dog Interaction

Growing evidence from both empirical research and families' personal experience suggests that children and youth with ASD respond to animals in general, and dogs in particular, with a marked increase in social behaviour and improved participation in everyday activities with family members and peers. Children with ASD exhibit a more playful mood, are more focused, and display more attention to other people in their social environment when a therapy dog is present than in 'no dog' social situations (see, e.g., Martin and Farnum 2002). They remain engaged in activities with other people for longer periods of time and their interactions with siblings and peers improve (Solomon 2010). Such use of human–canine interactions for children with ASD is a response to a particular kind of challenge inherent in autism intervention: to facilitate development-relevant experiences to address autistic impairments while at the same time offering experiences of ordinary childhood.

The language of 'we-ness', Lawlor (2003) argues, permeates developmental literature with such terms as attunement, mutuality, synchrony, and rhythmicity, describing how infants and children's social worlds are created through coordinated participation in activities and interpersonal events with other people. But what do the human–animal assemblages look like when children with ASD, therapy dogs and others come together in a joint activity?[2] The examples below describe processes and dynamics that support the sociality of children with ASD.

Example 1:
The Material-semiotic 'We' of Walking a Dog on a Leash

In the United States and other societies where dogs are positioned as companions, a dog's leash is often used as a material-semiotic artifact that physically links the human and the dog during a joint activity such as dog walking. The leash, however, is only a link but not a guarantee of a coordinated action: Laurier, Maze and Lundin (2006) illustrate the complex and intricate coordination of human–canine social actions in the spatially situated activity of dog walking in parks, on and off leash. The laborious process by which a child with ASD learns to walk a therapy dog on a leash and to recognize both the material-semiotic and the relational aspects of the connection between himself and the dog illuminates how the child–dog 'we' emerges in the context of ordinary everyday activities.

Boyone,[3] a seven-year-old diagnosed with autistic disorder, came for a dog-training session to work with his five-month-old Golden Retriever puppy in training to become his service dog. Besides Boyone and the animal trainer working with the puppy, the group consisted of the boy's mother, his older brother and sister, and his behavioural therapist who had been working with him for the past six months. In his everyday life, Boyone's limited ability to speak led to a struggle when he wanted to convey his wishes and intentions, and he often acted anxious and frustrated.

The animal trainer working with the family had extensive experience with children with disabilities. She took the group to a neighbourhood park, a grassy, shady place with old trees and a playground. Besides the family's puppy, two therapy dogs, both Australian Shepherds who belonged to the trainer, also came along, so that each child had a dog to walk. Boyone walked one of the Australian Shepherds, a white female.

The process by which Boyone eventually held the dog's leash independently and was able to walk her in a coordinated fashion unfolded over approximately 25 minutes. As the group was walking to the park down suburban streets, Boyone and his therapist walked together while the therapist pressed the dog's leash into Boyone's hand, facilitating the sense that he was also walking the dog. The dog was an attentive and patient walking companion for Boyone and his therapist. After a few minutes, the animal trainer, who was walking in front of the group, silently indicated to the therapist that she would like the dog's leash to be transferred to Boyone. When the therapist hesitated, the trainer waited and when Boyone and the therapist caught up with her, she inserted herself into the child–therapist–dog configuration between the therapist and the dog, also taking hold of the dog's leash.

Now at the park, three people – the child, the therapist and the trainer – were connected by the dog's leash to the dog and to each other. The therapist was holding the boy's hand that held the leash; the trainer held the part of the leash that was attached directly to the dog's collar. The therapist, who until this time was pressing the leash into Boyone's hand, let go of his hand so that only Boyone and the trainer were holding the dog's leash while the therapist was still touching the boy's arm (Figure 8.1).

Finally, the therapist let go of Boyone's arm and continued walking behind him. From that moment on, Boyone was holding the end of the leash while the trainer was holding the leash close to the dog's collar. Coordinated walking with the trainer and the dog while holding the leash was initially a challenge for Boyone because 'walking a dog' is not simply walking next to a dog but involves

Figure 8.1 Walking the dog, assisted by trainer and therapist.

precise coordination of speed, direction and orientation to physical and social environment by both human and dog. When Boyone was not looking, the trainer let go of the leash. There was a moment of startled surprise and hesitation when Boyone realized that he was the only one holding the leash. He lingered in mid-step but quickly recovered his composure and continued walking the dog next to the trainer.

After several minutes of walking next to Boyone and the dog, the trainer went ahead to join the others. Now Boyone walked the dog by himself. There was something new in his orientation to the dog: if previously he was holding the leash and walking next to the dog and the trainer, not visibly paying attention to either one of them, now he was looking at the dog while walking her. His apprehension, tangible at first, appeared to have diminished and he seemed curious watching the dog walking in front of him.

For a moment, he dropped the leash and stood uncertain looking at the ground. Then he bent down and picked up the leash (Figure 8.2 and Figure 8.3).

The moment when Boyone dropped the leash can be seen as the moment of an ontological crisis: the precarious child–dog 'we' 'came apart' (Haraway 2008: 230). After dropping the leash, Boyone hesitated for a second and then reached for the leash to pick it up. Here we see this child's embodied understanding of the material-semiotic link with the dog, his agency in maintaining the 'we', and his work at preserving the joint activity. Approximately ten minutes after the first 'leash drop', he dropped the leash again and then successfully regained it. When others around him celebrated his success in picking up the leash, he joined in the celebration, grinning widely and laughing.

His confidence had visibly grown, from walking with the therapist who pressed the leash into his hand, to walking the dog independently and regaining

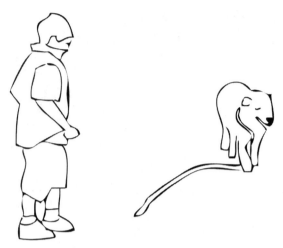

Figure 8.2 Dropping the leash.

Figure 8.3 Picking up the leash.

the child–dog 'we' by picking up the dog's leash. On the way back from the park to the trainer's house, Boyone walked the dog three long blocks, independently and confidently (Figure 8.4). 'Wow, look at you,' Boyone's therapist said to him as he was walking with the dog.

Haraway (2008) shares a 'coming apart' experience with her Australian Shepherd, Cayenne, during an agility exercise that may illuminate the inner workings of the human–dog figure connected by mutual response-ability and relatedness:

> Then at 9:25, we had our last run, one with only ten obstacles … We did fine until the last discrimination in the last run. In a nanosecond, we came apart, literally, and each went a different way. We each stopped instantly, no longer on the same course, and looked at each other with a blatantly confused look on her dog and my human face, eyes questioning, each body-mind bereft of its partner. I swear I heard a sound like Velcro ripping when we came apart. (ibid.: 230)

Figure 8.4 Walking the dog independently.

There are, of course, fundamental differences between these two 'coming apart' experiences. Haraway and Cayenne had shared years of life together and a deep attachment. In the example of Boyone and the Australian Shepherd, the two had just met and their relationship had not yet developed beyond Boyone's cautious curiosity and the dog's patient acceptance of the child as her handler. This makes Boyone's retrieval of the leash, and his confidence walking the dog on the leash even more remarkable: the child–dog 'we' was there to be preserved even in the absence of shared history.

What can such child–dog interactions tell us about the sociality of those with ASD? The reciprocal coordination of action with others appears to present a challenge for both individuals with ASD and the people interacting with them in everyday activities. Interested in experiences of children with ASD in such interactionally difficult circumstances, I recently examined the 'body in autism' to better understand the kinds of mutual orientation and coordination of actions that children with ASD achieve with others (Solomon 2011). Analysing school and home interactions of children with ASD with peers and adults, I identified ways in which the children's corporeal orientation was moulded by the others, not dissimilarly to the way in which Boyone's therapist moulded his hand so that he could hold the dog's leash. The practices of corporeal alteration – head-holding, body-scaffolding and hand-finger moulding – appeared to reflect what the children's communicative partners perceived as 'missing' in their social behaviour.

There has been little understanding of the children's experience as recipients of such corporeal reshaping and of its potential impact on children's agency and intentionality. Interactions involving therapy dogs seem to create a figured world with different rules of engagement with both dogs and people, than the human-only world. Such a world affords an interactional ground where agency and intentionality expressed through coordinated, embodied social action is enough for full participation.

Example 2: The Child–Dog 'We' as Facing One Another

A face-to-face orientation with other people, despite having been argued to be a significant dimension of human intersubjectivity (see, e.g., Schutz 1970) is usually challenging for, and is rarely initiated by, autistic children themselves. Additionally, children with ASD have an impaired ability to 'read' social information such as interlocutors' facial expressions and gestures (Dawson et al. 1998).

Consider the following example where thirteen-year-old Boytwo displays a mutual face-to-face orientation and 'response-ability' in his interaction with a therapy dog, a Golden Retriever. Boytwo has a limited ability to speak; however, since he was ten years old he has been communicating through a practice called 'Rapid Prompting' that involves tactile, visual and linguistic stimuli that focus the child's attention on written alphabetic and numerical symbols, which the child is prompted to indicate in response to specific questions (see Ochs et al. 2005). Boytwo's family includes his parents and his younger brother and sister.

The Golden Retriever and the Australian Shepherd (accompanied by the same trainer as in example 1) came to Boytwo's home for a therapy dog visit. Boytwo's mother was with him during the therapy dogs' two-hour visit. Boytwo spent approximately an hour slowly getting to know the dogs and the second hour playing fetch with the Golden Retriever. In the course of the second hour, Boytwo learned to throw a tennis ball to the dog and seemed to enjoy the dog's graceful, joyful running after the ball and retrieving it for him. Toward the end of the second hour, Boytwo stopped throwing the ball and, leaning forward, looked closely at the dog facing him and waiting for the ball to be thrown again. On Boytwo's face was a true fascination, with a particular interest in the dog's panting mouth. He even opened his own mouth as if imitating the dog's excited breathing. The dog's physicality and patient presence may have become, for Boytwo, 'a provocation to curiosity, ... one of the first obligations and deepest pleasures of companion species' (Haraway 2008: 7).

What might have contributed to Boytwo's desire for face-to-face orientation with the dog? Several observations may help understand the possible answers. First, Boytwo and this dog have been engaged in a successful mutual enterprise: a shared, exquisitely coordinated activity of throwing and fetching the tennis ball. Throughout the interaction, Boytwo, who had never thrown a ball before, exhibited a growing competence in this complex motor activity, including picking up the ball from the ground and throwing it in the desired direction. Throughout the interaction, both the dog and the child have been mutually intelligible, understanding each other's intentions and expected next actions. The range of these intentions and actions was limited by the activity at hand: child and dog playing fetch.

In the course of this activity, however, we can see that a certain kind of 'doing, being and becoming' is taking place (Wilcock 1999:10). In the course of the second hour of playing with the dog, Boytwo has become a skilled thrower of tennis balls. During his 'doing "playing fetch with the dog"', to paraphrase Harvey Sacks' (1984) notion of 'doing "being ordinary"', Boytwo became more confident, more in control of his actions, and increasingly appeared to be enjoying the activity. Thus in the course of the second hour he has become a kind of a social being who is competent in this kind of social interaction and confident in the execution of motor tasks necessary to engage in it. Additionally, Boytwo's engagement with the dog was accompanied by enjoyment, a sense of mutually enjoyable 'response-ability' (Stengers 2005; Haraway 2008), where both the boy and the dog were engaged with one another as bodies mindful of each other, in a relationship of response (Haraway 2008). This activity of playing fetch involved the boy and the dog in the work of 'articulating bodies to other bodies', 'in the language of non-mimetic sharing'(Haraway 2008: 84). Those who watched them – Boytwo's mother, his aide who momentarily passed by and saw him engaged with the dog – also became involved in his new way of 'being with'. In this sense, the boy's turn to face the dog may have been the result of his sense of a 'we' that comes from being well coordinated *with* another being in an ontological choreography, from being understood and related to through action. The face-to-face orientation with the dog may have also been a turn toward a more richly inhabited social world, where both dogs and humans were available for relationships of response. Moreover, on a practical level, the skill of throwing a ball was later incorporated into Boytwo's classroom environment and built upon to develop the relationship – and possibility – of response towards his teacher and fellow students.

Conclusion

In this paper I aimed to weigh theories of sociality against ethnographically informed understandings of sociality of children with ASD in order to problematize some theoretical assumptions about sociality: specifically, the primacy of language and theory of mind, and the 'humans only' attitude to what constitutes sociality. Autism presents a 'natural experiment' for such a task because both intersubjectivity and language use of those with autism appear to be affected by the disorder. Analysis of the social interaction of those with autism and non-human, not-even-primate, communicative partners is another opportunity for such problematization.

Several important conclusions emerge from this analysis. Firstly, not analytically prioritizing language as a vehicle for sociality opens a rich actional, phenomenological world in which sociality and action are indivisible. Sociality is almost never about *being* social, but is almost always about *doing* something together, and *becoming* different in the process. As Haraway recently observed, "'the social" as a noun is every bit as much a problem as "the animal" or "the human", but as a verb it is much more interesting' (Gane 2006: 143).

Secondly, not analytically prioritizing mental processes and theory of mind and looking for 'articulating bodies to other bodies' allows one to see a level of sociality that may be obscured by limiting the scope of interest to mentality. Reading bodies, rather than, or in addition to, reading minds, is another way to think of sociality, and it also bypasses the idea that the human mind is necessarily more worthy of 'reading' than the mind of an animal, in this case, a dog's mind. The final conclusion is quite compatible with Latourian philosophy regarding the role of 'assemblages of nature' in sociality. For a theory of sociality – premised by many upon language – Latour's concern with extending the boundaries of sociality to both human and non-human actors, acting together, illuminates certain kinds of sociality-in-action. In post-industrial societies, companion animals, and especially dogs and cats, along with some technological entities such as avatars, robots and other cyborgs, have entered into powerful 'figures' with humans, forming certain kinds of social worlds. In this sense, the world in which 'human-only' sociality is the only kind that counts is largely gone.

Such an analysis illuminates the tensions and the dialectical relationships between capacities for sociality, practices of sociality and ideas about sociality. In both examples of children with ASD engaged with therapy dogs, there is an identifiable dialectical process underway in which the activity on the way (doing) and the emerging relationship with the dogs and, through the dogs, with the people (being), produces new horizons of possibility (becoming) which in turn informs the practices of sociality between the children and the other people in their lives, even after the therapy dogs have gone.

Acknowledgements

I wish to express my gratitude to the children and their families who participated in this research, and to Susan Kraft, the professional animal trainer of The Learning Center for Dogs. The author gratefully acknowledges the University of Southern California Center for Excellence in Research for the James H. Zumberge Faculty Research and Innovation grant that supported this research.

Notes

1. The children were from middle-class, white families and all had a prior diagnosis of Autistic Disorder from medical institutions; two of the children were high functioning and three severely affected. Families with children of different ages and symptom severity were recruited to gain variation in children's responses and to explore challenges and potentialities of animal-assisted therapy. A professional animal trainer experienced in animal-assisted therapy for children with developmental disabilities brought one to four

therapy dogs to the children's home once a week. The number of visits varied among the children, with a maximum number of visits being six.

2. Dogs and humans have a long history of shared joint activities: by most historically generous archaeological estimates, dogs have shared a common evolutionary niche with humans for over 140,000 years. During this time, dogs have been attending to human social behaviour in a collaborative, reciprocal way in shared semiotic activities that resulted in dogs' proclivity for 'ontological choreography' (Haraway 2003: 50) and problem solving in coordination with humans (e.g., Hare and Tomasello 1999; Hare et al. 2002; Smuts 2008; Horowitz 2009).

3. Because of the Institutional Review Board's requirements the children are called 'Boy 1' (Boyone) and 'Boy 2' (Boytwo).

References

Abram, D. (2010). *Becoming Animal: An Earthly Cosmology*. New York: Pantheon.

Agamben, G. 2003. *The Open: Man and Animal* (trans. Kevin Attell). Stanford: Stanford University Press.

APA (American Psychiatric Association) 2000. *Diagnostic and Statistical Manual of Mental Disorders* (4th edition, revised text). Washington: APA.

Baron-Cohen, S., A. M. Leslie and U. Frith 1985. Does the Autistic Child Have a 'Theory of Mind'? *Cognition* 21, no. 1: 37–46. doi:10.1016/0010-0277(85)90022-8.

Berger, J. 2005. Falling Towers and Postmodern Wild Children: Oliver Sacks, Don DeLillo, and Turns Against Language. Publications of the Modern Languages Association (PML) 120, no. 2: 341–361. doi:10.1632/003081205X52446.

Carter, A. S., N. O. Davis, A. Klin and F. R. Volkmar 2005. Social Development in Autism. In *Handbook of Autism and Pervasive Developmental Disorders: Vol. 1, Diagnosis, Development, Neurobiology, and Behavior* (eds.) F. R. Volkmar, R. Paul, A. Klin, and D. J. Cohen, 312–334. Hoboken, NJ: John Wiley and Sons.

Clark, F. and M. Lawlor 2009. The Making and Mattering of Occupational Science. In *Willard and Spackman's Occupational Therapy* (11th edition) (eds.) E. B. Crepeau, E. S. Cohn, and B. A. Boyt Schell, 2–14. Baltimore: Lippincott, Williams and Wilkins.

———, D. Parham, M. E. Carlson, G. Frank, J. Jackson, D. Pierce, R. J. Wolfe and R. Zemke 1991. Occupational Science: Academic Innovation in the Service of Occupational Therapy's Future. *American Journal of Occupational Therapy* 45, no. 4: 300–310.

Dawson, G., A. N. Meltzoff, J. Osterling, J. Rinaldi and E. Brown 1998. Children with Autism Fail to Orient to Naturally Occurring Social Stimuli. *Journal of Autism and Developmental Disorders* 28, no. 6: 479–485.

Enfield, N. J. and S. C. Levinson (eds.) 2006. *Roots of Human Sociality: Culture, Cognition and Interaction*. New York: Berg.

Favareau, D. 2002. Beyond Self and Other: On the Neurosemiotic Emergence of Intersubjectivity. *Sign Systems Studies* 30, no. 1: 57–100.

——— 2008. Collapsing the Wave Function of Meaning: The Epistemological Matrix of Talk-in-Interaction. *Biosemiotics* (Special Issue: *A Legacy for Living Systems: Gregory Bateson as Precursor to Biosemiotics*) 2: 169–211. doi: 10.1007/978-1-4020-6706-8_12.

Feil-Seifer, D. and M. Mataric 2008. Robot-assisted Therapy for Children with Autism Spectrum Disorders. Proceedings of the 7th International Conference on Interaction Design and Children, Chicago.

Fiske, A. P. 1992. The Four Elementary Forms of Sociality: Framework for a Unified Theory of Social Relations. *Psychological Review* 99, no. 4: 689–723. doi: 10.1037/0033-295X.99.4.689.

Gane, N. 2006. When We Have Never Been Human, What Is to Be Done?: Interview with Donna Haraway. *Theory, Culture & Society* 23 no. 7–8: 135–158.

Gillette, D., G. Hayes, G. Abowd, J. Cassell, R. el Kaliuby, D. Strickland and P. T. Weiss 2007. Interactive Technologies for Autism. Proceedings of the Computer/Human Interaction Conference 2007, Extended Abstracts on Human Factors in Computing Systems. doi:10.1145/1240866.1240960.

Gintis, H. 2000. Strong Reciprocity and Human Sociality. *Journal of Theoretical Biology* 206, no. 2: 169–179. doi:10.1006/jtbi.2000.2111.

Glass, T. A. and M. J. McAtee 2006. Behavioral Science at the Crossroads in Public Health: Extending Horizons, Envisioning the Future. *Social Science & Medicine* 62, no. 7: 1650–1671. doi:10.1016/j.socscimed.2005.08.044.

Goodall, J. and M. Bekoff 2006. *The Ten Trusts: What We Must Do to Care for the Animals we Love*. New York: HarperCollins.

Gotham, K., S. L. Bishop and C. Lord 2011. Diagnosis of Autism Spectrum Disorders. In *Autism Spectrum Disorders* (eds.) D. G. Amaral, G. Dawson and D. H. Geschwind, 30–43. New York: Oxford University Press.

Grinker, R. R. 2010. Commentary: On Being Autistic, and Social. *Ethos* 38, no. 1: 172–178. doi: 10.1111/j.1548-1352.2010.01087.x.

Haraway, D. 2003. *The Companion Species Manifesto: Dogs, People, and Significant Otherness*. Chicago: Prickly Paradigm Press.

———— 2008. *When Species Meet*. Minneapolis: University of Minnesota Press.

Hare, B. and M. Tomasello 1999. Domestic Dogs (*Canis familiaris*) Use Human and Conspecific Social Cues to Locate Hidden Food. *Journal of Comparative Psychology* 113, no. 2: 173–177. doi: 10.1037/0735-7036.113.2.173.

————, M. Brown, C. Williamson and M. Tomasello 2002. The Domestication of Social Cognition in Dogs. *Science* 298, no. 5598: 1634–1636. doi: 10.1126/science.1072702.

Hearne, V. 1986. *Adam's Task: Calling Animals by Name*. New York: Knopf.

———— 1994. *Animal Happiness: A Moving Exploration of Animals and Their Emotions*. New York: HarperCollins.

Holland, D., W. Lachiotte Jr., D. Skinner and C. Cain 1998. *Identity and Agency in Cultural Worlds*. Cambridge: Harvard University Press.

Horowitz, A. 2009. Attention to Attention in Domestic Dog (*Canis familiaris*) Dyadic Play. *Animal Cognition* 12, no. 1: 107–118. doi: 10.1007/s10071-008-0175-y.

Jackendorf, R. and S. Pinker 2005. The Nature of the Language Faculty and its Implications for Evolution of Language (Reply to Fitch, Hauser, and Chomsky). *Cognition* 97: 211–225. doi: 10.1016/j.cognition.2005.04.006.

Kielhofner, G. 2009. *Conceptual Foundations of Occupational Therapy Practice*. Philadelphia: F. A. Davis Co.

Latour, B. 2004. *Politics of Nature: How to Bring the Sciences into Democracy* (trans. C. Porter). Cambridge: Harvard University Press.

———— 2005. *Reassembling the Social: An Introduction to Actor-Network-Theory*. New York: Oxford University Press.

Laurier, E., R. Maze and J. Lundin 2006. Putting the Dog Back in the Park: Animal and Human Mind-in-Action. *Mind, Culture, and Activity* 13, no. 1: 2–24. doi:10.1207/s15327884mca1301_2.

Lawlor, M. C. 2003. The Significance of Being Occupied: The Social Construction of Childhood Occupations. *The American Journal of Occupational Therapy* 57, no. 4: 424–434. doi: 10.5014/ajot.57.4.424.

Levinson, B. 1969. *Pet-Oriented Child Psychotherapy*. Springfield, IL: Charles C. Thomas.

Martin, F. and J. Farnum 2002. Animal-Assisted Therapy for Children with Pervasive Developmental Disorders. *Western Journal of Nursing Research* 24, no. 6: 657–670. doi: 10.1177/019394502320555403.

Miller Kuhanek, H. and R. Watling (eds.) 2010. *Autism: A Comprehensive Occupational Therapy Approach*. Bethesda, MD: American Occupational Therapy Association.

Ochs, E. and O. Solomon 2010. Autistic Sociality. *Ethos* 38, no. 1: 69–92. doi: 10.1111/j.1548-1352.2009.01082.x.

———, O. Solomon and L. Sterponi 2005. Limitations and Transformations of Habitus in Child-Directed Communication. *Discourse Studies* (Special Issue: *Theories and Models of Language, Interaction and Culture*) 7, no. 4–5: 547–584. doi: 10.1177/1461445605054406.

Park, M. 2008. Making Scenes: Imaginative Practices of a Child with Autism in a Sensory Integration–Based Therapy Session. *Medical Anthropology Quarterly* 22, no. 3: 234–256. doi: 10.1111/j.1548-1387.2008.00024.x.

Reilly, M. 1962. Occupational Therapy Can Be One of the Great Ideas of 20th Century Medicine. *American Journal of Occupational Therapy* 16, no. 1: 87–105.

Rorty, R. 1991. *Philosophical Papers: Objectivity Relativism and Truth*. Cambridge: Cambridge University Press.

Sacks, H. 1984. On Doing 'Being Ordinary'. In *Structures of Social Action: Studies in Conversation Analysis* (eds.) J. M. Atkison and J. Heritage, 413–429. New York: Cambridge University Press.

Sams, M. J., E. V. Fortney and S. Willenbring 2006. Occupational Therapy Incorporating Animals for Children with Autism: A Pilot Investigation. *The American Journal of Occupational Therapy* 60, no. 3: 268–274. doi: 10.5014/ajot.60.3.268.

Searle, J. 2010. *Making the Social World: The Structure of Human Civilization*. New York: Oxford University Press.

Schutz, A. 1970. *Alfred Schutz on Phenomenology and Social Relations*. Chicago: University of Chicago Press.

Smuts, B. 2006. Between Species: Science and Subjectivity. *Configurations* 14, no. 1–2: 115–126. doi: 10.1353/con.0.0004.

Solomon, O. 2010. What a Dog Can Do: Children with Autism and Therapy Dogs in Social Interaction. *Ethos* 38, no. 1: 143–166. doi: 10.1111/j.1548-1352.2010.01085.x.

——— 2011. Body in Autism: A view from Social Interaction. In *Language, Body, and Health* (eds.) P. McPherron and V. Ramathan, 105–141. Boston: De Gruyter Mouton.

Spitzer, S. L. 2003. With and without Words: Exploring Occupation in Relation to Young Children with Autism. *Journal of Occupational Science* 10, no. 2: 67–79. doi: 10.1080/14427591.2003.9686513.

Stengers, I. 2005. The Cosmopolitical Proposal. In *Making Things Public* (eds.) B. Latour and P. Weibel, 994–1003. Cambridge: MIT Press.

Strickland, D., L. Marcus, G. Mesibov and K. Hogan 1996. Brief Report: Two Case Studies Using Virtual Reality as a Learning Tool for Autistic Children. *Journal of Autism and Developmental Disorders* 26, no. 6: 651–659. doi:10.1007/bf02172354.

Weil, K. 2006. Killing Them Softly: Animal Death, Linguistic Disability, and the Struggle for Ethics. *Configurations* 14, no. 1: 87–96. doi: 10.1353/con.0.0013

Wilcock, A. A. 1999. Reflections on Doing, Being and Becoming. *Australian Occupational Therapy Journal* 46, no. 1: 1–11. doi: 10.1046/j.1440-1630.1999.00174.x.

9

Materials and Sociality

Susanne Küchler, University College London

We are surrounded, indeed overwhelmed, by new materials which flood in upon us at an ever-accelerating rate, often unnoticed for reasons that will become apparent. Yet we know little about how they come into being and tend to disregard their importance in shaping who we are and imagine ourselves to be, even though it is becoming clear that new materials frame everyday practice more subtly than law, cosmology and religion (Ball 1997; Barad 2003). While we know on one level that the material world we live in is not a natural one, for historical reasons set out below we still tend to assume that materials are a part of reality, a 'given', apprehended through experience while not being formed by it. Materials designed through engineering in laboratories and equipped with the ready-made functionality that was once exclusively tied to object forms and hidden technical devices, challenge this assumption. New materials unavoidably draw our attention to the social intervention at work in their selection, composition and take-up, compelling us to rethink long-standing premises that inform research and teaching into materials, society, science and innovation. This paper considers the problems new materials pose for social science today and what is at stake if we do not interrogate the boundaries that presently exist between social and materials sciences.

The idea that materials are socialized by being put to use in the making of things that extend the body's capacity for technical action as well as the cognitive effects of embodied skill, has been given much attention in anthropology against the background of Actor-Network Theory, which has drawn out the epistemic capacities of material and technological artefacts (Knappett 2005; Latour 1994). This recognition of the inherent sociality of materials, capable of mediating person–object relations and of distributing personhood across emergent networks, would suggest that anthropology as a discipline is positioned perfectly to be at the centre of work being carried out on a new class of materials that harbour the capacity for technical action and cognitive effect attributed previously only to things (Knorr-Cretina 1997). The problem, however, is that the Latourian approach to agentive materials emerging out of laboratory life

(Latour and Woolgar 1979; Latour 1996) assumes their mediatory capacity to derive from the sociality at work in material invention, technological inscription and take-up in society, while science assumes the pre-hermeneutic nature of the logic of materials emerging from laboratories and asks for the kind of sociality needed to meet such materials when they come to market (Bensaude-Vincent 2004). Not only is this clash of assumptions creating an impasse for collaboration between anthropology and science, but it also explains the dearth of ethnographic studies that explore the take-up of materials in society in ways that grant the logic implicit in materials a role in shaping the difference made by these materials in culture and society.

Like all new materials that become available for use, materials by design confound our senses through their apparent familiarity. Materials such as ladder-resistant tights, self-cleaning glass, and a plethora of responsive materials, now readily available in running shoes and high tech sports wear, look and feel much the same as materials that have surrounded us for some time, but they are fundamentally different in the way they perform. It is through what they make possible – extending the body and the mind to new limits, even constituting environments and objects in their own right – that such materials draw attention to themselves, demanding that we inquire into the potential fit between the capacity of these materials to work at a level prior to and independent of subjective intervention and the actions that such materials make possible in the everyday.[1] If science is correct in its estimation of the current situation in which most materials designed in the laboratory fail to be taken up, suggesting that social forces at work in the technical and knowledge-based action in the fashioning of materials by design are insufficiently priming such materials for social networks outside of laboratory, anthropology has found its new field of inquiry into the material face of sociality, searching for the dynamic of affinities between material and social worlds.

Compared to the wealth of literature dealing with the implications of a designed material world, ranging from the philosophical speculation surrounding the uses of artifice to the displacement of the human/non-human duality in a world fashioned in the laboratory, there is hardly any literature on the materials themselves and the processes that lead to their uptake or rejection. A notable recent example of an ethnography that inquires into the complex dynamic surrounding the uptake of materials is De Monchaux's (2011) detailed reconstruction of the selection of materials used in the construction of the Apollo spacesuits, whose image came to shape the way we think of the world we inhabit today and future worlds beyond. Rather than hard materials engineered for the purpose of space exploration which projected the image and mindset of the mastery of nature through technology, soft materials originally designed with very different uses in mind were chosen. De Monchaux shows that the membrane-like quality of this material, comprised of layered, additive composition rather than external reinforcement, embodied and perpetuated an accommodation between nature and technology, representing a literal extension of the astronaut's body, and setting the precedent for new ways of thinking about materials and their transformations. Another ethnography, of the invention and commercialization of Lycra by Kaori O'Connor (2011), reveals how social forces and cultural factors, far more than economic or technological ones, determine what new materials are taken up, and describes the complex ways in which materials interact with both the social and physical bodies over time.

The story of materials and sociality has barely been touched upon in the literature and yet we know that all societies have employed materials to erect everything from physical structures to imaginary edifices. From clay in fourth millennium Mesopotamia, to string among the ancient Inca, to coloured and printed cloth in the Pacific, the take-up of materials has made new forms of connectivity tangible and thinkable and left its trace in the history of civilizations (Boivin 2010; Colchester 2003; Quilter and Urton 2002; Wengrow 2010). And yet we find it hard as social scientists to ask questions of the materials that surround us today –what they are, how they came to be selected and how they became a central part of our cultural heritage.

Materials as Markers of Identity:
A Short History of an Idea

We tend to think that we know materials and recognize their potential on account of the sensorial nature of our encounter, tempered by the material's tactility, luminosity, acoustics and scent. This phenomenological framing of material knowledge has long informed our approach to material products of culture, an approach that was formalized in the mid-nineteenth century by the establishment of ethnographic museums as distinct institutional spaces devoted to the idea that the world is constructed from sensory impressions alone and that these impressions provoke patterns of distinction that enable stable identification and classification. Somatically arranged by their differing luminosity, acoustic and olfactory properties since the days of curiosity cabinets, nineteenth-century exhibitions began to classify materials with reference to form and technical function (Bensaude-Vincent and Newman 2007; Findlen 1996). Where antiquarians used to collect materials for the sake of knowledge accumulation, materials now receded into the background as qualisigns and as increasingly aesthetically framed means of identification and recognition of product worlds. Materials have since been perceived as end products and their technical functions, with the relations between materials and their potential manifold uses being lost amidst the overarching narrative of their application in relation to distinct object types. Thus, although their presence in collections surreptitiously served to sensitize a product-consuming culture educated by museums in ways of world-making, materials were left uncharted and profoundly aestheticized, their subtle role in museum collections contributing to the loss of a taxonomic knowledge of materials even as they were credited with the potential to enchant.

The sublimation of materials to object type and function took formal and public expression not just in mid-nineteenth-century museum exhibitions, but also in the home. The practice of aesthetically motivated collecting of materials to embellish the décor of homes, from wallpaper to furnishing textiles and clothing, is testified in the literature of the time, which describes authors as artistic collectors of sumptuous materials (Watson 1999: 63–75). Artists such as Matisse drew inspiration from decorative textiles he collected for his artworks that in turn came to be lastingly identified with the biographical narrative that placed materials and their collection both historically and culturally (J. Klein 1997; Spurling 2005). Ordinary homes were not left untouched by the drive to decorate with materials whose distinctiveness and aesthetic qualities came to matter as much as the functional specifications of the objects they clad. The art historian Ruth Phillips (1999) writes about the fascination with foreign materials in Victorian England as travel to, and souvenirs or gifts from, the colonies came to accessorize the home, the distinctiveness of the materials being carefully chosen for the fabrication of craftwork. Her tale of craft production in the North American Indian territories relays the story of French nuns who instructed the Huron on how to use moose hair for the fabrication of needle baskets, which became one of the most sought-after trading items exported from Canada to homes in England.

Materials are projected as capable of framing and plotting biographies, of staging identities and even of resonating with false memories of times and places. Their texture, luminosity and even their smell are suggested to conjure up complex synaesthetic images that will always be associated with Marcel Proust's (1913–22) flood of recollections evoked by a simple madeleine cake. Proust's writings, however, also signal the ending of a period in history when the preoccupation with the aesthetic potential of materials came to an end. This ending was prompted by the discovery and take up of a then 'new' material known as 'kautschuk', or rubber, which quickly became the material of choice for the making of new types of objects and product functions, from diving suits and hoses to girdles, electrical insulation and tires, bringing with them new social practices and new potential means of projecting identity through what we know today as 'life-style' (Semper 1854). One material now came to be the source of potentially infinite products and consumption practices, inspiring science to attempt not just to harness the properties of this material, but to emulate and indeed improve on its natural properties and behaviour through artificial means invented in the laboratory. The invention of Bakelite in the 1890s heralded the synthetic replication of rubber with plastic in the mid twentieth century and an array of polyethylene materials whose unstoppable emergent qualities continue to surprise us today (Bijker 1997; Meikle 1995; Mossman and Smith 2008).

It was this synthetic replication of materials and their growing status as 'potential' objects and, more recently, potential technology, which bifurcated the reception of materials into two components: 'things' and 'things material', collected and studied in their own right. This separation of a concern with materials and a concern with things, which continues to divide materials science and social science to this day, will be forever associated with the story of the divvying up of exhibits that marked the end of the Great Exhibition at London's Crystal Palace in 1851. The dismantled displays came to fill the halls of the newly created Victoria & Albert Museum, the British Museum and the Museum of Economic Botany at the Royal Botanic Gardens, Kew. No research has as yet been conducted on the criteria that allowed certain materials to be selected as decorative artefacts and placed in the V&A collection, and certain others as ethnographic specimens and thus worthy of the British Museum, while others retained their distinct material identity in the stores of the Jodrell Laboratory at Kew. But by the end of the process, the categories 'things' and 'things material' had been firmly established, and have been perpetuated ever since.

The Museum of Economic Botany at Kew is one of the forerunners of modern materials libraries and has remained the physical archive of the history of botanical collecting and of an expert culture of materials whose historical importance is only being unearthed today (U. Klein and Spary 2009; Schiebinger and Swan 2005). From its inception in 1847 to the 1930s, the Museum of Economic Botany at Kew facilitated the conversion of knowledge around new materials into political power and economic capital for the industrial world system. Next to artefacts made of plant materials from all over the world and samples that document the diversity of each plant material, there are also artefacts such as bark cloth made from the Paper Mulberry tree that one can equally find in ethnographic museums. Stored here for the 'non-woven' qualities of the bark, its technical transformation into a finished product testifies to the potential seen in the material in the late 1900s when it had become apparent that the height of British monopoly over textile production was ending (Mukerji 1983). The creation of a materials bank was the explicit aim of its founder, Sir William Hooker, who wrote that the Museum should contain:

> all kinds of useful and curious Vegetable Products and that such a collection would render great service not only to the scientific botanist, but to the merchant, the manufacturer, the physician, the chemist, the druggist, the dyer, the weaver, the cabinet-maker, and artisans of every description, who might here find the raw material (and, to a certain extent, the manufactured or prepared article) employed in their several professions, correctly named, and accompanied by some account of its origin, history, native country, etc., either attached to the specimens or recorded in a popular catalogue. (Desmond 2007)

The Museum collection (now known as the Economic Botany Collection) contains many thousands of biomaterials, dominated by rubber, gutta percha and other exudates, textiles and fibres, papers, timbers, adhesives and dyes – drawer after drawer of self-similar materials whose capacities and inherent relational matrixes befuddle the untrained eye and numb the unscientific mind.

The story of the fate of the displays of the Great Exhibition tells us how rapidly the bifurcation of materials, as markers of identity and as potential resources and products, was accepted by the public who only a few decades earlier, at the beginning of the nineteenth century, had been profoundly preoccupied with the morality assumed by materials. When in 1809 Goethe wrote his novel *Elective Affinities* about the analogy between chemical and human relationships, the notion of elective affinities captured a cultural moment when chemistry increasingly occupied the mind and leisure time of the European public (Adler 1990; Goethe 1809; Kim 2003). Chemical substances were said to unite 'like friends and acquaintances' or stay as 'strangers side by side' depending on their reaction to one another, transforming each in the process. Related chemicals were spoken of as 'families'. A whole array of moral lessons were drawn from the behaviour of chemical substances and their human analogues, making chemistry 'an authentic discipline' with prestige and public visibility well before the onset of the Chemical Revolution, nearly a century earlier than modern physics. At the close of the nineteenth century, the morality inhering in materials was not yet lost on a public that still could claim to know materials from experience. Yet this familiarity with materials came under increasing pressure as the number and variety of materials in peoples' lives increased, accelerated by the ever more rapid flow of new products and product functions. Product design and the consumer culture of the twentieth century demanded the delivery of materials whose functionality became increasingly open-ended, capable of being extended across distinct object categories. By 1990, the number of materials designed in laboratories had outstripped the number of discrete products and functions.

No longer merely stretchable across any shape, but able to take on forms and complex internal structures that defy mechanical processes of making, new material technologies such as rapid prototyping have realized the dream of creating material forms that are objects in their own right in the same way as we think of bone as both material substance and as structural component of the human body (Antonelli 1995; Bensaude-Vincent 2007; Hopkinson et al. 2005; Silberglitt 2001). Microenvironments in themselves, these material surfaces find their analogue in conceptions of architecture whose exteriorized interiority has been compared to an interactive and constantly unfolding and expanding second skin, an idea expressed by architects such as Neil Denari, whose buildings emulate continuous surfaces that wrap around the world like a ribbon with exchangeable inner and outer spaces. Such is the number of materials being invented, with manifold and often composite properties that are potentially good for everything we know or have not even thought of, that handbooks guiding selection are out of date within ever-decreasing time spans (Beylerian and Dent 2005).

The materials we surround ourselves with today are opaque to us and, in their self-similarity to one another, refuse to be readily known or distinguished in terms of distinctive properties or behaviours. The excitement that once met the arrival of unknown materials from the New World or, later, the capacity to synthetically replicate their modality and appearance, is now strikingly absent.

This disinterest in materials must be seen in relation to the impossibility of distinguishing and identifying materials on the basis of experience alone and it is this separation of materials from the phenomenal world that constitutes a great and growing problem for materials science and social science alike. Not only are the innovation and the crafting of materials uncertain, slow and costly processes, but, as materials come now as 'readymade' social actors, we are confronted with not knowing how to predict what kind of sociality will be required to meet materials in ways that will enable them to touch down and nestle into everyday worlds. Where we were once certain about the identity of materials and their function as markers of identity and as point of departure for narrations of past and future lives, we are left bereft today of all certainty over how to map out the social life of a material.

Making Materials Work

Ideas of what kinds of materials might 'work', in the double sense of technical functionality and social efficacy, tend to be developed against the background of twentieth-century preoccupations with two of the most entrenched cornerstones of Western thinking: the body and the unconscious. A famous, early and trend-setting study of the socializing capacity of materials is that of the anthropologist Marcel Mauss, whose publications in the first quarter of the twentieth century brought the cultural habituation that bodily techniques exerted on materials to lasting attention. Studying 'the ways in which from society to society men know how to use their bodies', his essay on the techniques of the body (Mauss [1935] 2006) turned to interactions between human bodies and everyday objects: diving boards, bugles, drums, shoes, wooden floats, hand axes, hammocks, poles and, in a recollection of his experience of serving with English troops during the First World War, spades, whose quite different design in France and England prevented the sharing of this simple object across national boundaries.

The idea that through an apprenticeship of repeated action and familiarity, individuals perceptually merge a sense of self with particular instruments and during subsequent use become a temporarily amalgamated subject-and-object are the foundation of much our understanding of the cognitive processes that inform the making and utilization of material artefacts. Most recently, neuroscientists have taken up this perceptual and emotionally driven extension of the mind through objects in their exploration of consciousness and in the devising of technical solutions to robotics. Thomas Metzinger (2009) in particular has advanced a so-called 'self-model theory of subjectivity' (SMT) based on experiments that reveal the possible infusion of objects with bodily perception and concepts of ownership, and an object-centred, spatial perspective that can be sustained over time. SMT explains and supports advances in robotics that seek to replicate technically the extension in objects of what is known as the 'theory of mind', that is the capacity to assign intentionality to the actions of others including objects. Much of this research has entered the design of 'smart' materials that anticipate and react to emotions as readily as they draw out and elicit thought implicit in movement.

The neuroscientist Vittorio Gallese has called this capacity of the mind to recognize shared intentionality through a process of 'filling in' movement by recreating and completing it neurologically, the 'relational nature of action' (Gallese 2001). The fact that action can be reconstructed in things that are made, as well as replicated in the movements of persons interacting with things, enables Gallese to conceive of a theory of agency that is shared by subjects and objects alike, and emulated in the properties and potentials of materials. The abandonment of an ego-centred model of agency implicit in Gallese's theory of mirror neurons has become a key issue in the philosophy of science. Philosopher Peter Hacker and neuroscientist Maxwell Bennett have recently taken up this debate by questioning the conceptual foundations of cognitive neuroscience that have insisted on retaining the relative, ego-centred and anthropomorphic description of mind (Bennett et al. 2007). In debate with Daniel Dennett and Jean Searle they dissect the assumptions underlying the biologically driven models of intentionality and consciousness, pointing up the need for new, non-perceptually driven models of agency.

The lingering trope of the body and bodily experience in the literature on technology, robotics and ambient, intelligent environments is perhaps not surprising given a language of mirroring, of mimesis and body-centred remembering that has dominated research into artificial intelligence and biotechnology since the 1980s. Throughout the twentieth century the study of social memory has remained synonymous with the study of the unconscious and a supra-human memory (perhaps internalized, but in a self-forgetting way) whose mechanism is used, but not controlled, by subject-centred remembering. Both the stability and the potential disruption to individual identity deriving from the social aspect of remembering became central issues in the philosophical thought of Bergson, the psychoanalytical writings of Freud and the autobiographical literature of Proust. The tension between them is invoked by the classical pairings of *mneme* and *memoria*, recalled by Marcel Proust as *mémoire involuntaire* and *mémoire volontaire*, by Walter Benjamin as *Eingedenken* und *Andenken*, by Aby Warburg as *Sophrosyne* and *Mnemosyne* and most recently by Aleida Assmann as *Gedächtnis* and *Erinnerung* (Assmann and Hart 1993; Eiland and Jennings 2006; Proust 1913–22; Warnke 2008). Common to the literature on social memory and its automation through the unconscious was the mediatory role assigned to objects, whose capacity to provoke shared associations and the mutual intersubjective anticipation of actions, was seen to bind words to concepts. As interlocutors between personal recall and shared recognition of what was thus recalled, objects accrued a value whose measure remained – often in spite of all appearances – unstable, requiring continuing reactivation through acts of social commemoration of which categorization and its institutionalization in libraries and their digital counterparts were an incremental part.

From remembering via things to things that remember was just a small step, made possible through the increasing technical sophistication of the replication of cognitive processes in different physical systems – not only organic ones, like the brain, but in inorganic ones such as computer hardware. An app on your mobile phone that remembers the names of your acquaintances and transmits them to you before you have recalled them yourself is now a realistic possibility. But this enhancement of the processes of recall by external devices is only part of the story: iPods, iPhones and iPads have begun to manifest social-memory work on a grand scale, signalling materially an intersubjective shared empathy with a knowledge of being connected at all times.

The spatial and temporal tropes that accompany our understanding of the duality of the 'work' of materials may appear resistant to change, and yet ironically it is the very functionality of designed materials that is undermining the basis of taxonomy which has until now facilitated the socially shared understanding of action. Bruno Latour has famously exploited the collapse of taxonomy in his actor-network theory, in which categorical distinctions and also mirroring relations between subjects and objects are lost (Latour 1994). In line with his argument that the very basis of the nineteenth-century theory of objectification is obfuscated by an emerging materiality that erases the tracing of distinctions in the material world as the basis for knowledge, leading historians of science note the increasing polarity between the natural and the artificial, re-creating new conceptual distinctions in the vacuum left by the collapse of old ones. Biotechnology, synthetic biology and new technologies of creating 'natural' forms such as bone structures through the additive processes of rapid prototyping have re-cast the theological foundations of the 'natural order' in ways not witnessed since the eighteenth century (Ball 2010).

If Latour and others are correct in interpreting our present situation, we may need to look beyond the body and the unconscious to understand the emerging new relation between materials and society. Perhaps even more importantly, we need to look beyond the first-person, perceptually driven model of ego-centred cognition. The new developments demand a new theory of material cognition that will allow us to comprehend decentred and third-person cognition as it is presented to us by the rapid advances in materials technology and materials by design today, and which will enable us to anticipate, at least in the imaginary, what kinds of social worlds might be required for future materials innovated by science to work.

Sociality beyond the Subject

The work on the recovery of a theory of sociality beyond the subject has already begun. Historians have started to unearth exciting data about the complex relation between materials knowledge, trade and commerce in early modern Europe that is waiting to be fully harnessed and extended (U. Klein 2003; Smith and Findlen 2002). Art historians such as Horst Bredekamp (2008) and Monika Wagner (2001) have started opening up the potential of pre-modern curiosity cabinets and modernist re-awakenings for a theory of a material threading of thought that promises to unsettle the institutional separations of science and humanities. It is ethnography, however, that may be uniquely placed to gather the data that will enable us to rethink the theories and methods that stand in the way of our realization of the challenge posed by materials today. This is because of ethnography's capacity for close observation of what the British historian of science Alfred North Whitehead has called the 'concrescence of things', attuned as famously remarked by Claude Levi-Strauss, to uncovering a logic that transcends the subject (Levi-Strauss 1962; Whitehead 1978). And it is this dialectic relationship between close observation and distanced comparative perspective that may enable ethnographers to be uniquely empathetic to the world of materials science, helping to translate and make apparent practices and assumptions that remain obscured in the hard graft and *long durée* of experimentation and crafting of materials.

We are awash with ready-made materials that matter briefly or whose capacity to attach themselves to a social imaginary appears to be the result of chance, and it is clear that explanations at the level of the subject are unlikely to yield results that will turn this tide. The present impasse could be the result of the inclination of materials science to take logic at the level of the material for granted. This, along with the tendency to think only in terms of scaling, proportioning and multiplication, culminates in a failure to extend through to the prototyping and design process at which materials are assigned object function. This oversight may itself be rooted in nineteenth-century disconnections between the space of the noumenal and the phenomenal which has left its legacy in the institutions of teaching and learning to this day. But whatever its origins, the time has come for us to relinquish the way we as social scientists have been accustomed to knowing and thinking about the material world. Opening up to this possibility would mean to take seriously the thought that materials science is not just for scientists, but crucial for those who seek to understand the nature of sociality today. In a world in which relations between persons and between persons via things are not mediated any longer in a simple manner by corporate institutions, but by processes unfolding in the uncharted territories of a digital world, we need to take stock of the implications of a new theory of material cognition for the practice and the teaching of science and sociality alike.

Notes

1. The case for such impact is made by Kaori O'Connor for Lycra (2011).

References

Adler, J. 1990. Goethe's Use of Chemical Theory in his Elective Affinities. In *Romanticism and the Sciences* (eds.) A. Cunningham and N. Jardin, 263–279. Cambridge: Cambridge University Press.

Antonelli, P. 1995. *Mutant Materials in Contemporary Design.* New York: Museum of Modern Art.

Assmann, A., and D. Hart. 1993. *Mnemosyne: Formen und Funktionen der kulrurellen Erinnerung.* Frankfurt: Fischer Tacshenbuch Verlag.

Ball, P. 2010. Critical Discussion Notes: Making Life: A Comment on 'Playing God in Frankenstein's Footsteps: Synthetic Biology and the Meaning of Life' by Henk van den Belt (2009). *Nanoethics* 4 no. 2: 129–132.

———— 1997. *Made to Measure: New Materials for the 21st Century.* New Jersey: Princeton University Press.

Barad, K. 2003. Posthumanist Performativity: Towards an Understanding of How Matter Comes to Matter. *Signs: Journal of Women in Culture and Society* 28, no. 3: 801–831.

Bennett, M., D. Dennett, P. Hacker and J. Searle (eds.) 2007. *Neuroscience and Philosophy: Brain, Mind and Language.* New York: Columbia University Press.

Bensaude-Vincent, B. 2004. *Le libérer de la matière? Fantasmes autour de la nouvelles technologies.* Paris: Inra.

———— 2007. The New Identity of Chemistry as Biomimetic and Nanoscience. In *The Evolving Identity of Chemistry* (ed.) Working Party on the History of Chemistry, European Association for Chemical and Molecular Sciences, 53–64. Belgium: Leuven.

Bensaude-Vincent, B. and M. Newmann (eds.) 2007. *The Artificial and the Natural: An Evolving Polarity.* Cambridge: MIT Press.

Beylerian, G., and A. Dent 2005. *Material Connexion: The Global Resource of New and Innovative Materials for Architects, Artists and Designers.* New York: Wiley and Sons.

Bijker, W. 1997. *Of Bicycles, Bakelites and Bulbs: Toward a Theory of Socio-Technical Change.* Cambridge: MIT Press.

Boivin, N. 2010. *Material Cultures, Material Minds: The Impact of Things on Human Society and Evolution.* Cambridge: Cambridge University Press.

Bredekamp, H. 2008. *Die Fenster der Monade: Gottfried Wilhelm Leibniz' Theater der Natur und Kunst* (2nd edition). Berlin: Akademie Verlag.

Colchester, C. 2003. *Clothing the Pacific.* Oxford: Berg.

De Monchaux, N. 2011. *Spacesuit: Fashioning Apollo.* Cambridge: MIT Press.

Desmond, R. 2007. *The History of the Royal Botanic Gardens Kew.* London: Kew Publishing.

Eiland, H. and M. Jennings 2006. *Walter Benjamin, Selected Writings Volume 3:1935–1938.* Boston: Harvard University Press.

Findlen, P. 1996. *Possessing Nature: Museums, Collecting, and Scientific Culture in Early Modern Italy.* Berkeley: University of California Press.

Gallese, V. 2001. The 'Shared Manifold' Hypothesis: From Mirror Neurons to Empathy, *Journal of Consciousness Studies* 8 no. 5–7: 33–50.

Goethe, J.W. von [1809] 2008. *Elective Affinities: A Novel* (trans. D. Constantin). Oxford: Oxford Paperbacks.

Hopkinson, N., R. Hague and P. Dickens (eds.) 2005. *Rapid-Manufacturing: An Industrial Revolution for the Digital Age.* Cambridge: Cambridge University Press.

Kim, M.G. 2003. *Affinity, That Elusive Dream: A Genealogy of the Chemical Revolution.* Cambridge: MIT Press.

Klein, J. 1997 . Matisse after Tahiti – The Domestication of Exotic Memory. *Zeitschrift für Kunstgeschichte* 60 no.1: 44–89.

Klein, U. 2003. *Experiments, Models, Paper, Tools. Cultures of Organic Chemistry in the Nineteenth Century.* Stanford: Stanford University Press.

Klein, U., and E.C. Spary. 2009. *Materials and Expertise in Early Modern Europe: Between Market and Laboratory.* Chicago: Chicago University Press.

Knappett, C. 2005. *Thinking Through Material Culture: An Interdisciplinary Perspective.* Philadelphia: University of Pennsylvania Press.

Knorr-Cetina, K. 1997. Sociality with Objects: Social Relations in Postsocial Knowledge Societies. *Theory, Culture & Society* 14, no. 4: 1–30.

Latour, B. and S. Woolgar. 1979. *Laboratory Life: The Construction of Social Facts.* London: Sage Publications.

Latour, B. 1994. On technical mediation. *Common Knowledge* 3, no. 2: 29–64.

—— 1996. *Aramis, or the Love of Technology.* Cambridge. Harvard University Press

Levi-Strauss, C. 1962. *The Savage Mind.* Chicago: University of Chicago Press.

Lyotard, J.-F. 1991. *The Inhuman: Reflections on Time.* New York: Polity Press.

Mauss, M. [1935] 2006. Techniques of the Body. In *Techniques, Technology and Civilisation* (ed.) N. Schlanger, 77–95. New York: Durkheim Press (Berghahn Books).

Meikle, J.L. 1995. *American Plastic: A Cultural History.* New Brunswick: Rutgers University Press.

Metzinger, T. 2009. *The Ego Tunnel. The Science of the Mind and the Myth of the Self.* New York: Basic Books.

Mossmann, S., and R. Smith 2008. *Fantastic Plastic: Product Design and Consumer Culture.* London: Black Dog Publishing.

Mukerji, C. 1983. *From Graven Images: Patterns of Modern Materialism.* New York: Columbia University Press.

O'Connor, K. 2011. *Lycra: How a Fiber Shaped America.* New York: Routledge.

Phillips, R. 1999. *Trading Identities: The Souvenir in Native North American Art from the North East 1700–1900.* Idaho: University of Washington Press.

Proust, M. [1913–22] 1987. *A la recherché du temps perdu.* 4 vols. Paris: Gallimard.

Quilter, J., and G. Urton 2002. *Narrative Threads: Accounting and Recounting in Andean Khipu.* Phoenix: University of Texas Press.

Schiebinger, L., and C. Swan (eds.) 2005. *Colonial Botany, Science, Commerce and Politics in Early Modern Europe.* Philadelphia: University of Pennsylvania Press.

Semper, G. [1854] 2004. *Style in the Technical and Tectonic Arts; or, Practical Aesthetics* (trans. H.F. Mallgrave). Santa Monica: The Getty Publications.

Silberglitt, R. (ed.) 2001. *The Global Technological Revolution: Bio/Nano/Materials Trends and their Synergies with Information Technology by 2015.* Santa Monica: Rand.

Smith, P., and P. Findlen (eds.) 2002. *Merchants and Marvels: Commerce, Science and Art in Early Modern Europe.* New York: Routledge.

Spurling, H. 2005. *The Unknown Matisse.* New York: Knopf.

Wagner, M. 2001. *Das Material der Kunst: Eine andere Geschichte der Moderne.* Munich: C.H. Beck.

Warnke, M. 2008. *Gesammelte Schriften. Aby Warburg: Mnemosyne.* Berlin: Akademie Verlag.

Watson, J. 1999. *Literature and Material Culture from Balzac to Proust: The Collection and Consumption of Curiosities.* Cambridge: Cambridge University Press.

Wengrow, D. 2010. *What Makes Civilisations: The Ancient Near East and the Future of the West.* Oxford: Oxford University Press.

Whitehead, A.N. 1978. *Process and Reality: An Essay in Cosmology.* New York: Free Press.

10

The Art of Slow Sociality
Movement, Aesthetics and Shared Understanding

Jo Vergunst, University of Aberdeen and
Anna Vermehren, Timespan, Helmsdale, Sutherland, UK

This chapter presents reflections on the theme of sociality from a mass-participation art event in the town of Huntly in north-east Scotland in 2009. Drawing on Alfred Schutz's notion of the 'consociate', our efforts are directed towards understanding the nature of sociality that the event created for the people involved in it. Two aspects should be noted: firstly, it was specifically a piece of art, and thus the involvement of art and aesthetics in sociality is of concern to us; secondly, it was art created on the move and through movement, and this encourages us to locate sociality in actual activity rather than in a pre-existing context or structure.

A biographical note is needed to explain our collaboration in this paper. Until 2012, Anna Vermehren was a curator at Deveron Arts, the organization in Huntly which produced the artwork under discussion here. Vergunst is an anthropologist at the University of Aberdeen and carried out ethnographic fieldwork focused on the event. Our working together comprises a contention that anthropology should not merely study art as if in a subject–object relation. Instead we find that there are questions of common artistic and anthropological concern that are most satisfyingly addressed by sharing authorship, though not entirely combining our voices. Schutz's perspective on the significance of co-presence in social relationships seems pertinent to our joint attempt to move beyond the usual modes of art criticism, and indeed anthropology, in which the critic/researcher constructs a relationship of distance towards the objects of concern.

We now turn to how the notion of sociality has shaped our work. As the introduction to this collection points out, scholars have tended to use the term to denote a concern with the nature of social relations rather than social structure or 'society'. Sarah Pink gives a definition: 'By socialities I refer to different sets of concrete (and in this case face-to-face) social relationships that develop around actual activities' (Pink 2008: 172). We share Pink's concern to link 'sociality' to ongoing social action rather than any free-floating or a priori context of social relations, and by 'concrete' we take Pink to mean substantive rather than fixed or structural. Nonetheless, a more philosophically grounded approach to sociality could help specify what analytical insight is being gained beyond the well-rehearsed criticisms of the structural concept of 'society'. Alfred Schutz's *The Phenomenology of the Social World* (1932) provides one such approach. He gives weight to the phenomenal co-presence of people already immersed in shared worlds of meaning, taking us beyond the mere fact of a relationship based on activity.

Schutz was broadly concerned to form a response to the methodological premises of Max Weber, which he found flawed due to Weber's manner of disassociating objective sociological meaning from subjective experience (Schutz [1932] 1972: 31–33). He sought instead to pursue the nature of intersubjective knowledge in a public, shared world, or, as he puts it: 'The world is now experienced by the individual as shared by his fellow creatures, in short, as a *social* world' (ibid.: 139). How then are experience and understanding linked? 'In the living intentionality of this experience, I "understand" you without paying attention to the acts of understanding themselves' (ibid.: 140). People who share the same world can understand each other without reflecting on that understanding. Occasionally, attention is directed explicitly towards understanding – for example, when we need clarification in a conversation, or even, if we happen to be social scientists, when we are struggling to interpret what is going on around us (ibid.: 140–141). Schutz identified the starting point of social science in ordinary life. Researchers in real-life interactions with people do not make enquiries from a position of ignorance, but from some shared understanding in a social world.

People who gain a sense of shared understanding and meaning by way of directly experiencing social reality are termed 'consociates' by Schutz (or initially 'fellow-men', *Mitmenschen*) – as opposed to 'contemporaries' (*Nebenmenschen*) whose social world one may live 'with' but not share or live 'through' (ibid.: 142), and whose creation of subjective meaning can merely be inferred rather than directly experienced. Schutz goes on to argue that the consociate face-to-face relationship, the 'pure We-relationship' (ibid.: 164) is basic and most meaningful to being human. Relations conducted indirectly, such as through letters posted from afar, he says, do not have the same quality of interaction. It is perhaps harder to read Schutz now as digital communication is blurring the boundaries between social time and space ever more effectively, although he also recognized a 'spectrum' between consociate and contemporary relations rather than a single boundary line (ibid.: 177). And yet ethnographically we still find claims for the significance of shared direct experience, not necessarily posed in philosophical terms but nonetheless resonant with them.

The argument of this paper is that sociality may be usefully conceived of as the experience of immersion in a shared world of meaning and understanding, most readily and richly apparent in consociate relations. This is to be distinguished from a simpler concept of sociality in which a relation between people in and of itself would be seen as evincing it. Two questions come to the fore here. Can we conceive of sociality-as-immersion as learned or purposively engendered? We might thus usefully enquire into moments when the course of sociality shifts, expands or contracts. Secondly, Schutz's thesis is relatively unconcerned with notions of place and movement. If these social worlds are at the same time material places experienced on the move and rarely with the isolated stability of a literally face-to-face relationship, what difference would it make to our notion of sociality? We want to ask these questions of our fieldwork material, while also recognizing the contribution of Schutz's ideas in theoretical discussions of experience (e.g., Throop 2003; Ho 2008). Examining these issues through the lens of an art project allows us to straddle the sense of enduring social worlds and the possibility that they can be created anew.

In methodological terms, both art and anthropology involve visual practices that have commonalities that could be further explored. Referring in particular to Gell's *Art and Agency*, Schneider and Wright (2006: 5) write: 'Recent proposals have called for anthropologists to focus on the performative aspects of artworks, but these have been applied to the cultures that anthropologists study, and not to anthropology's own visual practices.' They seek to encourage a 'methodological dialogue' centred around practice in art and anthropology, which is altogether different from the study of one by the other. Cycling, meanwhile, has also provided an impetus towards new visual methodological practices in the social sciences, for example through head and bike-mounted cameras where the emphasis is on engaging with experiential aspects of the activity (Brown et al. 2009; Spinney 2011). Our methodology has involved tracking the process by which a particular art project came to happen, and participating in and reflecting upon it when it did. In what follows we describe how the project situated itself amongst the social worlds of the town in which it was set and, for a short while at least, re-made them into something slightly different.

Slowing Down Huntly

At the time of the project, Deveron Arts was run by Claudia Zeiske and Anna Vermehren, with occasional administrative support and interns. With a motto of 'The town is the venue', it has no formal exhibition space but specializes in art projects and events that involve the residents and the environment of Huntly. While Deveron Arts' practice could be understood as 'socially engaged art', that can also connote a top-down approach to community art as a tool for social change (Finlay 2008). Instead we look elsewhere for synergies in theoretical approaches to art and sociality, specifically to the concept of 'relational art'. Coined by Nicolas Bourriaud, this refers to 'an art taking as its theoretical horizon the realm of human interactions and its social context, rather than the assertion of an independent and private symbolic space' (Bourriaud 2002: 14). Bourriaud is concerned with the way that contemporary art works as 'a state of encounter' (ibid.: 18) and while his discussion draws on Marxist theories of the interstice as a space of non-profit transaction, there are also connections with Schutz in the emphasis on social interaction rather than individuality. Although for Schutz, the social is not so much the 'context' for interaction as the thing itself (i.e., the enduring process of immersion in a shared world of experience), in drawing on Bourriaud we follow a different path for anthropological engagement with art to that of a reading of the agency of the finished artefact (Schneider and Wright 2006; cf. Gell 1998). Nonetheless, what the art 'does' for the people involved in it, and in its own terms, continues to be significant.

The 'Slow Down' project was part of Deveron Arts' wider three-year residency programme, funded by Aberdeenshire Council, the Scottish Arts Council, the LEADER programme of the EU, the Scottish Government's Climate Challenge Fund and the Forestry Commission, and focused on four topics: heritage, environment, intergenerational connections, and identity. 'Slow Down' was the first of a series of environmental projects, followed by '21 Days in the Cairngorms' with walking artist Hamish Fulton and 'Red Herring' by French artist Stefanie Bourne in 2010. Between 2009 and 2011 Deveron Arts' residencies were devised in the following way. Before the on-site residency, director Claudia Zeiske would choose and invite an artist whose practice suited one of the four given topics. The artists submitted proposals in response which were then collaboratively developed by Zeiske and the artist. At the beginning of each residency, the artist was introduced to selected members of the local community considered by Deveron Arts to be important for the project. During the first month the artist then conducted research and extended his or her network within the community. The second month was spent developing the ideas and working on a marketing and outreach programme while the last month concentrated on an event-based public artwork and a discussion event with invited speakers.

Slow Down itself evolved from a long-planned residency based on the artist Jacqueline Donachie's idea to do a project on cycling in Huntly. Her proposal involved using the central square of Huntly, historically a market square but today mostly taken up by roads and a car park. The idea was to ban vehicles from the whole town centre for a weekend, but eventually just the Square was closed off. The festival came to be themed around the concept of environmental awareness in conjunction with non-motorized transport, and links were made with the Cíttaslow initiative ('slow towns', which emerged from the Slow Food movement in Italy). During the final event the 'slow' theme provided the focus for a whole range of activities. While many of these took place in the Square itself – a snail race, a slow bike race, a tai chi session, together with Slow Down deck chairs and the encouragement to simply sit down, chat or read – others were in the wider vicinity, including an excursion to the nearby Bin Forest, a guided history walk around town, a foraging walk with a herbalist to gather natural foods and remedies, and two curated walks by walking artist Tim Brennan.

In describing these events, we are concerned to convey a sense of what participating in a 'slow' art event was like. Pink (2008) describes the emergent and specific social relationships formed through the Cíttaslow movement elsewhere in the U.K. as a contrast to what she sees as an uncritical approach to 'community' taken by other scholars of the Slow movement. Wendy Parkins, for example, tracks the more recent rise of a generalized discourse of 'care' in the Slow social movement (2004: 377). In our case, however, there was an experiential aspect to slowness in a literal sense that was integral to how the Slow Down Festival was devised by the artist: moving slowly rather than just a Slow movement.

This raises the possibility that sociality might have a particular pacing associated with it, which we could also understand as 'cadence' or rhythmical tempo. Social relationships were generated and played out through the very pace at which things happened, rather than cultivating a collective adherence to the idea of a slow social movement in a sociological sense. Specifically, the notion of cadence for us approaches more closely the human experience of pace, rather than objective speed. Walkers moving their legs rapidly, at a high cadence, may feel they are rushing regardless of the fact that they are likely to take longer to cover a distance than the slowest car. Similarly, a cyclist turning the pedals quickly and strenuously may still be travelling more slowly than another rider on a different bike or in a higher gear. While cadence in this sense is most often used in bio-mechanical or engineering research, the bodily experience of cadence can also generate a pacing in social interactions.

Donachie was clear from the beginning that she wanted to present an alternative to the transport system of roads and parking spaces that the Square is today by creating (indeed recreating) a kind of informal commercial space. Aided by a warm sunny day, the Square took on a very relaxed, sociable feel – more akin to the Latin American plazas described by Setha Low (2000). The tai chi group slowly moved their arms and torsos in unison. The deckchairs were full of people doing not terribly much. Vergunst flicked through a book on fruit growing bought from a charity book stall in one corner while Vermehren was organizing the start of the parade. As a counterpoint to the participants' slowness, most of her day had been hectic, organizing the Deveron Arts team, closing the roads, setting up gazebos and tables, bringing out bikes and building a stage in the middle of the car park. Now people gathered around the stalls, and bought coffee and burgers from the Huntly Hotel. The artist created an opportunity for new interactions in an area where much 'public life' is otherwise composed of or is secondary to vehicle movement.

A call went up for entrants to the slow bike race and Vergunst joined in. About a dozen racers went off, slowly, in heats where the last person to cross the finish line of the ten-metre course was the winner. Here, slowness had an intensity to it. The cycling was about balance and control and momentum needed to be resisted rather than created. One cyclist in particular demonstrated remarkable skill on a fixed-gear bike, holding a track stand by angling the wheels and shifting weight on the pedals while standing up in the saddle and periodically holding the brakes on. Vergunst ended up using the same bike but could not remotely get the hang of it. In the head-to-head final, one contestant heroically kept his feet off the ground for a couple of minutes while only progressing about five metres, but on looking round he saw the track stand cyclist having barely moved from the start line at all.

One noteworthy aspect here was that the participants were trying something new with their bikes. Learning different ways of cycling was, to us, an unexpected outcome of the event. In amongst the deckchairs all kinds of bicycles weaved with various degrees of steadiness. A bicycle collector, 82-year-old Doug Smith, had brought an 1890 Penny Farthing and later expressed to a local newspaper his happiness at seeing it being ridden around the Square (*Press and Journal*, 22 June 2009: 14). Two student companions, one of whom was the skilful slow cyclist, had brought double-frame 'tall bikes' along – one frame welded to the top of another, making the saddle roughly the height of the Penny Farthing – and also offered rides to the crowd. As in the slow bike race, Vergunst appreciated the skill in keeping the right amount of momentum in going forward while not turning too sharply, and finally leaping bravely down from the saddle. Other cyclists had, at the invitation of the festival, decorated their bikes with paper, flags, plants and flowers. In all this, the sharing of bikes went with the learning and sharing of skills in riding them, and, evocative of Schutz, this was the course by which a sharing of worlds of experience and meaning took place.

The centrepiece of the festival was a collective drawing made by around a hundred cyclists who took part in the Slow Down parade on the Saturday afternoon. In an interview Donachie explained to Vergunst that she got the idea for a device for making a bicycle drawing from the internet. But the image she had initially found turned out not to be what it seemed:

> We realized it was only ever this one image that was coming up, then we started thinking 'this has been photoshopped'. It's on my computer, it's lots of cyclists and pink and white and yellow lines and stuff, and that's been made up. So we based the project on something we'd seen on a website. I'd always said I wanted to visualize a cycle lane, and I thought about using chalk, because it had to be temporary. And I thought 'that's perfect, that's what we'll use'. Then we spent about a month trying to get it, or finding out how to use it, and then 'it doesn't exist'. It's just an idea. But now Allen's made it with bottles and duct tape.

This illuminates the creativity engendered during the project. During Donachie's residency, Deveron Arts had engaged two interns, Allen Breed being one, assisting the project. In the final phase they mostly worked on designing a device that could be attached to the bikes to leave a trail of coloured chalk behind them. Before the weekend, they spent most of their time trying out designs in the street. From various prototypes they progressed to Irn Bru bottles cut in half and pieces of plastic tub and rubber, held together with duct tape. All in all they produced over 120 of these chalk bottle devices and attached about 100 of them

Figure 10.1 The Slow Down cycle parade. Photo courtesy of Deveron Arts.

to the bikes, some of which had been donated for use in the festival, made fit for use, and painted bright blue.

Setting off to the playing of bagpipes, the parade rolled out from the Square east towards the train station, then north-west through residential areas towards the Gordon Schools. Pausing at the golf club on the edge of town, chalk bottles were refilled and the parade re-gathered before continuing through the school grounds – symbolically significant, as cycling to school had been a contentious issue locally. The drawing devices worked brilliantly, leaving smooth curved trails of chalk behind each bike. Each line became intertwined with others and became a colourful flow along the road. At one point the route crossed itself and we saw where we had been earlier: the lines swept up a slope straight over two 'stop' signs and white lines painted on the road. The drawing was somewhat less elegant in sonic terms, as the devices made a racket as the plastic and rubber scraped along the road, and Donachie had handed out dozens of Slow Down whistles for us to blow as we went along. She later joked that she would not do the whistles again.

Donachie's intention was that the parade should happen slowly, and she emphasized this in several planning meetings beforehand. As it turned out, people chatted as they cycled. Vergunst found the sociality of the parade very much like the sociability engendered by a group going on a walk together, in which social interaction and shared bodily orientation reinforce and find expression in each other (Lee and Ingold 2006). In most urban parts of the U.K., talking while cycling is not a common occurrence, as cycling infrastructure is not good, bike lanes if present are narrow and cyclists are almost always in close proximity to vehicular traffic. Here, however, the slow pace together with the overall sense of fun in the collective venture led to a good deal of conversation and banter as we went along. Vergunst talked to a woman who worked in the Nordic Ski Centre in Huntly. Vermehren chatted to her close friends and enjoyed no longer having to be organizing anything. Vergunst heard a young child yelling to his friend: 'My house was just back there! Douglas, my house was just back there', seemingly a surprise moment of familiarity in the midst of an unfamiliar way of moving around, yet experienced at a pace that enabled its sharing with a consociate.

It was nonetheless tricky to keep together as a large and disparate group of cyclists. There was a number of very small children and parents who went at the pace of the youngest, and as we went up and down the hills there was a tendency for gaps in the parade to appear. Donachie rode at the front and she had a task in preventing some of the older young people speeding off. Vergunst asked her at the end if she had enjoyed the parade. 'I don't know if that's quite the right word. Cos I was at the front with all the boy racers, because I was the only one that knew the route. I kept on having to go "*slowwww down, slow down!*"' Jackie's visceral efforts to maintain the group bike ride contrasted somewhat with the overall tone of slow and easy social interaction. She had anticipated some of these difficulties in advance and stopped the parade every now and again to bring the group back together.

The Socialities of Cycling

Phil Jones' (2005) account of cycling to work in Birmingham reaches towards the 'non-representational' aspects of his experiences of moving in the city, in contrast to the technoscientific discourses of cycling policy and urban planning. In describing the 'thrills and chills' of a daily commute, his cycling skills are linked to his knowledge of the city and the choices that need to be made along the way. It is nevertheless a distinctly individualist account. Although the skills are generated and mediated socially, in his reading it is the cyclist's individual experience, his experience of the streets and architecture of Birmingham as a lone cyclist, which is most constitutive of the bike ride.

As Jones suggests, cycling, like walking, is an activity that people constantly adjust and improvise as they go along. As people move in new environments, each step or turn of the pedals, itself indivisible from the last, is a form of adjustment in understanding the environment and a performance in relation to it. The interaction of the ground and the shoe or bike tyre produces sensations of texture which are central to how the movement takes place and the journey proceeds (Vergunst 2008; Spinney 2006). On a bike, sensitivity towards incline or decline and wind speed and direction increase. As familiarity with an environment increases (though is never fully achieved), adjustments take place more tacitly, through 'muscular intelligence' (Bachelard 1958), or 'thinking in movement' (Sheets-Johnston 1999): not a prior cognitive process, but a dispersed, bodily-led activity where the 'mind' may only later gain some understanding of what the body has done.

The Slow Down project was an experiment into what it would be like if we all cycled together, and moreover in a slow and sociable way. The familiarization with the environment, the movement and coordination of oneself within the group of the other cyclists was a shared social world encompassed by the parade. Cycling in the group offered participants an increased level of awareness about the activity itself and the environment one was in, moving perhaps towards Schutz's moments of 'paying attention to' rather than immersion in the flow of social experience.

What Donachie created in Huntly was a challenge to bodily *habitus*, remade from the personal to the collective, and social space. A theme of the artwork was of having the opportunity to cycle – indeed to move – in unfamiliar ways, together. In other fieldwork Vergunst has seen similar challenges amongst walkers in unfamiliar or difficult environments, trying to deal with loose or slippy rocks, steep slopes, stretches of water, wind, snow or ice (Vergunst 2008). In one respect the difficulties of movement are ultimately part of the overall progression of the journey, the minor or major adjustments in rhythm that one makes in order to deal with the environment being moved through. Purposively moving in an unfamiliar way relates to distinctive kinds of sociality. Like participating in a parade on foot, cycling slowly means not overtaking, while also not falling too far behind. Cycling downhill results in a faster speed, and uphill one goes much slower. The pace of the family groups differed to that of the older children. There were, therefore, a variety of movements and rhythms of cycling during the parade, and we could think of all of these as engendering particular socialities – amongst families and close friends as consociates in Schutz's terms, or amongst people meeting each other for the first time who, by virtue of their involvement, were already contemporaries and could yet become closer. It is therefore not so much that a way of moving produces a way of being social, but rather that sociability and the cadences of travelling resonated with each other through immersion in a common stream of experience. The 'cycle lane' drawing became a trace of the sociable activity of the riders, rather than a route connecting two abstract points of start and destination (Ingold 2007).

For Vergunst in particular the enchantment of the artwork was the feeling of being together and being engaged in the same activity over a certain amount of time. Riders had an incentive to adjust and to learn how to cycle together, in order to create the parade and the drawing. The broad purpose pulled the riders together, and with the help of Donachie's efforts, kept the cycling rhythms from diverging too much. The collective, unfamiliar movement in time through what was for most a very well-known space, while at the same time leaving behind a memory of that very action with the chalk trace, was what Vermehren perceived as the core of the artwork. Using Bourriaud's terminology, we agree that Huntly became a social interstice, an example of contemporary art that is 'a space in human relations' that 'creates free areas, and time spans whose rhythm contrasts with those structuring everyday life' (Bourriaud 2002: 16). The relational space created through co-movement contrasted with the usual experience of the Square and surrounding streets.

Sociality and Sociability

While this new relational space could be seen by anthropologists as engendering distinct forms of *sociality*, the artist herself framed her work as an opportunity to engender *sociability* (see also Bourriard 2002: 16). Indeed, in previous research on walking in north-east Scotland, Vergunst has also noted the significance of 'sociability' (Lee and Ingold 2006; Vergunst 2010). Many people walked as a way of being sociable, a practice of sociality and its experiential reality. Walking together does not reflect general 'social relations' so much as create an ability to get on with someone through a shared rhythm of movement. On the other hand, where walking rhythms are very different in direction, pace and demeanour, even though walkers may be in the same vicinity, sociability is resisted. By such means walkers can achieve the feeling of being alone in a crowd in a busy street – to which we could contrast the feeling of togetherness or sociability created by a crowd walking together through the streets to a football match, which was an example used by Donachie in conversation with Vergunst.

Since the beginning of this fieldwork, Vergunst has started to notice other occasional moments of sociability between cyclists. Occasional waves and nods go beyond the standardized signalling before shifting position, and such gestures occasionally happen amongst vehicle drivers too. On his cycle commute to work, spoken contact with other cyclists usually happens at traffic lights, commenting on the weather or the traffic. However, conversations amongst cyclists can sometimes allow for a little more shared experience. Just before the Slow Down weekend Vergunst took his bike to Huntly on the train, and at Huntly station he helped a young Polish man, who had also brought his bike by train, to find an address in the town where he hoped to get work. Heading in the same direction the two cycled together and chatted a bit. From the town centre Vergunst sent him off down the road and wished him good luck with the job. He would no doubt have found his way there by himself, but through sharing a way of moving, they opened up a way of being sociable for a few minutes.

Before and during the weekend, there were also points of tension and dissent amongst the townspeople. Very soon after Donachie had arrived in Huntly and publicized the initial plans for the event, there was an adverse reaction from local businesses. In a story headlined 'Roads Closed Threat to Business' published in a local newspaper, one shop-owner complained: 'The reality of the situation is that every time there is a road closure for something in the town centre or the Square my business loses money.' In Huntly town centre, shopkeepers battle against not just one but two enormous out-of-town supermarkets and they perceive car access to their shops as vital. Claudia Zeiske sent Donachie around all the local businesses and while in the end they came up with the compromise of limiting the extent of the road closures, most businesses did not seem to fully buy into the idea and did not join in the discussion symposium at the end of the festival.

During the main events, the sense that some communities had not become involved also became apparent. The symposium was held in a function room above a social club, and during a break in the proceedings a young man came up from the social club bar, a pint in his hand, to complain vigorously about the chalk all over the roads around the Square that had caused his 'bike' (motorbike) to skid the previous evening, and which he thought had been the result of children playing.

Some of the walking events associated with the festival also put participants themselves in rather awkward, unfamiliar situations which were not straightforwardly enjoyable for participants – trooping collectively into a pub to look at a piece of art commissioned by Deveron Arts, for example. In line with Allan Kaprow's call for the artist to enact the 'transformation of the public consciousness' (Lacy 1995: 33), Donachie was quite upfront about enabling 'disruptions' of the everyday. The socialities of Slow Down were not just about creating convivial sociability. Other currents circulated, encompassing those who saw their activities in the Square being encroached upon through to those unwilling to share in quite the same kind of movement as Donachie was suggesting. Yet we also have to look beyond the immediate social relationships to understand what kind of activism was being created.

Art and Efficacy:
Cycling as a Continuing Spectacle in Huntly

In practice, arts organizations like Deveron Arts need to be entrepreneurial to operate in a competitive funding environment, and they draw attention to the more-than-artistic value of their work. They have to demonstrate 'impact'. The Scottish Government, meanwhile, has a National Cultural Strategy in which culture refers to the arts, and has a brochure entitled 'Culture Delivers' that sets out for local authorities and 'culture bodies' how the arts can contribute to 'local and national well-being and prosperity' (Scottish Government 2008). In a sense this fits well with a relational approach to art. If art becomes interesting not through what it is but through the interactions and encounters it enables, we might expect the value of art to be sought and circulated through a variety of discursive and material realms.

A few weeks before the festival, Vergunst asked Claudia Zeiske what she felt would make for a successful project, and her answer foregrounded artistic achievement, but also connected up a series of different outcomes:

Of course, my first ambition is that it's a success as an art project. That it looks visually interesting and makes people talk about it. And talks about it means that people talk about it locally. And that maybe a significant amount of people would come to Huntly that day. And, er, that it is discussed in the media, if there are articles stuck on to that as well. And then in a nutshell, I would hope to see people walking and cycling after this. That would be nice. Very few people cycle here, given how such an easy place to cycle it is.

In this face-to-face conversation, the 'efficacy' and intent of the art is placed in immediate and experiential terms, and to some extent a tension can be discerned between this and the way that funding was secured. The sociable and space-transforming aspects of the project were not the same as the long-term practical outcomes many of the funders were interested in. The Climate Challenge Fund, for example, was introduced by the Scottish Government in 2007 to encourage community-led responses to the climate change and environmental sustainability agenda. Finding evidence for actual mitigation or adaptation to climate change through this art project would be difficult, yet the mix of artistic quality and ecological imperative in the funding package was part of the 'encounter' designed into it.

Donachie consulted locals about which routes in and around Huntly they would like to cycle on. Deveron Arts' staff and friends created small cycling groups during lunch time to try out the suggestions. Cycling the streets of Huntly in groups for the first time, Vermehren was well aware of 'cycling together' as people commented on the rare sight of cyclists in Huntly. Pedestrians waved and greeted, school children pointed and shouted, and we joked about the impact our small group of five or so made in town. Recently, Vermehren cycled from the centre of Huntly to the train station together with a friend sitting on the same bike, and felt it was again something of a spectacle in the town. While no quantitative research has been carried out, an impression has been gained of there being more cyclists in Huntly since the project. People in Huntly remember Slow Down, and often associate it with Deveron Arts: 'Ah, you're from Deveron Arts – was that the cycling thing?' Deveron Arts' artists in residence are still encouraged to cycle around town and are given a bike at the beginning of their residency.

Jackie Donachie's answer to the question on what would make for a successful project emphasized the lead-up and overall community involvement in the event:

Well, one element of the success is that people had a good time making it. For me, I have to gauge if it works as an artwork, and that means if I get good photographs of it. And if it does make some kind of temporary imprint on the town, visually. That's how I gauge it. But also, you gauge it if people enjoy taking part. Cos the idea is what people picked up on, the idea is the most important part of using, thinking, using people on their bikes to draw a cycle lane around town. That is the most important part of it. And that idea is there, it could almost not happen. But then you get another level of success if you get people to turn up and they kind of enjoy themselves, and then the Square takes on a – it looks different, we turn it, we stop making it a car park and we start making it into a – like a place filled with deckchairs.

Donachie specified 'good photographs' as one important outcome. Photographs here seem to signify a documentary image-making capacity, literally a snapshot of how the art looks to create a transferable, representational object. Together with the social aspects, it was a priority to create an artwork with an aesthetic value. But like Zeiske, Donachie moves on from the visual aesthetic to an almost Platonic ideal – the idea of cycling as art – and from there to 'another level' again, the involvement of people in changing the public space of Huntly. Both Zeiske and Donachie demonstrate an unwillingness to compromise or to choose between these outcomes. They would rather see a proliferation of affects and effects, somehow combining a representational object with a material trace, an idea and a social process, which we feel is captured well by Bourriaud's notion of relational art. This is a critique of any single grand narrative in art, and in the end an idealist rejection of any dilemma between aesthetics and an environmentalist agenda. Donachie's art is not so much about aesthetics, or ways of knowing, as it is about a way of being – and, we can suggest here, sociality. Or then again, it is not 'about' anything; rather, it is an immersion in sociality in itself.

This was not lost on the participants. At the end of the parade, Jackie, along with co-artists Merlyn Riggs and Norma D. Hunter, had set up a 'Slow Down Soup Kitchen' at the disused Battlehill Quarry. A trailer tent – an artwork Donachie had exhibited in gallery spaces before – was a kitchen-base to feed and water the cyclists. Vergunst asked another participant what he thought of the art: 'The art? Um, well I think the whole thing was art, wasn't it, or do you mean the lines on the pavement?'

While others enjoyed the event, it was less clear whether they felt they were creating an artwork, although we do not think this was a major concern for Deveron Arts or the artist. These participants enjoyed the cycling without seeming to ponder much on what it might 'mean' on a more abstract level as 'art'. However there was some quirkiness in the parade created by the devices attached to the bikes that left a trace on the road as they went along – a reminder, perhaps, that there was something else going on besides a group bike ride. At one point, Zeiske said that Deveron Arts rarely suggested to local people that they should take part in 'art', with its connotations of high culture – rather, they would let it be known that a certain artist was coming to Huntly to work on a project that people might find interesting and/or useful. On the other hand, public organizations are more and more involved in explicitly promoting art as a demonstration of the more-than-economic or intangible impact of their own activities – at the same time as requiring art practices to show tangible and economic outcomes. These tangled webs of impact and cause and effect are one result of the accountability and audit culture that we live in (Strathern 2000). Yet what public, relational art can best demonstrate as 'impact' is not so much measurable and attributable changes in behaviour but, in the language of sociality, an offering up of the possibility of immersion in certain kinds of social relations or relations with the environment. People's participation in that offering, although temporary, would be the marker of success.

The Ephemerality of Slow Sociality?

> It was never going to be a permanent work I was going to do here, it was always going to be a temporary work – so the idea of doing something that was fairly disruptive almost, just for a day, was always part of it. Cos, as an artist, you're kind of able to do that, cos you're kind of coming in and go away again.

This was Donachie's own approach to the question of having to do a time-limited project. Her residency lasted three months. The parade itself lasted about an hour. There were two days of action over the weekend itself. Carbon emissions in Huntly were, according to the original funding proposals for the Deveron Arts residencies, to be reduced over three years. Any slow sociality could emerge only within these time-limited parameters. The artwork was created specifically as a brief, though slow, activity that everyone could be involved in, move on from, but hopefully also remember and return to in the future. By giving out whistles and badges, Donachie created an afterlife in memorabilia for everyone taking part. She felt able in her identity and role as an artist to make an intervention that would not permanently change the Square or the streets of Huntly but would broaden the range of possibilities of what they could be again in the future. Indeed, what the Slow movement in general does rather well is propose an alternative temporal mode where time is not 'lost' but rather 'taken', in the sense of gathered, or 'made' in the sense of cooking a meal – the effort put into making time for a meal is productive of further social benefits (Pink 2008). Slow sociality, as we have conceived of it here, contradicts the timescales imposed by project-outcome dispositions in the governance of funding.

The results of the artwork in this rendering are not orientated to the future as a particular scenario (in which carbon emissions are cut by a certain amount by a specific date), but to the future as a range of possibilities informed by past experience. This is also rather resonant of Horton et al.'s comments on the relationship between cycling, a wider social context and time: 'Is cycling of the past, the present or the future?' In some places, cycling is 'something to be left behind in the rush to modernity' but on the other hand 'the most mobile and affluent societies appear increasingly willing to re-embrace the bicycle' (Horton et al. 2007: 4). Although Huntly would fall into the latter category of relative affluence, the artwork becomes the mode of action, as Morphy (2009) puts it, to provide a different kind of possibility for the future.

Donachie herself took time out shortly after the event to reflect on the ephemeral work she had created. She described in writing her experience of the visual imprint of her work:

A walk around the town later that evening (after a very frantic take-down) was very satisfying – whole streets covered in ribbons of coloured chalk that showed our route – sometimes clearly, sometimes just faint marks on busier roads, but enough to navigate a route round the town that we had made as a community. (Donachie 2009: 4)

For her, the best way to consider the art was to take another journey around town, and even slower this time through being on foot rather than cycling. The walk allowed her to reflect on the piece in its entirety, even though it was never visible at the same moment or in a single photographic frame, before all the chalk traces of it were washed away by rain several days later.

Conclusion

The themes we have touched on here are about sociality as encompassing both the convivial, sociable, immediate relationships between people and the tenser and more political engagements they are involved in, all of which can be understood better through attention to process rather than structure, as the concept of sociality encourages. Schutz's perspective on the sharing of worlds of experience has helped us move beyond the 'mere' social relationship (as if such a thing could exist) and towards a sense of meaning, yet one that we have described as also necessarily emplaced, embodied and mobile. The distinction of consociate and contemporary, moreover, is not drawn according to a strict boundary but describes shifts in sociality. And understanding our art project as a 'relational' aesthetic further tracks common philosophical grounding in contemporary art and anthropology.

We have considered slowness as an actual experience through pacing and cadence but equally through the tensions between experience and the requirements that art has measureable 'impact'. The work endeavoured to create a dialogue between aesthetic achievement through art and sociopolitical efficacy. Finley (2008) argues that 'arts-based enquiry' is ideally combined with a radical and even revolutionary, politically active social science that responds at the same time to crises of representation in art and social sciences and to pressing social and environmental problems. In this respect, sociality has as much to do with an alternative politics of change as it does with sociability; a politically charged sociality, perhaps.

Finally, different kinds of pacing and movement can clearly be savoured in different ways. This was brought home to Vergunst at the end of the day at Battlehill Wood where the parade had ended. Four young folk on mountain bikes came spinning out of the wood, at high speed and high cadence, following each other in a line wheel-to-wheel. Down the entrance to the car park, then onto the main road and gone in an instant. They looked like a cycling pursuit team embodying speed, finesse and concentration. They clearly knew the woods and the tracks and they seemed to mock the slowness that the bike parade had created, and they may well have been the boys Donachie was yelling at to slow down. While we have affiliated ourselves to 'slowing down' in this paper, we can still admire these boys' demonstration of a high speed sociality – although we hope that bike lanes will one day be established permanently in Huntly, and other places like it, and that the boys will not rush to exchange their bikes for cars at the first opportunity they get.

Acknowledgements

We would like to thank Jacqueline Donachie, Claudia Zeiske and the participants of the Slow Down Festival for enabling us to write this paper.

References

Bachelard, G. [1958] 1969. *The Poetics of Space*. Boston: Beacon Press.
Bourriaud, N. [1998] 2002. *Relational Aesthetics* (trans. S. Pleasance and F. Woods). Paris: Les Presses du Reel.
Brown, K., R. Dilley and K. Marshall 2009. Using a Head-mounted Video Camera to Understand Social Worlds and Experiences. *Sociological Research Online* 13, no. 6. <http://www.socresonline.org.uk/13/6/1.html> (accessed 7 February 2012).
Donachie, J. 2009. *Slow Down Huntly. A Residency with Deveron Arts, Huntly, April–June 2009*. Unpublished report for Deveron Arts.
Finley, S. 2008. Arts-based Inquiry. Performing Revolutionary Pedagogy. In *Collecting and Interpreting Qualitative Materials* (eds.) N. Denzin and Y. Lincoln, 681–694. London: SAGE.
Gell, A. 1998. *Art and Agency. An Anthropological Theory*. Oxford: Clarendon Press.
Ho, W-C. 2008. Writing Experience: Does Ethnography Convey a Crisis of Representation, or an Ontological Break with the Everyday World? *Canadian Review of Sociology* 45, no. 4: 343–365.
Horton, D., P. Cox and P. Rosen 2007. Introduction. Cycling and society. In *Cycling and Society* (eds.) D. Horton, P. Cox and P. Rosen, 1–23. Aldershot: Ashgate.
Ingold, T. 2007. *Lines*. London: Routledge.
Jones, P. 2005. Performing the City: A Body and a Bicycle Take On Birmingham, UK. *Social and Cultural Geography* 6, no. 6: 813–830.
Lacy, S. 1995. *Mapping the Terrain. New Genre Public Art*. Washington: Bay Press.
Lee J. and T. Ingold 2006. Fieldwork on Foot: Perceiving, Routing, Socializing. In *Locating the Field. Space, Place and Context in Anthropology* (eds.) S. Coleman and P. Collins, 67–86. Oxford: Berg.
Low, S. 2000. *On the Plaza. The Politics of Public Space and Culture*. Austin: University of Texas Press.
Morphy, H. 2009. Art as a Mode of Action. Some Problems with Gell's Art and Agency. *Journal of Material Culture* 14, no. 1: 5–27.
Parkins, W. 2004. Out of Time. Fast Subjects and Slow Living. *Time and Society* 13, no. 2–3: 363–382.
Parkins, W. and G. Craig 2006. *Slow Living*. Oxford: Berg.
Pink, S. 2008. Re-thinking Community Activism: From Community to Emplaced Sociality. *Ethnos* 73, no. 2: 163–188.

Schneider, A. and C. Wright 2006. The Challenge of Practice. In *Contemporary Art and Anthropology* (eds.) A. Schneider and C. Wright, 1–27. Oxford: Berg.

Schutz, A. [1932] 1972. *The Phenomenology of the Social World*. London: Heinemann Educational.

Scottish Government 2008. *Culture. Culture Delivers.* Edinburgh: Scottish Government.

Sheets-Johnstone, M. 1999. *The Primacy of Movement*. Amsterdam: John Benjamins.

Spinney, J. 2006. A Place of Sense: A Kinaesthetic Ethnography of Cyclists on Mont Ventoux. *Environment and Planning D: Society and Space* 24: 709–732.

―――― 2011. A Chance to Catch a Breath: Using Mobile Video Ethnography in Cycling Research. *Mobilities* 6, no. 2: 161–182.

Strathern, M. (ed.) 2000. *Audit Cultures: Anthropological Studies in Accountability, Ethics and the Academy*. London: Routledge.

Throop C. 2003. Articulating Experience. *Anthropological Theory* 3, no. 2: 219–241.

Vergunst, J. 2008. Taking a Trip and Taking Care in Everyday Life. In *Ways of Walking. Ethnography and Practice on Foot* (eds.) T. Ingold and J. Vergunst, 105–121. Aldershot: Ashgate.

―――― 2010. Rhythms of Walking: History and Presence in a City Street. *Space and Culture* 13, no. 4: 376–388.

Notes on Contributors

Anne Allison is Robert O. Keohane Professor of Cultural Anthropology at Duke University. Her books include *Nightwork: Pleasure, Sexuality, and Corporate Masculinity in a Tokyo Hostess Club* (1994, University of Chicago Press), *Millennial Monsters: Japanese Toys and the Global Imagination* (2006, University of California Press), and – on the subject of precarity and sociality in twenty-first century Japan – *Precarious Japan* (2013, Duke University Press).

Adam Yuet Chau is University Lecturer in the Anthropology of Modern China in the Department of East Asian Studies at the University of Cambridge. He is the author of *Miraculous Response: Doing Popular Religion in Contemporary China* (2006, Stanford University Press) and editor of *Religion in Contemporary China: Revitalization and Innovation* (2011, Routledge).

Peter Geschiere is Professor of African Anthropology at the University of Amsterdam (earlier at Leiden University). Since 1971 he has undertaken historical-anthropological fieldwork in various parts of Cameroon and elsewhere in West Africa. His publications include *The Modernity of Witchcraft: Politics and the Occult in Post-colonial Africa* (1997, University of Virginia Press), and *The Perils of Belonging: Autochthony, Citizenship and Exclusion in Africa and Europe* (2009, University of Chicago Press).

Susanne Küchler is Professor of Anthropology at University College London, specializing in the study of material culture. She has conducted long term field-research in Papua New Guinea and Polynesia and has published widely on issues ranging from art and memory in political economies of knowledge, to innovation and the take-up and transformation of cloth and clothing as new material and new technology across the Pacific, charting the dynamics of societal impact. Over the past five years she has begun to take this topic to new materials designed in laboratories and their selective take-up and transmission.

Sian Lazar is a University Lecturer in Social Anthropology at the University of Cambridge. As well as her monograph, *El Alto, Rebel City: Self and Citizenship in*

Andean Bolivia (2008, Duke University Press) she has written extensively on the anthropology of citizenship and collective organization.

Nicholas J. Long is a Lecturer in Anthropology at the London School of Economics and Political Science, where he is presently completing a British Academy Postdoctoral Fellowship. He is the co-editor of *Southeast Asian Perspectives on Power* (2012, Routledge) and author of *Being Malay in Indonesia* (forthcoming, NUS/KITLV/University of Hawai'i Press).

Henrietta L. Moore is the William Wyse Chair of Social Anthropology at the University of Cambridge. Her most recent book is *Still Life: Hopes, Desires and Satisfactions* (2011, Polity Press).

Olga Solomon is an Assistant Professor of Occupational Science and Occupational Therapy at the University of Southern California. An applied linguist with a background in clinical psychology and linguistic anthropology, she is interested in the mutually constitutive relation of activity, experience and meaning, and in ways in which engagement and participation in everyday activities intersect with both personal experience and family life. Her research examines the sociocultural, psychosocial and structural phenomena that support engagement and participation with an eye for mediating potentialities of social practices, innovations and technologies.

Christina Toren is Professor of Anthropology and Director of the Centre for Pacific Studies at the University of St Andrews. She is the author of numerous papers and two monographs *Making Sense of Hierarchy: Cognition as Social Process in Fiji* (1990, Athlone Press) and *Mind, Materiality and History. Explorations in Fijian Ethnography* (1999, Routledge). She co-edited (with Deborah James and Edie Plaice) *Culture Wars: Contexts, Models and Anthropologists' Accounts* (2010, Berghahn) and (with Joao de Pina Cabral) *The Challenge of Epistemology* (2011, Berghahn).

Jo Vergunst is a Lecturer in the Department of Anthropology at the University of Aberdeen. His interests are in landscape, movement and creativity, and he has carried out fieldwork in Scotland and Greenland. Along with Tim Ingold he is co-editor of *Ways of Walking: Ethnography and Practice on Foot* (2008, Ashgate).

Anna Vermehren is Director of Timespan in Helmsdale, and former Project Manager at Deveron Arts in Huntly. With a background in Art History and Sociology her current focus is on contemporary art that invests in social relations and investigates local heritage. Vermehren is interested in the way the concept of North shapes Scottish identities.

Index